YALE STUDIES IN POLITICAL SCIENCE, 12

DAVID HORNE, EDITOR

PUBLISHED UNDER THE DIRECTION OF THE
DEPARTMENT OF POLITICAL SCIENCE

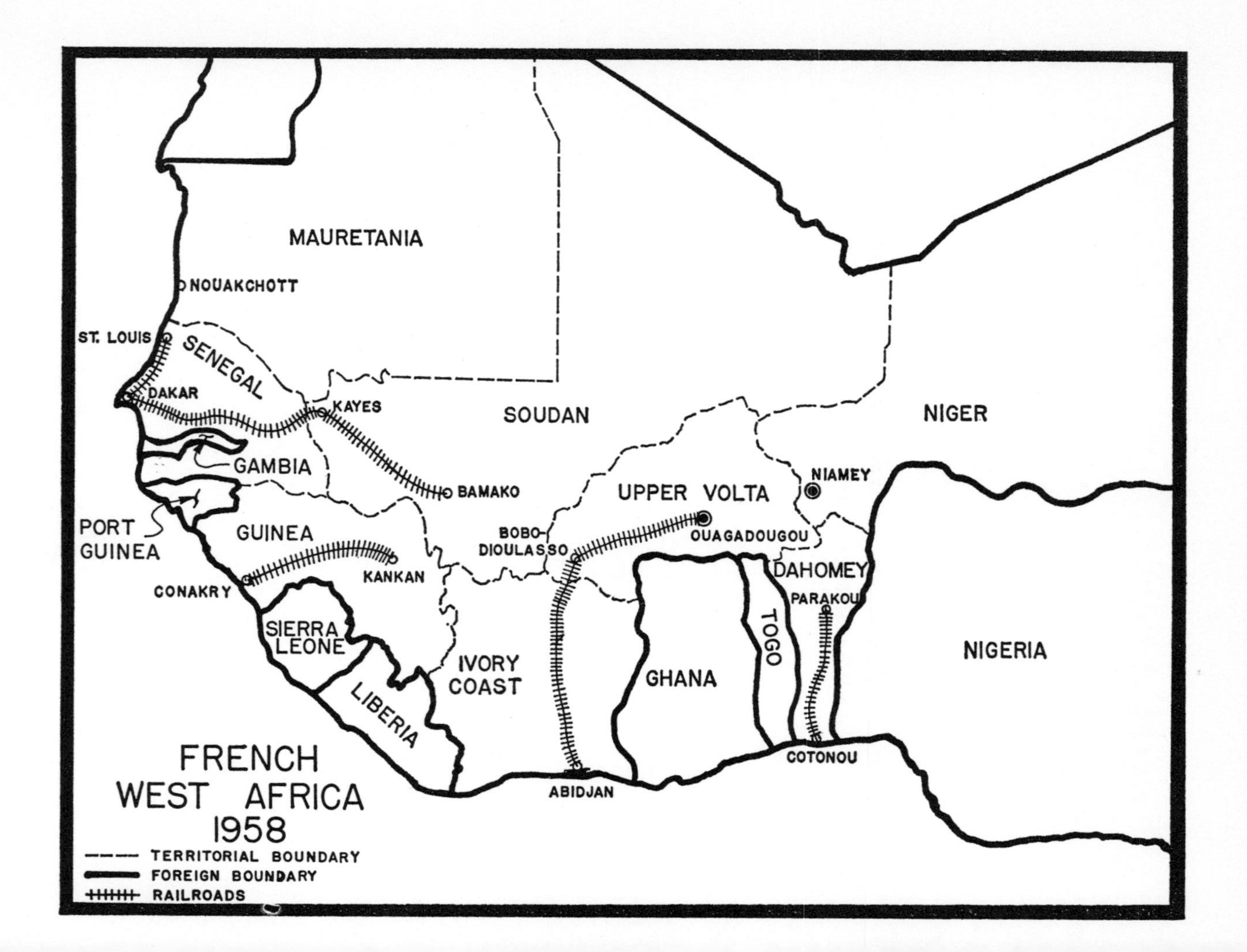
MAURETANIA
NOUAKCHOTT
ST. LOUIS
SENEGAL
DAKAR
KAYES
SOUDAN
NIGER
GAMBIA
BAMAKO
NIAMEY
UPPER VOLTA
PORT GUINEA
GUINEA
BOBO-DIOULASSO
OUAGADOUGOU
CONAKRY
KANKAN
DAHOMEY
PARAKOU
TOGO
SIERRA LEONE
IVORY COAST
GHANA
NIGERIA
LIBERIA
ABIDJAN
COTONOU
FRENCH WEST AFRICA 1958
TERRITORIAL BOUNDARY
FOREIGN BOUNDARY
RAILROADS

FROM FRENCH WEST AFRICA TO THE MALI FEDERATION

by William J. Foltz

New Haven and London, Yale University Press

Second printing, February 1967.
Designed by John O. C. McCrillis,
set in Caledonia type,
and printed in the United States of America by
The Murray Printing Company,
Forge Village, Massachusetts.

Library of Congress catalog card number: 65–11178

Published with assistance from the foundation
established in memory of Philip Hamilton McMillan
of the Class of 1894, Yale College.

For Anne-Marie

"Bolo fla be gnouan ko ka dye."

Preface

THIS BOOK seeks to answer two specific questions: Why was the Mali Federation formed? Why did it fail? Through these answers, in themselves primarily of historical interest, the book tries to throw light on two problems of a more general and contemporary nature: What are the chances for future African political unions? How do the conditions for federation in the underdeveloped world differ from those in Western Europe and North America?

The decision to found the Mali Federation was taken by a few African political leaders. As things turned out, it was a poor or at the very least inadequate decision, based on assumptions, perceptions, and expectations that were out of line with reality. I shall try to show what went wrong: on the one hand what the opportunities for federation actually were, and on the other hand what preconceptions the African politicians held about them.

The Mali Federation grew out of the colonial federation of French West Africa, and both opportunities and preconceptions were in large part determined by the colonial experience. This book will be particularly concerned with the contributions of the colonial period to institutions and patterns of behavior that affected the area's capabilities for federation, and its effect on the way Africans think and act about the whole issue of federation.

A well-worn truism has it that generals are usually best equipped to fight the war that has just ended. The same, alas, is often true of politicians. At the risk of falling into that trap, I hope that this study of the recent past may contain some useful lessons for Africa's future.

The main documentary sources used in this study are African political party programs, records, speeches, and newspapers. In addition, I have relied on regular African and French newspapers and press services, particularly *Afrique Nouvelle, Le Monde,* and *Agence France Presse,* for transcripts and citations of speeches and statements. French and African government publications, particularly the various *Journaux Officiels* and several economic and statistical publications, have been most helpful.

Beyond these written sources, I derived most of my information from interviews and conversations with African, French, and foreign political participants and observers. Because of the unsettled political situation (I began my work in Africa four days after the Mali Federation's breakup), I was unable to employ the systematic interview schedule I had hoped to give to a comparable sample of Senegalese and Soudanese political leaders. My interviews were structured as much as possible, considering the particular person with whom I was talking and the sometimes difficult conditions under which the interview took place. Although I tried to include comparable questions in most interviews, the lack of comparability of contexts in which these questions were brought up prohibited any meaningful statistical presentation of results. To get around this handicap, I did a detailed comparative content analysis of Senegalese and Soudanese party newspaper editorials, the results and methods of which are described in Appendix II. Finally, because of the conditions imposed on many of the interviews and even more in consideration of the use to which such information might be put, I have, as a general rule, not identified my respondents. Similarly, I was granted privileged access to some private, governmental, and party documents not normally available to the public, and have felt obliged not to reveal these sources. I am certain that anyone who has done recent political research in Africa will appreciate the need for such reticence, and I trust that the reader will not object to some statements contained herein which are not supported by specific references.

My field research was made possible by a generous Ford Foundation Area Training Fellowship, and I am grateful to the Foundation and its staff for additional favors and good advice. This study owes much to the teaching, criticism, and advice of Professors Karl W. Deutsch and Harry R. Rudin of Yale University. George Brooks provided needed criticism of Chapter 1, and Nathan Leites dissected and greatly improved Chapters 7 and 8. Gabriel d'Arboussier's reading of the final version saved me from several errors, as did the comments of Claude E. Welch, Jr. I am especially grateful to the Rector and faculty of the University of Dakar and to the directors and staff of the Institut Français d'Afrique Noire in Dakar and its offshoots in Bamako, Ouagadougou, Abidjan, and Porto Novo for living quarters, research facilities, and many hours of pleasurable and profitable conversations.

Jean Ramseier, Patricia Lloyd, and Lavon Saunders typed drafts of various chapters, and Doris Peterson prepared the final manuscript. Ruth Davis has proved an unusually understanding editor. Above all, I owe a vast debt to my wife, Anne-Marie, whose preparation of the index is her smallest contribution to this study.

Finally, I wish to thank the many people of Africa who helped me at all stages of my research, those who answered my interminable questions and those who taught me much in not answering. Although most must remain unnamed in these pages, I shall always remember their hospitality, kindness, and friendship. None of these people or organizations is in any way responsible for the opinions, errors, or shortcomings found in this study. Those are mine.

W. J. F.

New Haven
24 November 1964

Contents

Spellings and Abbreviations

I HAVE, as a general rule, retained the French spelling of proper names, except where the English equivalent is well-known. Thus, I have used Ségou (not Segu) and Ouagadougou (not Wagadugu), but Timbuktu (not Tombouctou). In one case, at least, the spelling makes some difference. I have used "Soudan" and "Soudanese" to refer to the territory formerly known as French Soudan, now the Republic of Mali. "Sudan" and "Sudanese," as used here, refer only to the geographic areas immediately south of the Sahara, stretching from the Atlantic to the Red Sea. At no time does either form refer to the Republic of Sudan, formerly Anglo-Egyptian Sudan.

I use the following abbreviations:

AOF	*Afrique Occidentale Française* (French West Africa)
J.O.	*Journal Officiel*
J.O., A.N.	*Journal Officiel, Assemblée Nationale* (French National Assembly)
J.O., A.U.F.	*Journal Officiel, Assemblée de l'Union Française* (Assembly of the French Union)
J.O., C.R.	*Journal Officiel, Conseil de la République* (French Council of the Republic)
CFA	The West African franc, worth .02 French new francs. Since 1958, approximately 246 CFA francs have equaled one dollar.

1

The Western Sudan and Its Conquerors

"PAYS DE DÉMESURE," the early French explorers called the western bulge of Africa—"A land without limits or order." Limits and order there were, of course, but they were those that nature imposed on man, and only rarely those that man imposed on his environment.[1]

In the Saharan interior and in the coastal forest belt, nature was at its most extreme and inhospitable. The desert was inhabited only by small bands of nomads, mostly Arabs and Berbers mixed with Negroid stock, who drew their rude livelihood from herds of camels, cattle, sheep, or goats. Except around scattered oases, with their date palms and gum trees, agriculture and permanent settlement were unknown. The strongest bond between the Sahara's inhabitants was their common adherence to Islam. Although they acknowledged membership in large tribes, like the Touareg, effective political and social authority was usually exercised by the lineage or nomadic band.

At the other extreme, the rain forest gave rise to discrete and compact settlements of farmers. The poor soils of the forest and the lack of large domestic animals for traction or fertilizer severely limited the range and yield of crops. The dense forest itself restricted contact between close neighbors. Kinship ties and traditions of common descent were the bases of social, political, and religious organization. Even when centralized governmental institutions arose in some areas, political organization was formally just an extension of kinship ties. Not until European trade along the coast provided the means and impetus to unite did great states of forest peoples come into being west of Nigeria.

Between the extremes of desert and rain forest lay the area of high savanna grass and scattered trees known today as the western Sudan. Although the temperatures and the alternating dry and

1. For the geography of the area see Jacques Richard-Molard, *Afrique Occidentale Française* (Paris, Berger-Levrault, 1956).

rainy seasons might have seemed extreme to a European, the Sudanic region offered the greatest opportunities to men with limited technology to experiment with diverse patterns of social and economic organization. Abundant and relatively fertile farmland permitted a variety of crops, and freedom from the tsetse fly of the forest zone allowed complementary herding and farming economies to exist side by side. The relative ease of communications across the grasslands permitted trade to develop. Before the coming of the Europeans, the Sudan gave West Africa what internal communication and unity it possessed.

The basis of the Sudan's trade was the export of gold, hides, and slaves to the Muslim north in exchange for cloth and artisan-manufactured goods and, most important, salt from the Saharan mines.[2] This export trade gave rise to the many great "port" cities on the edge of the Sahara, like Djenne, Timbuktu, and Gao, from which caravans set out for the long journey north to the Mediterranean. South of these cities the routes extended on to Ségou and Bobo-Dioulasso, and down to the trading cities near the forest zone, like Kankan, Kong, and Kumasi, where gold could be procured and goods could be sold in exchange for slaves or kola nuts, an important item in local African trade. The trade within West Africa was carried out almost exclusively by peoples speaking languages belonging to the great Mande family. From the core group of Malinke (or Mandinka) centered in what is now upper Guinea, the Mande family dispersed over a period of several millennia to form distinct ethnic groups which nevertheless preserved similar customs, religious traditions, and languages.[3] The traders, virtually all Muslims, developed a common Mande language for trading purposes which, like the traders themselves, came to be called Dioula. Like the trade routes, this common Mande tradition and the Dioula language gave some basis of unity to the hundreds of ethnic

2. On this trade see E. W. Bovill, *The Golden Trade of the Moors* (London, Oxford University Press, 1958); Raymond Mauny, *Tableau géographique de l'Ouest Africain au Moyen age* (Dakar, IFAN, 1961), pp. 227–441, esp. 426–41; and Benjamin E. Thomas, "Trade Routes of Algeria and the Sahara," *University of California Publications in Geography, 8* (1957), 165–288.

3. On the dispersion of the Mande peoples see George Peter Murdock, *Africa, Its Peoples and Their Culture History* (New York, McGraw-Hill, 1959), pp. 64–77; and M. de Lavergne de Tressan, *Inventaire linguistique de l'Afrique Occidentale Française et du Togo* (Dakar, IFAN, 1953), pp. 167–77 and Carte 9.

groups inhabiting the western bulge of tropical Africa.[4] The trading routes and the Mande cultural sphere extended as far east as the Volta River in present-day Ghana. East of this dividing line, Hausa and Yoruba became the trading languages and the dominant cultural influences.[5] While it would be incorrect to speak of a division of West Africa into different culture areas—the trading systems only rarely dominated the various ethnic groups—the patterns of trade did create certain unifying predispositions which were exploited and reinforced by the builders of multitribal empires.

The Western Sudan's geography facilitated the creation of large-scale political units. Some, like the Mossi kingdom which still exists in present-day Upper Volta, were based on the same principle of ethnic homogeneity that was the dominant mode in the forest zone, although in the Sudan ease of communication permitted a much larger political community under a single political authority than was possible until recently in the coastal region.[6] More important to the development of large-scale political organization, however, was the early growth of the multitribal conquest empire in the Western Sudan. The conquest empires differed from the ethnically homogeneous kingdoms in that they evolved formal techniques for subjugating and administering large and disparate populations. In this, they have particular relevance to the problem of today's Africa. The medieval period, from about the ninth to the sixteenth century, produced three great conquest empires in the Western Sudan—Ghana, Mali, and Songhai—and the nineteenth century gave rise to two others, led by El Hadj Omar and Samory Touré.

The similarities in the structure and organization of the three medieval empires are striking.[7] Each of them was based on a core

4. For a fascinating, though highly speculative, discussion of the religious and social aspects of this tradition see Germaine Dieterlen, "Mythe et organisation sociale au Soudan Français," *Journal de la Société des Africanistes, 25* (1955), 39–76; "Mythe et organisation sociale en Afrique Occidentale," ibid., *29* (1959), 119–38.

5. Roland Oliver and J. D. Fage, *A Short History of Africa* (Baltimore, Penguin Books, 1962), pp. 104–07.

6. Elliott P. Skinner, "An Analysis of the Political Organization of the Mossi People," *Transactions of the New York Academy of Science,* Ser. II, *19* (1956–57), 740–50.

7. On the medieval empires see Mauny, *Tableau géographique;* Maurice Delafosse, *Haut-Sénégal-Niger* (Paris, Larose, 1912), *2;* Cheikh Anta Diop, *L'Afrique Noire pré-coloniale* (Paris, Présence Africaine, 1952); Jean Rouch, "Contribution

ethnic group: the Soninke for Ghana, the Malinke for Mali, and the Songhai for the empire of that name. Under the leadership of a dominant lineage (the Keita of Mali and the Askia of Songhai are among the names that are known), the core ethnic group spread from its native habitat to conquer its neighbors and extend its dominion. We can only guess at the precise reasons for this expansion, but certainly the desire to promote and secure trade, both within West Africa and with North Africa, was a prime motive. Each of these empires was centered around one or more of the main port cities of the Saharan fringe. As the Saharan caravan routes were forced eastward by desert raiders and discovery of new salt mines in the Sahara, so the core of succeeding empires shifted in the same direction. Through trade, the ruling group could accumulate the wealth necessary for peaceful or enforced expansion. The acquisition of cavalry horses from North Africa was particularly important. Furthermore, through its control of the distribution of salt, the government wielded a powerful lever over recalcitrant populations.[8]

Each of the medieval empires owed a considerable debt to Islam.[9] Although the Soninke rulers of Ghana were pagan, trade was largely in the hands of Muslims. The Soninke also relied extensively on the Muslims for councillors, and probably granted them formal administrative positions. The Keita lineage of the Malinke was itself Muslim, and the expansion of the Malinke apparently followed closely on their conversion. Although the Malinke did not impose Islam on their conquered peoples, Islam almost certainly gave both the impulsion and a rationale for Malinke aggrandizement. The Songhai people were more thoroughly Islamized, and it was under their aegis that Timbuktu attained its greatest fame as a center of Islamic culture and learning. Islam also contributed new military techniques, particularly the disciplined horse cavalry.

Finally, Islam, as a universal religion, separated governmental and political roles from tribal religious offices and facilitated the

à l'histoire des Songhay," *Mémoire de l'Institut Français d'Afrique Noire, 29* (Dakar, 1959), 141–259, esp. 179–224; J. S. Trimingham, *A History of Islam in West Africa* (London, Oxford University Press, 1962); and Diedrich Westermann, *Geschichte Afrikas* (Cologne, Greven-Verlag, 1952).

8. M. R. Bloch, "The Social Influence of Salt," *Scientific American, 209* (July 1963), 89–98.

9. Alphonse Gouilly, *L'Islam dans l'Afrique Occidentale Française* (Paris, Larose, 1952), pp. 41–82; J. S. Trimingham, *Islam in West Africa* (London, Oxford University Press, 1959), pp. 138–43.

administration of disparate populations and their inclusion under a central secular authority. This ability to create a bureaucracy for territorial administration gave the medieval empires their strength and durability.

Nevertheless, the empires' territorial administrations were limited in a number of ways. Except for the core ethnic groups, the central government interfered little in local social, religious, economic, or even political procedures.[10] Imperial government imposed the minimum of order necessary for trade, provided a system of settling disputes between different subject peoples, collected taxes, and maintained roads. It did not, so far as one can tell, interfere regularly with the conduct of local affairs or attempt systematic social integration of the diverse peoples. Local communities were left to choose their leaders and to administer their village life according to local customs. By thus limiting interference in their subjects' lives, the conquerors limited causes for revolt. Under the Songhai, the largest and least integrated of the three empires, whole kingdoms continued to exist in a vassal relationship to the central government, whose representative acted more as an influential ambassador than a provincial governor.

A good example of such tenuous control at the periphery of the Mali and Songhai empires was the state of Tekrur in the west.[11] Ruled first by the Muslim Tukulor people, and after about 1350 by the Wolof whose leaders the Tukulor had converted, Tekrur was more a competitor than it was subservient to the larger empires. With independent access to marine salt, but with little gold or trade with the north, Tekrur was strong enough to maintain its individuality, but not to extend itself. To the southeast of the Sudanic empires the Mossi kingdom presented a more formidable obstacle to imperial expansion. Its centralized government was able to mobilize sufficient military strength to discourage invasion, although the kingdom allowed Muslim, Mande-speaking traders to operate across its territory.

10. "The introduction of Islam did not upset the equilibrium of the Sudan states . . . [The emperors] did not attempt to spread it among subjects other than state servants, for that would have meant their downfall. Village life followed the same pattern as before." Trimingham (1959), p. 139. See also Trimingham (1962), pp. 34–37.

11. André Villard, *Histoire du Sénégal* (Dakar, Maurice Viale, 1942), pp. 37–52; and Kurt Wolff "Die Entstehung der frühen ful-staaten in Senegambien," *Beiträge zur Gesellungs– und Völkerwissenschaft: Professor Dr. Richard Thurnwald zu zeinen Achtzigsten Geburtsdag gewidmet* (Berlin, Gebr. Mann, 1950), pp. 435–45.

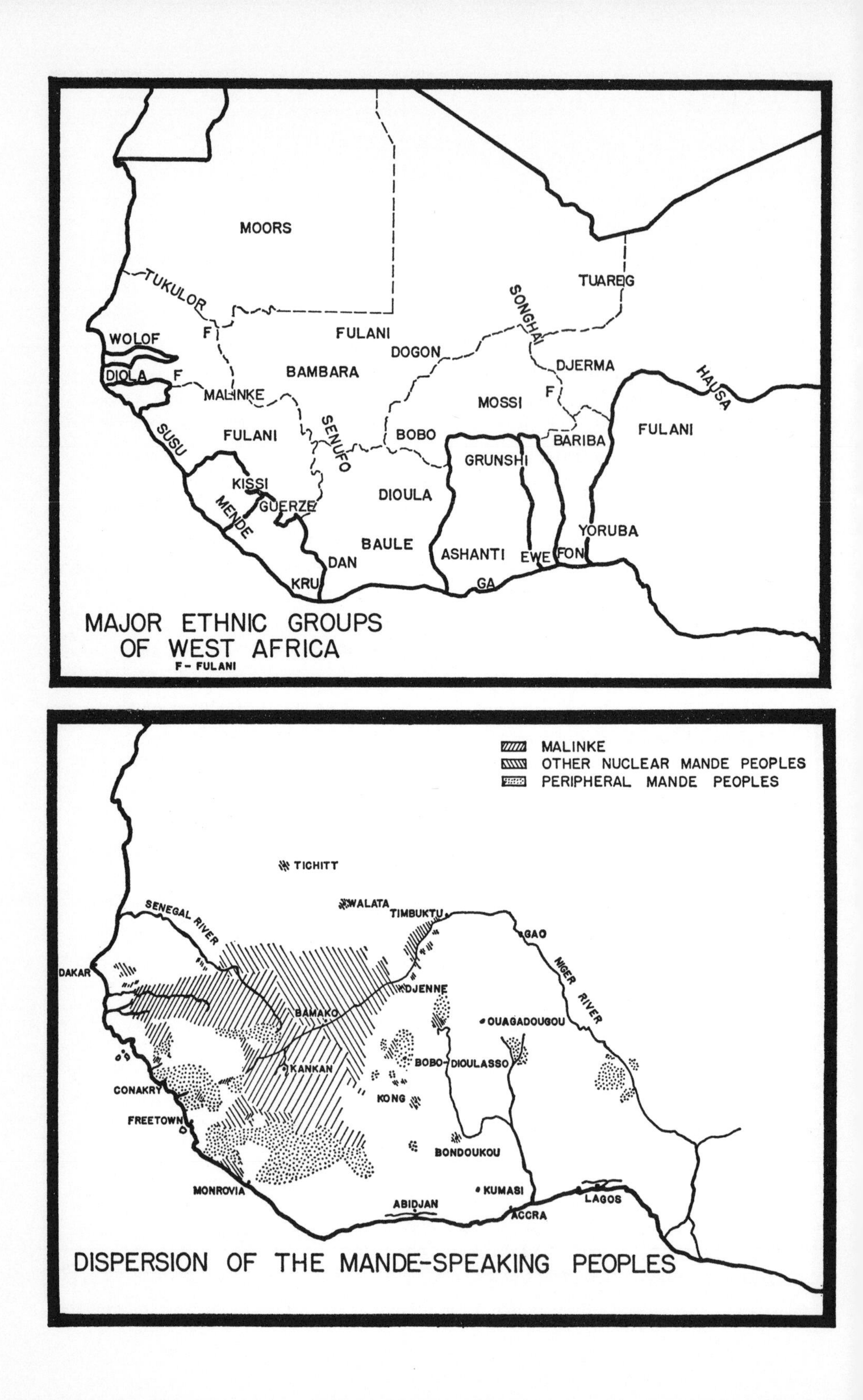
MOORS
TUKULOR
TUAREG
SONGHAI
WOLOF
F
FULANI
DOGON
DIOLA
BAMBARA
DJERMA
HAUSA
MALINKE
MOSSI
SUSU
FULANI
SENUFO
BOBO
BARIBA
FULANI
GRUNSHI
KISSI
MENDE
GUERZE
DIOULA
YORUBA
BAULE
DAN
ASHANTI
EWE
FON
KRU
GA
MAJOR ETHNIC GROUPS OF WEST AFRICA
F - FULANI
MALINKE
OTHER NUCLEAR MANDE PEOPLES
PERIPHERAL MANDE PEOPLES
TICHITT
WALATA
TIMBUKTU
SENEGAL RIVER
GAO
NIGER RIVER
DAKAR
DJENNE
BAMAKO
OUAGADOUGOU
KANKAN
BOBO-DIOULASSO
CONAKRY
KONG
FREETOWN
BONDOUKOU
MONROVIA
KUMASI
ABIDJAN
LAGOS
ACCRA
DISPERSION OF THE MANDE-SPEAKING PEOPLES

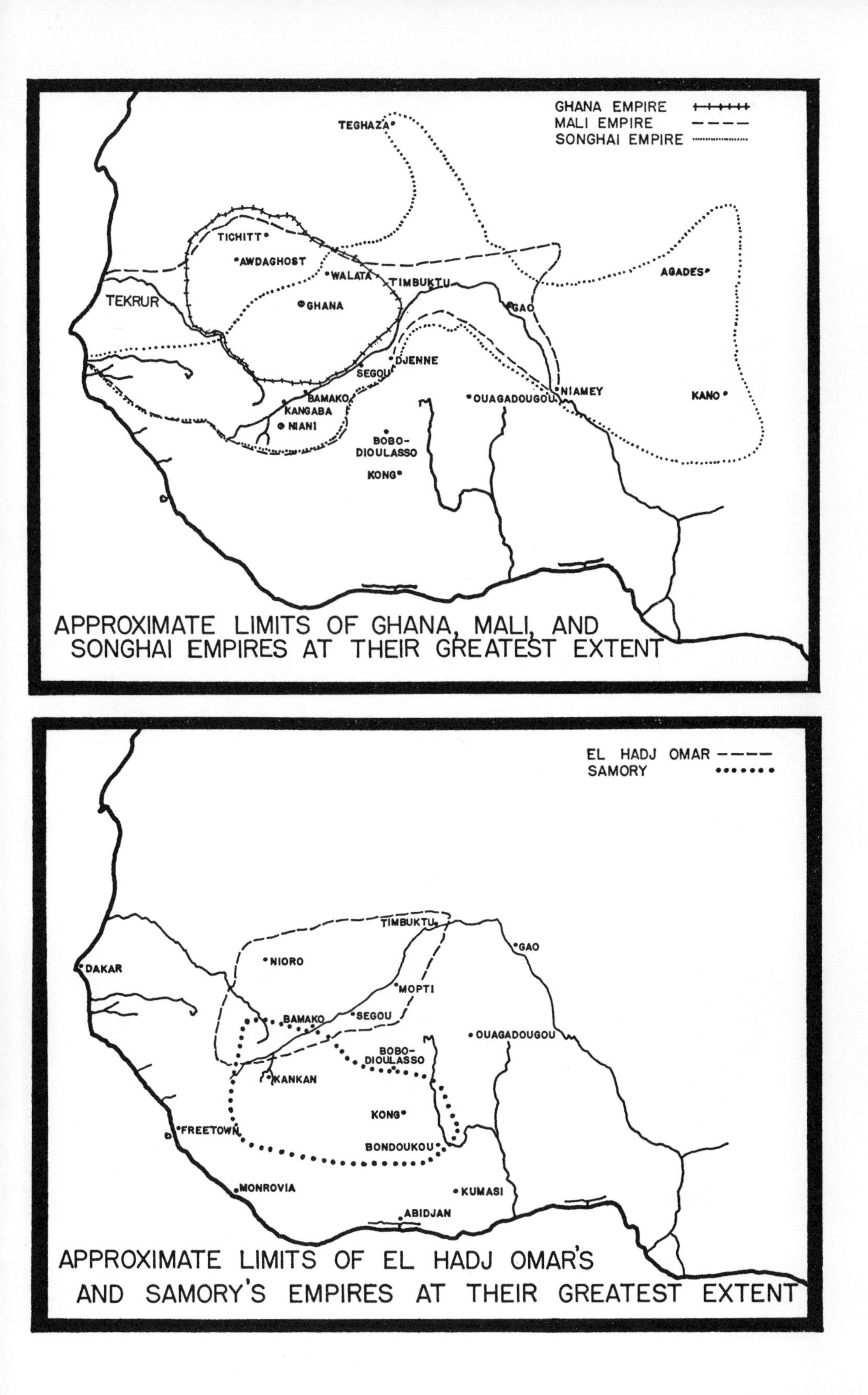

APPROXIMATE LIMITS OF GHANA, MALI, AND SONGHAI EMPIRES AT THEIR GREATEST EXTENT

APPROXIMATE LIMITS OF EL HADJ OMAR'S AND SAMORY'S EMPIRES AT THEIR GREATEST EXTENT

A Moroccan invasion in 1591 ended the Songhai empire which soon broke up into its component tribal groups or small, warring states. By this time the trans-Sahara trade had already begun to decline under pressure from the coastal trade, and the caravan routes shifted eastward to Hausaland and the Lake Chad area. No new conquest empires arose in the Western Sudan until the nineteenth century. By that time, however, political organization had new complexities to contend with. Europeans controlled much of the coast and at isolated points were moving into the interior. New tribal states had arisen in the forest zone, and the greatest volume of trade flowed toward the coast, rather than across the Sahara. Gunpowder had replaced the horse as the most potent military weapon.

The first "modern" attempt at a multitribal empire west of Nigeria was that of the Tukulor, El Hadj Omar Tall.[12] A man of considerable learning and ferocious piety, El Hadj Omar used his religious prestige to mobilize Muslims from a wide area of West Africa. After his return from a pilgrimage to Mecca, he went to the Fouta Djallon in northern Guinea where he opened a school and military training center, drawing mainly Tukulor and Fulani, but also Muslims of many tribes. From this base he set out to spread Islam among the pagans and to fight the white interloper. He was more successful in the first than in the second. At its height in 1862 the Omarian empire reached from near the present-day Mali-Senegal border to Timbuktu and Bandiagara. Despite his Tukulor origins, Omar was unable to extend his empire to the Senegalese area, even to the Fouta Toro, the Tukulor's homeland. The Wolof of Senegal had long been in contact with the French—some were even agents of French trading companies—and wanted no interference from anyone they regarded as an outsider, even for the cause of Islam. The Tukulor contributed men and money to the cause, but their rulers were careful to keep Omar at arm's length politically.[13]

12. This account is based principally on Delafosse, 2, 305–38; Gouilly, pp. 72–76, and Westermann, pp. 112–16. See also John D. Hargreaves, *Prelude to the Partition of West Africa* (New York: St. Martin's Press, 1963), pp. 9–14, 121–25. Further east, Hausaland had been conquered by the Fulani leader, Usuman dan Fodio, whose jihad was a precursor of Omar's. Omar had visited the Fulani capital of Sokoto and married the daughter of Usuman's son.

13. Hargreaves, pp. 12, 102. The Tukulor colonies that Omar's armies left strewn along its path of conquest have for the most part become integrated into the local population and have today few contacts with their homeland.

Until his death in 1864 El Hadj Omar was never at peace. His insistence on reorganizing his conquered lands on territorial rather than tribal principles, and the social disruption resulting from enforced conversion of pagan peoples, provoked revolt after revolt—occasionally aided by the French. Omar conquered no new trade routes that would not otherwise have been open to him and his people, and although he relied heavily on the slave trade to provide him with military equipment, he left such matters to the already established trading groups. It is possible that, given enough time, the spread of Islam would have provided a solid base for a long-lasting empire, although it must be noted that many established Muslim groups reacted as violently as did the pagans against Omar's rule. In any case, French conquest prevented the experiment from taking place. At his death El Hadj Omar's empire was divided among his sons, who added their family quarrels to the already confused course of empire.

The empire that the Malinke, Samory Touré, founded in the second half of the nineteenth century had much in common with El Hadj Omar's.[14] Like the Tukulor conqueror, Samory battled in the name of Islam, although for Samory this may have been more a tactical appreciation of Islam's charismatic power than a matter of deep conviction. Like Omar, Samory started out in northeastern Guinea, but while the Omarian path of conquest was along the Niger River trading axis, Samory headed east along the trade routes of the Dioulas who supported and profited from Samory's activities. Like Omar's army, Samory's was based on a nucleus of his own countrymen, and also picked up recruits through the area of its operations. Samory, too, divided his conquered territories into territorial administrative districts, not tribal units, under Muslim almamys who, like their leader, backed their military power with religious fervor. The shifts from ethnic to cross-tribal territorial units and from tolerance of local political and religious customs to the imposition of centralized direction by a reforming conqueror most clearly distinguish the nineteenth-century empires from their medieval precursors.[15]

14. This account is based primarily on André Arcin, *Histoire de la Guinée Française* (Paris: Challamel, 1911), pp. 123–28 and passim; L. G. Binger, *Du Niger au Golfe de Guinée par le pays de Kong et le Mossi (1887–1889)* (Paris, Hachette, 1892), passim; and Delafosse, 2, 341–51.

15. It should be noted, however, that neither Omar's nor Samory's empire was, properly speaking, a theocratic state. As Watt observed, "It must be emphasized

Finally, like Omar, Samory was continually at war against recalcitrant chiefdoms and finally against the French, who became his dominant problem. Alternately conciliating and attacking him for twenty years, the French drove Samory further and further east before capturing him and destroying his army in 1898. The destruction of Samory Touré's power removed the last serious obstacle to French control.

The main thrust of French penetration was along the Senegal river from their historic base in St. Louis.[16] The French had steadily expanded their trading operations up the Senegal throughout the nineteenth century, and it was along this axis that the French colonial armies marched to the Niger at Bamako, where they fanned out along the major Dioula trading routes. At the same time smaller forces penetrated inland from coastal bases in Guinea, the Ivory Coast, and Dahomey to link up in the Sudanic interior, leaving the coastal colonies of Sierra Leone, the Gambia, and the Gold Coast in the hands of the British. By the end of the nineteenth century the French colonial armies had carved out a new conquest empire in West Africa.

French conquest and administration of West Africa brought drastic changes in political organization. The "assimilation policy" that France sought initially to apply assumed that the greatest good French rule could bring to the backward peoples of Africa was to make Frenchmen of them, and that imperial expansion found its ultimate justification in France's *mission civilisatrice*.[17]

---

that [the empires of El Hadj Omar and Samory], though properly called Islamic states (since the authority of the ruler was based not on animism but on his qualifications, charismatic or otherwise, as a Muslim), owed little of their organization to Islam. . . . The acceptance of Islam did not involve the acceptance of any political system which could at once be put into operation in West Africa." W. Montgomery Watt, *Islam and the Integration of Society* (London, Routledge, 1961), pp. 134–35. Gouilly, p. 78, states that both conquerors were inspired vaguely by the government of the Ottoman empire, but produces no evidence.

16. For an interesting viewpoint on this path of conquest, see Richard-Molard, pp. xii–xiii. Hargreaves' *Prelude to Partition* provides the best discussion of the conquest and division of West Africa between the European powers.

17. Among the vast literature on the assimilation policy, see Raymond F. Betts, *Assimilation and Association in French Colonial Theory (1890–1914)* (New York, Columbia University Press, 1961); L. G. Cowan, *Local Government in West Africa* (New York, Columbia University Press, 1958), pp. 36–61; R. L. Buell, *The Native Problem in Africa* (New York, Macmillan, 1928), *1*, 946–1001, *2*, 77–96; Hubert Deschamps, *Méthodes et doctrines coloniales de la France* (Paris, Colin, 1953); Robert Delavignette, *Freedom and Authority in French West Africa* (London, Oxford University Press for the International African Institute, 1950).

France planned ultimately to integrate its African charges fully into the French political system as soon as they were culturally ready to accept the privileges and responsibilities of full French citizenship. With this in mind the agents of French colonial rule felt little concern to preserve the traditional system of political authority within the areas they acquired, and in many places simply removed the traditional rulers above the village level or let the office disappear with the incumbent's death.

As many Frenchmen with colonial experience were aware, the policy of assimilation was unlikely to stand the test of large-scale colonization in Africa.[18] It was one thing to accord modern representative institutions to the inhabitants of Senegalese coastal settlements, some of whose families had been in contact with the French for two hundred years; it was quite another to attempt to make good Parisians or Marseillais out of several million Africans from the interior. Accordingly, by the time the French thought of establishing permanent administrative institutions in the vast interior regions, the policy of assimilation was replaced by the more supple policy of "association" which retained some of the indigenous authority structure while integrating it into the structure of the colonial administration.[19] While the association policy did not make Frenchmen of Africans, it did destroy traditional society as a focus for political integration. In part this resulted from the persistence of assimilationist modes of thought in the men both in Paris and Africa who made and applied colonial policy;[20] in part it resulted from the sincere attachment to the ideals of assimilation

18. See the attack on assimilation by Jules Harmand, *Domination et Colonisation* (Paris, Flammarion, 1910). Some French intellectuals also attacked assimilation on the grounds that science had shown the primitive mind to be incapable of assimilating modern civilization. See Lucien Lévy-Bruhl, *Les Fonctions mentales dans les sociétés inférieures* (Paris, Alcan, 1910).

19. Association became the official policy after World War I. The best exposition of the association policy in practice under the Third Republic is Delavignette's *Freedom and Authority*.

20. As one contemporary critic of French colonial policy charged, "The word assimilation has disturbed the assimilationists in recent years, and so they have thought up another, 'association' . . . But what do they mean by it? . . . There is no doubt that the secret views of the 'associationists' are very close to those of the 'assimilationists.'" Louis Vignon, *Un Programme de politique coloniale* (Paris, Hachette, 1919), pp. 201–02, cited Cowan, *Local Government*, p. 43. Wistful traces of assimilationist sentiment could still be detected in the speech of former Minister of Overseas France, Paul-Henri Teitgen, on African affairs, March 20, 1956, *J.O., A.N. Débats*, p. 1072.

by some members of the African elite who had been favored by the old policy.[21] More immediately, it resulted from the French attempt to impose a uniform and efficient administrative structure on a vast country with widely different forms of indigenous political authority.

The delineation of administrative boundaries was the source of much difficulty. The French divided every colony into between fifteen and thirty *cercles* each under the direct control of a French administrator. The *cercles* were in turn divided into subdivisions, each also under a Frenchman. The major geographic and administrative unit within which native authorities were allowed to function was the next smallest unit, the canton. Although intended to reflect some ethnic or geographic homogeneity, in practice the canton reflected principally the convenience of the occupying power. This was especially evident in the regions near the coast where populations were most ethnically mixed and where long European presence had broken down traditional areas of authority, but was frequently the case also in the Sudanic regions. The first cantons created in the Sudan were based on the administrative areas established by the empires of Samory and El Hadj Omar. As we have seen, however, these divisions were themselves arbitrary, and at the time of the French conquest they neither had real meaning for the majority of the populations involved nor reflected an accepted political community. Only in areas where pure tribal influence remained great—either because of the remoteness of the region, the intrinsic strength of preexisting institutions, or simply the fortunes of conquest—did the canton have any true meaning. Examples of this are the Mossi state in Upper Volta, the Saharan tribes, and to a lesser extent the Fulani regions of Macina in Soudan and the Fouta Djallon in Guinea. In most places, while the French were able to impose an African "chief" on a canton, he had little or no support from indigenous tradition. Although he might be of upper or even noble caste, and personally a dynamic and intelligent individual, he was not regarded by the populations under his control as being chief by any right other than that of French conquest.

This problem persisted even at the village level. For a variety of reasons, the legitimate chief was seldom brought forth and presented to the conqueror. Usually a younger man or an elder of in-

21. This was certainly the case of the Senegalese who occupied subaltern positions in the administration of the interior regions.

ferior caste or status was put up by the people themselves as a "straw chief" to deal with the white man and be invested as chief.[22] Even where the real chief was presented to the French, he was frequently discarded in favor of a younger man known to them, even if only as an interpreter or houseboy. The resultant confusion or division of authority so weakened the chiefs that the French generally responded by incorporating all the chiefs into the administrative structure, appointing them to tours of duty sometimes in areas far from their place of birth, and indeed, in Senegal where the deviation from tradition was most marked, giving them regular civil service grades through which they progressed as they gained experience in their duties or rendered significant services to the state.[23]

Aside from a few ephemeral *conseils des notables* set up to advise French administrators and a generally unsatisfactory attempt to include chiefs in a territorial legislature in Senegal, the French never established regular machinery for traditional rulers to participate in political decisions (such as the Houses of Chiefs in the Gold Coast and Nigeria). The only regular participation of traditional political figures in colonial political affairs was as local administrative agents for the colonizing power charged with collecting taxes, choosing men for the *corvée* (obligatory communal labor on public works projects), administering a foreign judicial code, and the other unpleasant aspects of colonial administration.

The French administrative system thus effectively undercut the use of preexisting traditional political units as major bases for political activity during the colonial period. Only in rare cases, like that of the Mossi where early agreement was reached with a solidly entrenched chief, or like the Saharan tribes, which the French (like most of their African successors) left strictly alone, did a tribal unit continue to exercise significant political functions.[24] By interfering thus on the local level, in a manner quite contrary to

22. Delavignette, *Freedom and Authority*, pp. 71–78.

23. Buell, *The Native Problem*, *1*, pp. 990–91.

24. Under the French Fourth Republic some individual chiefs successfully transferred a heritage of chiefly authority to electoral backing for their activities within the arena of territorial politics. This did not mean, however, a return to the tribal level as a focus for political organization, as did, for example, the political activities of the Ashanti chiefs in Ghana before and immediately after independence. If the chiefs ran for public office they did so at the territorial not the local level and, at the most, represented the interests of a particular ethnic group within the greater context of territorial politics.

that of the medieval empires, the French continued the dissolution of traditional political life that El Hadj Omar and Samory had begun. Omar and Samory interfered in the name of Islam, France in the name of its own *mission civilisatrice.*

Nor did French rule give Islam the politically unifying role it had played indirectly under the medieval empires and more directly under the Muslim governors of Samory and Omar. French colonization did, certainly, create conditions favoring the spread of Islam among the masses, principally by promoting trade controlled by Muslims and the growth of an urban population cut off from traditional religious life.[25] However, the colonial administrative structure broke down the association of religious and governmental structures in Muslim areas and destroyed the temporal political power of the almamys. Having won much of their empire by defeating Islamic conquerors, the French were in no mood to continue the political privileges of Muslim rulers.[26] Furthermore, many French administrators viewed the problem of Islamic rulers in the perspective of the anticlerical fight of the Third Republic and sought to impose a separation of church and state in Africa. As a result, the Muslim political authorities were downgraded in favor of the cantonal chiefs, while those who operated or were persuaded to operate outside the political realm met with little interference. Indeed, where the system of cantonal chiefs proved particularly weak, as in Senegal, the French frequently used the Muslim authorities as agents of social control over their followers. In return, the cooperative marabouts, as the Muslim religious leaders are known, were given substantial symbolic and financial rewards by the colonial authorities and frequently developed intense loyalties to the colonial regime.[27] Because of their loyalty to France, and also

25. As an estimate, probably over one half of French West Africa was Muslim by the end of the colonial regime, as compared to about 30 per cent in 1900. See also Vincent Monteil, "L'Islam noir en Afrique," *Le Monde,* June 14, 1960. On reasons for Islam's growth, see Gouilly, pp. 239–44 and Trimingham (1959), pp. 190–92. As M. Gosselin has observed for the Soudan, "The acquisition of the status of city-dweller is accompanied by a formal conversion to Islam." "Bamako, ville soudanaise moderne," *L'Afrique et l'Asie, 21* (1953), 36.

26. The French military who had primary responsibility for organizing the colonies in the early days were particularly vehement against Islam. See L. G. Binger, *Le Péril de l'Islam* (Paris, Hachette, 1906), and the biography of Colonel Archinard, E. Requin, *Archinard et le Soudan* (Paris, Berger-Levrault, 1946), p. 166.

27. As one of the great marabouts of the early twentieth century, El Hadj Malick Sy, urged his followers, "Give your total allegiance to the French Government. . . . God had chosen them to protect our person and our property." Cited in Paul Marty, *Etudes sur l'Islam au Sénégal* (Paris, Leroux, 1917), *1,* 208–09.

because of the rivalries between Islamic sects and between individual marabouts, the Muslim leaders never banded together into a cohesive political force to attempt to recreate a political unity based on common allegiance to Islam. Nor, later, did they lend their religious support to secular nationalists who sought to unite against the French. When under the Fourth Republic some did dabble in politics, they did so usually within the context of existing territorial political movements and almost always from behind the scenes. No more than tribal or local sentiment was Islam able to provide a basis for a new political community during the colonial period.

For better or for worse, French conquest destroyed the fragile preexisting bases for political community in West Africa. Although, as we shall see, factors like ethnic identification, religion, and trading links continued subtly to influence the development of political unity in West Africa, the political and administrative system that the French imposed has to this day been the primary determinant of the organization of political power in French-speaking West Africa.

2

Political Organization in French West Africa

The Third Republic

At the end of the nineteenth century France's West African holdings consisted of four coastal settlements—Senegal, Guinea, the Ivory Coast, and Dahomey—separated one from the other and united principally by coastal steamer, and a vast hinterland initially under military command. These coastal territories were governed by civilian administrators reporting directly to Paris and assisted in their decisions by an informal council of subordinate administrators, representatives of the local Chamber of Commerce (a semiofficial organization in each territory that throughout the colonial period exercised considerable influence on governmental policy) and whatever local notables the governor considered advantageous or politic to include.

The first serious modification of this system came in 1895, when a governor-general was appointed to St. Louis to oversee the organization and administration of all the West African possessions. Initially his presence had little effect on the autonomy of the individual colonies, given the primitive state of communications, and it was not until the reforms of 1902–05 that the federation became an administrative and political reality. The crucial step was the promulgation of a constitution for French West Africa (AOF) which gave the governor-general the power to raise money for the federal government by taxing the imports and exports of the individual territories.[1] By this and subsequent decrees, the interior land was established as a vast colony bearing the name Haut-Sénégal-Niger, later shortened to French Soudan, with its capital in Bamako, flanked on the west by the colony of Mauretania administered from St. Louis and on the east by the military district of Niger which became a full colony in 1922. Their interior borders were altered several times under the Third Republic, notably by

1. Decree of October 18, 1904.

the creation in 1919 of the predominantly Mossi state of Upper Volta, and its subsequent division between the Ivory Coast, Niger, and Soudan in 1932.

The 1904 constitution and the decrees of March 30 and April 20, 1925, established the basic form of colonial government for French West Africa. The regimes under which each of the colonies was governed differed according to circumstances, but the relations between the colonies and the federal and "greater French" levels were similar. Each colony was headed by a lieutenant governor (after 1937 he became a full-fledged governor) "under the high authority of the Governor-General."[2] Except in Senegal, the lieutenant governor was assisted by a *Conseil d'Administration* with only advisory powers. This Council was composed of appointed senior civil servants, and in the Ivory Coast, Dahomey, Guinea, and Soudan included unofficial representatives chosen by the colony's Chamber of Commerce and by a restricted African electorate. The electorate, aside from the cantonal and provincial chiefs, consisted of Africans with five years' service in the administration, licensed traders, and owners of urban property or large rural holdings. In 1939 these categories were further liberalized to include veterans of the colonial army and holders of certain licenses. Thus, despite the limitations on the Council's power, it did draw those categories of Africans most likely to exercise influence in a modern setting into some sort of regularized relationship with government on the territorial level.[3]

For Niger and Mauretania this Council was composed entirely of official members. Senegal was under a more complicated regime. The four coastal communes, St. Louis, Dakar, Gorée, and Rufisque, had been granted limited self-government in the 1870s. Their elected representatives, along with those chosen by the administration-appointed chiefs of the interior populations, formed the Colonial Council with quasi-legislative powers over financial matters, like those of a French department's *Conseil Général.* Except for Senegal the colonies were in no sense self-governing units. The "governments" of the colonies were, like the *cercles* with their com-

2. Ibid., Article 6.

3. Lord Hailey, *An African Survey* (London, Oxford University Press, 1938), p. 201. Cowan, *Local Government*, pp. 52–53, points out that this electorate was in fact more extensive than that of the local government councils in the British territories, although the latter enjoyed more real power of decision.

mandant and advisory group of notables, part and parcel of an administrative system with its headquarters in Paris.

Immediately superior to the lieutenant governors in this hierarchy was the governor-general of the federation. He alone in West Africa was the "repository of the Republic's powers" and alone had the right to correspond with Paris.[4] Every right the territorial administration possessed was a delegation of the governor-general's powers, and he accordingly had the right to intervene at any level he saw fit. Since, with few exceptions, the governor-general was a man of considerably greater prestige and ability than his subordinates, his effective power was enormous. Like his subordinates, he was assisted by a purely consultative body, the *Conseil de Gouvernement,* whose advice he was never obliged to accept; in fact most of this Council's work was done by its permanent commission, composed entirely of the governor-general's own men. The governor-general's position between Paris and the individual colonies was of the utmost strategic importance for a vigorous administrator. No ministerial decree could be put into effect in West Africa without his promulgating an *arrêté d'application* explaining the circumstances in which it was applicable and indicating, as specifically as he saw fit, how it was to be put into effect. Likewise, no colonial budget could be submitted to Paris without his approval.

The governor-general's power was further consolidated by the system of taxation. Under the 1904 decree all indirect taxes (customs, export taxes, port charges, excise taxes, as well as receipts from federal services such as the post office) went to Dakar. This meant that the individual colonies had to rely on direct taxes on real estate, cattle, and the like, which, particularly in the interior with its poor populations and high administrative overhead, left them dependent on rebates from the federal government for most public works funds. The governor-general controlled the treasury, and men like Roume (1902–08), Van Vollenhoven (1917–18), and Carde (1923–30) used their position to call the tune throughout the federation.

According to the Third Republic's constitution, final decision-making power on all matters concerning the colonies—as concerning France—lay with the French Chamber of Deputies; however,

4. Decree of October 18, 1904, Article 2.

this power was usually delegated to the Colonial Minister, who could rule by decree. The Colonial Minister was assisted in his deliberations by a *Conseil Supérieur des Colonies* (after 1937 the *Conseil Supérieur de la France d'Outre-Mer*) with the same advisory powers as the councils assisting the governor-general and the lieutenant governors. The Superior Council was composed of representatives elected by the French citizens and a few native notables from each colony, the senators and deputies of those colonies with parliamentary representation, and several nominated members representing metropolitan and colonial commercial interests. Since most of the colonial representatives were linked to the major commercial interests, and many were permanent residents in Paris with only tenuous ties with the colony they represented, commercial interests dominated the Superior Council. In West Africa the major counter influence was that of the governor-general, who spoke usually in the name of administrative efficiency.

Although the Superior Council had only advisory powers, its importance was greatly increased by the instability of tenure of the Colonial Minister, whose post was "almost invariably viewed . . . as an unwelcome *pis aller*, the alternative to being excluded altogether from the Cabinet."[5] Thus, although the Minister was never bound to accept the Superior Council's recommendation, there were few men with enough tenure in office or real interest in colonial problems to buck the wishes of the commercial interests in the Council. The example of one African deputy from West Africa, Blaise Diagne, the representative of the Senegalese communes from 1914 until 1934, is particularly instructive. Originally violently opposed by the commercial interests, Diagne soon found that his personal policies could best be advanced by cooperating with them so as to obtain reciprocal advantages within the Superior Council, something which won him the opprobrium of many African intellectuals.[6] Against these colonial commercial interests, the governor-general of the federation was the only man with the prestige and access to the Minister to maintain a different point of view, should he care to.

The Third Republic thus united French West Africa under a

5. S. H. Roberts, *History of French Colonial Policy* (*1870–1925*) (London, King, 1929), p. 644.

6. Buell, *The Native Problem, 1,* 956, and oral information.

complex political hierarchy, but one which operated virtually without African political participation and indeed almost without reference to the Africans' wishes or needs. Most Africans had no chance to participate in government and indeed were but little affected by the colonial political order, usually only by demands the system made upon them.[7] Traditional political authority had been weakened or distorted, and little had been put in its place. Where tribal or village allegiance remained strong, it represented primarily allegiance to a social, not a political, order. If a focus for political loyalties was open to the Africans, it was that of a "Greater France," a distant, vague idea unlikely to survive the shock of increased direct African participation in the political process.[8]

From the Third to the Fourth Republic

The Third Republic had not offered significant opportunities for Africans to participate in politics, but it had begun the training of a potential nationalist elite. Although educational opportunities were meager compared with those in most of British West Africa, 71,000 students were in schools of some sort in French West Africa by 1938. This represented a mere 3.2 per cent of potential students, but they were concentrated in the urban areas, and particularly in Senegal, Dahomey, and the Ivory Coast, where they were able to acquire positions demanding modern skills both in the administration and in private business. While very few French West Africans attended university in France before World War II, many more attended the federal Ecole Normale William-Ponty, near Dakar,

7. The importance of the experience of political participation for the establishment of political loyalties is amply illustrated by the four Senegalese communes. Unlike tribal units or rural villages the communes early developed distinct and often separatist political sentiments. Although their municipal government was dominated by the old inhabitants of the towns, Wolof and *métis* in St. Louis, and Lébou in Dakar and Rufisque, government and political organization was neither tribally nor traditionally based. These communes have played in French West Africa the politically separatist role played by tribal political units under the British system of indirect rule.

8. As a measure of the attraction and difficulties of full incorporation into the "Greater French" political community, it is significant that at the end of the interwar period few more than 2,000 West Africans had availed themselves of the privilege of exchanging subject status for French citizenship. The term "Greater France" enjoyed considerable popularity among the most ardent advocates of French colonial expansion. See Joseph Chailley-Bert, "La France et la Plus Grande France," *Revue politique et parlémentaire* (August 1902), pp. 230–62.

which trained teachers, civil servants, and African assistant doctors. Ponty granted only about 2,000 degrees between 1918 and 1945, but it was very much the "nerve center" of the new African elite. As Leopold Senghor and Modibo Keita noted in 1959, "All the [French West] African elite for the last half century have received the same training. Whatever may have been their origin, all the *cadres* of the former colonial civil service went through William Ponty. This experience of rubbing shoulders together has created strong ties, a single will, and common aspirations."[9] Alumni associations of Ponty students were formed throughout the federation and provided natural forums for unofficial political discussion and for the development of leaders in every territory. Participation in the federal civil service, in the African corps of the French army, and in the veterans' organizations provided other means of association and fundamental training in modern skills for a new elite.

The Popular Front government of Léon Blum gave impetus to these associations, and leftist Frenchmen frequently provided new leadership and guidance.[10] The Popular Front government also permitted the formation of the first labor unions which, although hedged about with formidable restrictions (an elementary school diploma was required for membership) again permitted organization of an African elite.[11] Although the Vichy government prohibited all such suspect organizations in 1940, they burgeoned again after the Free French forces took over in 1943. The *Groupes d'Etudes Communistes,* with sections in all the major West African cities, reestablished contact between the African elite and the French Left. A decree of August 7, 1944, abolished the literacy requirement for union membership, and two years later the Labor Inspectorate of French West Africa registered 175 trade unions.[12]

9. Modibo Keita and Leopold Senghor, "Conférence de Presse" (Paris, May 21, 1959, mimeo.), p. 3. See also Thomas Hodgkin and Ruth Schachter, "French-Speaking West Africa in Transition," *International Conciliation,* No. 528 (May 1960), 385.

10. As one Vichy administrator for the Soudan reported disapprovingly in 1941, "During the last years of the republican regime, committees of popular union (*rassemblement populaire*) developed in centers such as Kayes, Toukouto, Bamako and Ségou—and also Communist committees—in which Europeans and natives sat side by side. . . . In 1937 a section of the Communist-line Republican Association of Veterans functioned in Bamako, organizing the former native soldiers." (Private source.)

11. Decree of March 11, 1937.

12. E. J. Berg, "French West Africa" in Walter Galenson, ed., *Labor and Economic Development* (New York, Wiley, 1959), p. 205.

By the end of the Second World War the political climate of French West Africa, like that of France, had changed radically. The development of an educated African elite combined with the anticolonialist tenor of pronouncements like the Atlantic Charter and the liberal euphoria of victory over the Nazis made it impossible to return to a regime like that of the Third Republic.[13] The conference of colonial administrators and "technicians" called at Brazzaville early in 1944 set the liberal tone for the establishment of new political rights, although the ultimate right—to independence—was ruled out.[14] While explicitly denying the label, French colonial thinking was still functioning within a vague, renovated assimilationist perspective in which all political and especially executive power would still emanate from the government in Paris, although African assemblies would be permitted to discuss matters of local economic—not political—interest. The basic principle admitted was that Africans should be granted increased representation in the councils in Paris.

Pursuant to the Brazzaville agreements, West Africa sent five delegates to the two constitutional conventions of 1945–46. Initially, the argument over Africa's political institutions was framed in terms of assimilation versus association on the political level, and centralization versus decentralization on the administrative level. In fact, as became clear both at Brazzaville and at the two constitutional conventions, these categories of thought were now outmoded. Liberal administrators like Félix Eboué and Africans like the canton chief, Fily Dabo Sissoko, made it perfectly clear that pure assimilation could not even be considered by the Africans, and younger members of the educated African elite insisted that association, with its connotations of perpetuating old administrative elites, could not continue either.[15] Administrative organization could no longer be separated from political organization. The conflict was thus transposed to that of the unitary state as against some form of federalism, and around this issue much of the

13. *Le Rassemblement Démocratique Africain dans la lutte anti-impérialiste* (Paris, 1948), pp. 12–13.

14. *La Conférence Africaine-Française, Brazzaville, 30 janvier–8 février, 1944* (Algiers, 1945), p. 35.

15. Félix Eboué, *La Nouvelle politique indigène pour l'AEF*, text found as appendix to Jean La Roche and Jean Gottmann, *La Fédération Française* (Montreal, 1945). Fily Dabo Sissoko, communiqué in *La Conférence Africaine-Française, Brazzaville*, pp. 95–101.

debate of the constitutional conventions took place. In general, the parties of the right favored reinforcing the *République une et indivisible* while those of the left, supported by the African delegates, fought for a federal structure. The resulting compromise settled few problems and satisfied no one, although each side saw a possibility for the system to evolve in his preferred direction.[16]

The system of political representation elaborated by the Fourth Republic's Constitution was an extension to the rest of the West African territories of the privileges enjoyed by Senegal before the war. Each territory was granted a territorial assembly with power to raise and dispose of territorial revenue, but the French governor held the executive power and French citizens chose a fixed minority of the members. Senegal continued to enjoy special privileges by choosing its territorial assembly on a single electoral roll. Each territory also elected directly two or three deputies to the National Assembly in Paris, and the territorial assemblies chose representatives (*sénateurs*) to the Council of the Republic and councillors to the Assembly of the French Union. This last organ, originally conceived by the "federalists" as the great decision-making body for the French Union, was in fact virtually powerless, being granted only the right of debate with the possibility of formulating *voeux*, or suggestions, which the National Assembly was not required to accept. The territorial assemblies also chose delegates to the Grand Council of French West Africa which would have legislative power over interterritorial receipts and expenses analogous to that of the territorial assemblies over territorial financial and budgetary questions. As at the territorial level, all executive power was to remain in the hands of the French administration in the person of the governor-general.[17]

16. It will be recalled that the constitution won a bare majority of adherents in the October 1946 referendum and was actually rejected by the voters of Overseas France. Michel Devèze, *La France d'Outre-Mer 1938–1947* (Paris, Hachette, 1948), pp. 221–70, and Gordon Wright, *The Reshaping of French Democracy* (New York, Reynal and Hitchcock, 1948), pp. 99–230, give good accounts of the activities of the constitution makers and the problems of elaborating a statute for the overseas possessions.

17. On the territorial assemblies, see P. F. Gonidec, "Les Assemblées locales des territoires d'outre-mer," *Revue juridique et politique de l'Union Française, 6* (1952), 317–55, and *6* (1953), 443–91. On the Grand Council, Robert Bourcart, *Le Grand Conseil de l'Afrique Occidentale Française* (thesis, University of Paris, 1955). The best general study in English is K. E. Robinson, "The Public Law of Overseas France Since the War," *Journal of Comparative Legislation, 32* (1950), 37–57.

Africans were now associated with the government at the territorial, interterritorial and French Union levels, which otherwise seemed destined to function much as before. This increase in popular participation in government, however, brought several unforeseen consequences, the first of which was a growing dissatisfaction with the role of the federal Government-General. The Government-General, or, more precisely, its legislative branch, the Grand Council, had neither the power nor the prestige of the Parisian assemblies nor the direct contact with the African masses that the territorial assemblies had. From the point of view of the overseas deputies, the National Assembly and the Council of the Republic did not often take up problems directly relevant to their immediate constituents, nor indeed did most of their metropolitan colleagues consider such problems of great moment; however, when the parliament did reach a decision on an African question, it was usually on a point of crucial interest, for only from Paris, not from either the territorial or the federal level, could come the initiative to change the system.[18] Only in Paris could new powers, new degrees of self-government or autonomy for the lower organs be voted. For this reason the Parisian focus of politics was of primordial importance for the political leaders of West Africa. As all the major politicians of French West Africa made clear from the beginning, the local institutions established in 1946 were considered only a starting point, and it was only by participation in the deliberations of the government of metropolitan France that the Africans could bring about any change.[19]

In Africa, the new institutions permitted the indirect participation of great numbers of people in the modern political process. One of the major concessions extracted by the African representatives from the constitutional conventions was the provision that the franchise requirements for the African populations should be left to an electoral law and not inscribed in the constitution.[20] As expected, the extension of the franchise to the African populations proceeded rapidly. The electorate increased from 171,500 for the

18. Title VIII, Article 72 of the French Constitution: "In the overseas territories, the legislative power belongs to the [French] Parliament in the domains of . . . civil rights and political and administrative organization."

19. See, for example, Leopold Senghor, "L'Avenir de la France dans l'Outre-Mer," *Politique Etrangère*, No. 4 (October 1954), 419–26, "The truth is that the present system no longer fits the requirements of the day . . . that in the overseas territories the formula of the Republic 'one and indivisible' is a hypocrisy" (p. 420).

20. Title VIII, Article 77.

elections to the first Constituent Assembly to 3,062,600 for the National Assembly elections of 1951, and 6,054,300 for the National Assembly elections of 1956, representing over one third of the total population, of whom over half actually cast ballots.[21] Such electoral participation took place on the territorial level. Except in municipal elections the electorate chose directly only the representatives to the territorial assembly or the territory's representatives to the French National Assembly. Representatives to the Grand Council in Dakar, to the Council of the Republic, and to the Assembly of the French Union in Paris were chosen by the territorial assemblies. This put a premium on control of the territorial assembly, which in turn meant that political parties organized along territorial lines and oriented their propaganda to a specific territorial audience.

The new institutions inducted a large proportion of the new West African elite into parliamentary roles. The territorial assemblies had a total of 384 members of whom 277 were elected by Africans either in a separate electoral college or on a common electoral roll with French colonists. The Grand Council had forty members, five from each territorial assembly, and sixty-seven West African representatives sat in the three Parisian assemblies.[22] This, too, worked to reinforce the long-range political importance of the territorial level, as the territorial assemblies became the parliamentary training ground for most of the political elites. It also reduced the importance of the interterritorial level, for all the Grand Councillors were also territorial legislators, and one fourth of them were also members of the Parisian assemblies. This meant that the most prestigious of the Grand Councillors were preoccupied with affairs on the Parisian level while the others were too few to offset the territorial legislators' drive for political influence.

At first, the trend toward the Government-General's domination of the territorial authorities, which had been initiated by the reforms of 1904 and reached a high point under Vichy, seemed fated to continue under the Fourth Republic. As Table 1 shows, federal income from taxes increased much more rapidly than did the income of the territories.

In fact, a more detailed analysis of governmental performance

21. Ministère de la France d'Outre-Mer, *Inventaire sociale et économique des territoires d'outre-mer* (Paris, 1957), p. 7.

22. Ibid., p. 8, and Haut Commissariat de la République, *AOF 1957, Tableaux économiques* (Dakar, 1958), pp. 42–66.

TABLE 1. Gross Revenues of General and Territorial Budgets (Millions of CFA Francs)

	1905–1912	*1937–1943*	*1946–1953*
General budget	201.9–30%	4,907.9–47%	163,939.0–61%
Territorial budgets	467.1–70%	5,583.0–53%	103,345.0–39%

Source: Colin Newbury, "The Government General and Political Change in French West Africa," *African Affairs,* No. 1, St. Antony's Papers No. 10 (Carbondale, Southern Illinois University Press, 1961), p. 46.

and of the relations among the three levels of government will show that the Government-General and particularly the Grand Council were considerably weakened by the new institutions.

A substantial portion of the Government-General's revenue from indirect taxes was redistributed to the individual territories for their own use. In the 1946–53 period this was about 26 per cent of the general budget's gross revenues, which meant that direct federal expenditure was about 121 billion CFA and combined territorial expenditures about 146 billion CFA. In 1951, for example, the Government-General employed a total of 14,600 people of whom over 12,000 were Africans, while the territorial governments employed a total of 24,194 of whom more than 21,205 were Africans.[23] In the following years the trend was toward an extension of territorial employment at the expense of federal. Thus in 1956 the total spent on civilian salaries by the territories was almost double that spent by the Government-General.[24] Senegal, with the highest percentage of Government-General employees, had only 9,426 federal employees as compared with 14,381 employees of the territorial government. Soudan, whose ratio was more typical, had only 1,604 federal employees and 6,840 territorial government employees.[25] Government-General expenditures on goods and services were also not well distributed throughout the federation. In 1956, out of total federal expenditures of 41.05 billion CFA, 21.54 billion

23. Gouvernement-Général de l'A.O.F., *Annuaire statistique de l'Afrique Occidentale Française, 1950 à 1954, 5, tome* 3, 98–101.

24. Haut Commissariat Général à Dakar, *Comptes économiques de l'Afrique Occidentale Française en 1956, 5,* 96.

25. Banque Centrale des Etats de l'Afrique de l'Ouest, *Comptes économiques du Mali, 1956,* Etudes économiques ouest-africaines, *1* (February 1960), 42. By way of comparison, the United States Federal Government employs some 2,421 million civilians, while the state governments employ only about 1,592 million. U.S. Bureau of the Census, *Statistical Abstract of the United States 1961* (Washington, GPO, 1961), Table 550, p. 421.

were spent in Senegal and Soudan, and at least four fifths of that in Senegal alone.[26] Since Senegal was the seat of the Government-General, most federal expenditures for equipment and buildings were made there, and Senegal furnished the major contingent of federal employees.

Even when the Government-General did act as the primary redistributive agency for major expenditures, its role was often obscure or equivocal and was frequently resented by the territorial legislatures. This was particularly evident in the case of the developmental aid offered by France through the *Fonds d'Investissement pour le Développement Economique et Social* (FIDES). FIDES aid to French West Africa was divided into three sections: the general section administered projects involving all or much of the French Union; the common section administered projects involving more than one West African territory; and the territorial section established in 1955 handled projects within a single territory. Of these three, the common section was by far the largest. In principle its financing was to come 45 per cent from the general budget and 55 per cent from the metropolitan budget. Since the general budget borrowed most of its share from another metropolitan agency, the *Caisse Centrale de la France d'Outre-Mer* (CCFOM), metropolitan France in fact paid about 90 per cent of the total.[27]

The Grand Council was given the right to decide the distribution of FIDES aid among the territories on the basis of reports by the administration, but it required the approval of the directing committee of FIDES, made up of administrators, and representatives from the Ministry for Overseas France, from the Parisian assemblies, and from the CCFOM, unless the general budget were to pay its full 45 per cent. The result was a series of time-consuming and rather ludicrous *navettes,* or bickering back and forth, between the Grand Council and the metropolitan agencies, which frequently led the parliamentary representatives of the territories interested to intervene directly in Paris on behalf of their respective electorates. To avoid continuing the *navette* the FIDES directing committee took most of the final decisions without return-

26. *Comptes économiques de l'AOF, 1956, 5,* 116, and *Comptes économiques du Mali, 1956,* p. 42.

27. Marcel Capet, *Les Economies d'AOF?* (Paris, Librairie Générale de Droit et de Jurisprudence, 1958), pp. 198–99.

ing the matter to the Grand Council for final approval.[28] FIDES money was presented by the French as a metropolitan contribution to the development of the individual territories and was viewed primarily as such by the territorial assemblies and administration.[29] In the case of the FIDES allocations for the second four-year plan, 1953–57, the Grand Council was called on to deliberate on some 39 billion francs of expenditures, of which all but 1.8 billion were finally allocated directly to the territories.[30]

The Grand Council was in a shaky position. Much of the actual planning and coordination for federal activities was carried out in Paris while, conversely, the Council often had to pass on matters which more directly concerned the individual territories. When conflicts arose, the territorial assemblies unquestionably took precedence over the Grand Council, the Minister for Overseas France having ruled that the territorial assemblies should be consulted first in all matters in which their jurisdiction might overlap that of the Grand Council.[31] At the executive level the Governor-General retained most of his personal powers and prestige but continued to rely for advice as much on his own *Conseil de Gouvernement* (the only advisory organ continued from the Third Republic) as on the Grand Council. "The Grand Council, then, found itself inconveniently placed between the Government-General which it could advise, the Territorial Assemblies which conducted their own business with the territorial Governors, and the Ministry for Overseas France and the Council of State which could overrule its decisions."[32] In this situation the Grand Council appeared increasingly, to many French and Africans alike, to be at best ineffectual and possibly even unnecessary. There seemed to be two possible solutions—either reinforce the power and competence of the Grand Council or eliminate it altogether.[33]

As if this were not enough, the very principle upon which the Government-General had been established, that of spreading the

28. Ibid., p. 199; Bourcart, *Le Grand Conseil*, pp. 120–27 and 217–21.

29. See for example the territorial emphasis in *AOF 1957*, pp. 316–80 and in Ambassade de France, Service de Presse et d'Information, *French Africa, a Decade of Progress, 1948–1958* (New York, 1958), pp. 7–27.

30. *AOF 1957*, p. 344.

31. *Interprétation ministérielle* No. 2142 of March 10, 1949; cf. Bourcart, *Le Grand Conseil*, p. 194.

32. Colin Newbury, "The Government General and Political Change in French West Africa," p. 55.

33. Bourcart, *Le Grand Conseil*, pp. 208–24.

wealth of the coastal territories to the less favored interior regions, proved a constant source of conflict. The distribution of funds from the general budget to the individual territories was supposed to be based on two principles—the amount of federal tax revenue collected from each territory, and relative need. The relevant section of the law[34] was drawn in so ambiguous a manner, however, as to render the determination of these rebates and subsidies an exceedingly complicated matter, which all too often degenerated into undignified horse-trading. The rebates and subsidies were worked out in secret session among the grand councillors generally acting by territorial block rather than by party.

The redistributive principle had been opposed ever since the inception of the federal budget by those coastal states who thought they had the most to lose, but by the end of World War II opposition had become centered in the Ivory Coast, the most prosperous territory of French West Africa.[35] As Table 2 shows, the burden of

TABLE 2. Territorial Contributions to Federal Budget, 1949 and 1954

	Net contribution of territories to federal budget (*Millions of francs*)		*Per capita contributions to federal budget* (*Francs*)
	1949	*1954*	*1954*
Senegal	4,810	10,240	4,590
Mauretania	–170	170	28
Soudan	–220	530	15
Guinea	650	1,940	1,773
Ivory Coast	2,270	10,180	4,560
Upper Volta	–110	350	11
Dahomey	510	1,170	670
Niger	–40	500	21

Source: E. J. Berg, "The Economic Basis of Political Choice in French West Africa," *American Political Science Review, 54* (1960), 403; compiled from data in *Annuaire Statistique de l'Afrique Occidentale Française*, 5 (1956), tome 3, pp. 83, 106 ff. All francs are CFA francs.

34. Law of August 29, 1947, Article 38, Section 24b.

35. As Senator Djaument of the Ivory Coast protested, "The Governments-General are the tombs of our territories. All our resources are bled dry and we are obliged to crush our people with head taxes." *J.O., C.R., Débats*, p. 1719 (Meeting of August 11, 1947).

federal expenditure was borne by the Ivory Coast and Senegal; however, Senegal received from the presence of the Government-General in Dakar many indirect advantages, which were indeed magnified in the mind of many West Africans, and was among the staunchest supporters of federal power.[36] Thus, while the Government-General was supported by important sections of African political opinion and did perform useful work, it was almost constantly a bone of contention and the one political forum in which political issues tended to polarize by territories. It was the weakest and most uncertain link in the political hierarchy of the Fourth Republic.

36. See the speech of Ivory Coast Senator Lagarosse, *J.O., C.R., Débats,* p. 1718 (meeting of August 11, 1947), protesting the possibility of the Government-General's having a "slight tendency to favor Senegal somewhat." This attitude seems to have been common also under the Third Republic, as witness the testimony of Villard, the semiofficial historian of prewar Senegal. "The proximity of Dakar, it was said, led the Governor-General to recall frequently that Senegal was the essential colony and to surround it with an excessive solicitude—something that the colonies of deserts and lagoons judged harshly. It is evident that . . . the Government-General cast a more understanding eye on Dakar's suburbs, and those suburbs extended sometimes to the Falémé [Senegal's Eastern border]." André Villard, *Histoire du Sénégal,* pp. 180–81.

3

Economic Integration in French West Africa

In our examination of precolonial political units we saw the important role internal and foreign trade played in reinforcing political cohesion. The new orientation of the monetary commercial economy brought by the colonial era had an equally great effect on political cohesion in modern French West Africa.

French West Africa has long been considered to rank among the lowest of the African regions in terms of the development of an exchange economy. A 1954 United Nations study estimated that only approximately 19 per cent of the cultivated land area was used for commercial production (as opposed to 75 per cent in the then Gold Coast) and that 23 per cent of the active male population was engaged in commercialized production (as opposed to 79 per cent in the Gold Coast).[1] In fact, this seriously underestimates the number of people directly touched by the operations of the exchange economy. As a 1956 study of the economy of French West Africa shows, out of an active male population of 5,762 million, 1,055 million are engaged in work in the secondary and tertiary sectors of the exchange economy, while a strict minimum of 2 million more are engaged in agriculture, entirely or principally for commercial production.[2] This tallies fairly closely with the official estimate that commercial production made up 69 per cent of French West Africa's gross domestic product for that same year.[3] Such a high degree of involvement in the commercial economy means that very few groups are not touched in some way by commercial exchange.

Nor can one assume that this is limited to an exchange of goods and services within a given community or tribal area. A study of

1. United Nations Department of Economic and Social Affairs, *Enlargement of the Exchange Economy in Tropical Africa,* Doc. E/2557/ST/ECA/23, p. 14. All figures are for 1950 except the first, which is for 1947–49.

2. *Comptes économiques de l'AOF 1956,* 2, 34–37 and estimates based on information from the Dakar, Bamako, and Abidjan Chambers of Commerce and the Senegalese Statistical Service.

3. *Comptes économiques du Mali 1956,* p. 54.

consumption patterns within one of the most isolated, most tradition-bound, and poorest groups of Senegal and Soudan, the Tukulor of the Senegal River valley, reveals that over 40 per cent of a family's food budget alone is spent on "imports and products from other regions."[4] The popular image, then, of the isolated, self-sufficient African village unfamiliar with the use of money and out of contact with the outside world has little foundation in fact. Those that did exist in West Africa before the coming of European administration were irrevocably changed by the imposition of the head tax, which the African was obliged to pay in cash. Today it is safe to say that any groups isolated from participation in the exchange economy are also isolated from participation in any form of national political life.

The exchange economy in French West Africa may be divided into two parts—the traditional and the modern. The traditional exchange economy involves the two-way exchange of African services or products (dried fish for kola nuts, day labor for a share of the crop), or the exchange of an African service or product for an imported product (rice for sugar, maize for flashlights) through commerce organized and controlled by Africans. Exchange may be on a barter basis, although this is becoming rarer, and even where no money is exchanged on the retail level, relative values are generally calculated in monetary terms. The modern exchange economy involves the exchange of African services or products for imported products through commerce organized and controlled by non-Africans. The basis of this trade is the export of the major African cash crops—peanuts, coffee, cocoa, mineral ore—and the import of a wide variety of manufactured articles or the production and distribution of a few articles manufactured in French West Africa by European-controlled firms. The foreign groups controlling this commerce may be European or Levantine; the retail level, except in the major cities, is usually in the hands of Levantines or Africans and thus merges with the traditional exchange economy when African entrepreneurs either buy or trade for imported goods, and then distribute them through their own commercial networks.

The modern sector of the exchange economy occupies the pre-

4. Mission Socio-économique du Fleuve Sénégal (MISOES), *Les Budgets Familiaux* (Dakar, 1959), Table 6, p. 26. On the importance of markets in Africa for communication of all sorts see Leonard W. Doob's book, *Communication in Africa* (New Haven, Yale University Press, 1961), pp. 143–45.

dominant position. While statistics are only approximate, in 1956 the modern sector handled a turnover of 220 billion CFA francs as opposed to 94 billion for the traditional sector.[5] The distinction between the two sectors cannot be sharply made, for they are closely linked at several stages of their operations. This is particularly true as regards the provision of credit for capital expenditures by African entrepreneurs, who generally obtain advances directly from a European commercial house rather than from a bank. Thus, an African trader might buy a new truck on credit from the commercial house whose products he retails in the bush and to whom he sells African cash crops he has collected, while the commercial house uses its own credit to obtain the money for the truck from the European banking system.

The simplest way to separate the two sectors is by area covered. In general, the European-controlled modern circuit deviates little from the established main lines of communications, usually the railroads, while the African commerce branches out from these primary commercial axes. Most trade from Dakar to Bamako is in the modern circuit, while between Bamako and Bobo-Dioulasso it is in the African circuit. This difference is important for our study since the African traders would not necessarily have the same stake in retaining the major communications links that the European traders have.

In examining the economic structure of French West Africa under the colonial regime, we shall take 1956 as the sample year. As a whole, the French West African territories exhibited all the usual signs of colonial economic dependence. Foreign trade predominated over domestic exchange and consisted principally in the exchange of raw materials for manufactured goods. There was little domestic capital accumulation and an excess of imports over exports, with the deficit being made up by cash transfers from the metropolitan country. The organization of foreign trade was almost entirely in the hands of non-Africans, usually from the metropolitan country, which was by far the greatest buyer and supplier of goods.

Table 3 presents the interterritorial and foreign trade of French West Africa for 1956; Table 4 represents the same trade minus

5. *Comptes économiques de l'AOF 1956, 5,* 81. This figure includes most of the Levantine operations under the traditional sector and thus slightly underestimates the role of the modern sector as here defined.

TABLE 3. French West African Interterritorial and Foreign Trade, 1956[a]

	IMPORTERS								
EXPORTERS	*Senegal*	*Maure-tania*	*Soudan*	*Guinea*	*Ivory Coast*	*Upper Volta*	*Dahomey*	*Niger*	*Rest of world*	*Total exports*
Senegal		1,585	17,229	1,329	1,998	—	446	—	21,102	43,689
Mauretania	1,091		1,400	—	—	—	—	—	—	2,491
Soudan	5,586	61		501	894	2,050	—	118	20	9,230
Guinea	303	—	209		244	—	11	—	5,392	6,159
Ivory Coast	370	—	1,098	341		4,831	88	—	26,842	33,570
Upper Volta	—	—	454	—	1,908		67	—	1,000	3,429
Dahomey	165	—	—	23	88	—		1,240	3,638	5,154
Niger	—	—	81	—	—	—	988		3,943	5,012
Rest of world	34,780	370	50	7,003	18,519	1,661	4,718	1,796		
Total imports	42,295	2,016	20,521	9,197	23,651	8,542	6,318	3,154		

Source: *Comptes économiques de l'AOF 1956*, 6, 44.
a. Millions of CFA francs.

TABLE 4. French West African Interterritorial and Foreign Trade, 1956, Not Including Transit Trade[a]

	IMPORTERS								
EXPORTERS	*Senegal*	*Maure-tania*	*Soudan*	*Guinea*	*Ivory Coast*	*Upper Volta*	*Dahomey*	*Niger*	*Rest of world*	*Total exports*
Senegal		549	6,968	710	1,223	—	291	—	16,000	26,341
Mauretania	847		1,400	—	—	—	—	—	244	2,491
Soudan	1,196	61		364	846	2,050	—	118	4,278	8,913
Guinea	151	—	192		193	—	1	—	5,392	5,929
Ivory Coast	339	—	1,089	153		3,016	38	—	25,653	30,288
Upper Volta	—	—	438	—	587		67	—	2,189	3,281
Dahomey	135	—	—	11	64	—		220	2,658	3,088
Niger	—	—	81	—	—	—	8		4,923	5,012
Rest of world	22,280	1,406	10,036	7,541	17,644	3,328	3,847	2,816		
Total imports	24,948	2,016	2,024	8,779	20,557	8,394	4,252	3,154		

Source: *Comptes économiques de l'AOF 1956*, 6, 44 and passim.

a. Millions of CFA francs.

transit trade and with all exports and imports computed for the territory of origin or destination. The amount of trade among the territories of French West Africa is perhaps slightly underestimated—particularly that between Soudan and the Ivory Coast—since some of the traditional commerce inevitably escapes control by government statisticians. Even making allowances for such lacunae, however, the predominance of the external sector is evident. If we include transit trade as part of internal trade, trade between territories equals 46,767 million CFA francs,[6] while the average of French West Africa's exports and imports is 65,417 million CFA.[7] If we make the more rigorous assumption, as in Table 4, that all exports go directly to the country of destination, thus discounting transit trade, we see that for the same average of imports and exports from the outside world, commercial exchange between French West African territories amounted to only 23,406 million CFA francs or approximately 36 per cent as much. Only Soudan and Mauretania traded as much with other French West African territories as with the outside world, a situation explained partly by their geographical positions and partly by their lack of exportable commodities and their low purchasing power.

Not only did the external sector predominate in French West Africa's commerce, but this sector was controlled by the metropolitan country. In 1956, 66 per cent of French West Africa's foreign trade was with metropolitan France. This figure has been remarkably stable, although the proportion accounted for by imports tended to rise (as the French domestic economy gained the capacity to supply Africa's needs) and the proportion accounted for by exports fell somewhat (as Britain, the United States, and the Netherlands increased their purchases of fats, oils, coffee, and cocoa). Within this same period another 8 to 12 per cent of foreign trade was with other countries within the franc zone.[8] While such a continuation of "imperial preference" may have been justified by the need to conserve scarce foreign exchange, it reflected and perpetuated French dominance of the French West African economy.

Structurally, this dominance was completed through the inter-

6. Computed as the sum of total imports minus the sum of the imports from rest of the world. See Table 3.

7. Computed as the sum of total exports minus exports from rest of the world, plus total imports minus imports from rest of the world, divided by 2. See Table 3.

8. See *AOF 1957*, pp. 125, 136.

locking holdings of the great commercial houses of Marseilles and Bordeaux, which combined their commercial activities with ownership or control over the principal shipping lines and freight-carrying airline. In addition they maintained close relationships with the principal banks serving French West Africa. Their position was reinforced by preferential import duties, exchange and commodity quotas on imports from outside the franc zone, and governmental regulations obliging the use of French bottoms for transport between points within the French Union.[9]

Since these commercial groups made most of the major economic decisions from their headquarters in France, and in particular since many of them operated throughout the French Union or throughout Africa, economic decisions were taken not only in terms of French West African economic conditions, but also in terms of world market prices for Africa's agricultural and mining exports. The sense of economic community within French West Africa was thus reduced. Prices of basic imported commodities, such as cloth and certain foodstuffs, bore little relation to prevailing wage rates and demand within French West Africa, but rather varied closely with those in metropolitan France. The great commercial firms continued the practice followed under the Third Republic of lobbying and directing other forms of political action primarily at the Parisian level, where basic policy was set on matters as diverse and essential as minimum wage rates, shipping charges, workers' family allocations and fringe benefits, import quotas, and subsidies for establishing new commercial or productive enterprises.

As a result of restrictions on competitive imports and of the high prices of French domestic agriculture, industry, and transport, prices in French West Africa were considerably above world levels. In the period 1950–56 prices paid for cotton cloth, for example, ranged from 20 to 25 per cent higher than the cost of cloth supplied by Dutch and English firms, and the price of sugar, a major West African import, has been as much as 85 per cent above the standard Cuban export price. One French authority calculated the overall difference at about 15 per cent, although this is probably conservative.[10] Richard Harding's estimate of 20 to 30 per cent seems

9. Capet, *Les Economies d'AOF,* pp. 123–30, 146–50.

10. Pierre Moussa, *Les Chances économiques de la Communauté Franco-Africaine* (Paris, Colin, 1957), p. 79.

more nearly correct.[11] These high prices have in part been compensated by the higher prices that France has been willing to pay for basic West African exports, such as Senegal's peanuts and the Ivory Coast's coffee, although these subsidies, varying between 8 and 12 per cent, do not entirely compensate for the difference.[12]

The structure of high prices worked particularly to the disadvantage of the interior territories. They had few exports to be subsidized, but the price of all imported goods was increased by the costs of transportation and the profits of innumerable middlemen. While this made little difference in the average African's purchase of foodstuffs, it affected seriously those items of equipment, machinery, and construction materials necessary for economic development. Thus the price of gasoline in Bamako or Ouagadougou was from 25 to 30 per cent higher than in Dakar, galvanized iron roofing sheets about 50 per cent higher, and cement about 250 per cent higher.[13] The cost of living for urban Africans in the interior, particularly for those employed in the government administration or modern sector of the economy, was notably higher than in the major coastal cities. This imbalance was further aggravated by differential wage rates which tended to favor salaried workers in the coastal cities. Basic wage rates were determined by governmental decree, and within each territory most wage rates varied in proportion to the minimum wage; wages outside of the major cities would be lower, while prices would be higher.

The foreign commerce of French West Africa consistently ran a deficit, occasionally reaching as high as 22 per cent of the total volume of foreign trade. This deficit was financed by monetary transfers from the metropolitan treasury.[14]

From the above it is apparent that, as a whole, French West Africa existed in a sort of economic never-never land in which major economic decisions could rarely be taken on the basis of French West African factors alone. The usual laws of the marketplace seemed to have little effect on the conduct of business. The French West African economy was an integral part, and a minor part at that, of the overall economy of the French Union and of the

11. Richard Harding, "The Survival of the French Community in West Africa" (unpublished seminar paper, Yale University, May 1960), p. 45; cited by permission.

12. Ibid., pp. 46–47.

13. Ministère de la France d'Outre-Mer, *Inventaire*, pp. 284–85.

14. See *AOF 1957*, pp. 135–39.

TABLE 5. Average Urban Minimum Wage in French West African Territories, 1956

Territory	*CFA francs/hour*	*Index*
Senegal	29.31	100
Ivory Coast	26.73	91
Guinea	21.83	74
Dahomey	21.60	74
Mauretania	20.00	68
Soudan	19.90	68
Niger	16.13	55
Upper Volta	16.08	55

Source: *Comptes économiques de l'AOF 1956, 3,* 69.

franc zone and as such was subject to decisions made in Paris. These decisions affected both the governmental and private sectors of the economy through decisions on developmental aid, wages, working conditions, subsidies, and allocations of foreign exchange. Above all, the French government was always there "*pour boucher les trous,*" to provide stopgap aid and to bail out the French West African economy—or individual parts of it—when it was in difficulty. This situation could hardly encourage the development of a sense of economic interdependence within the federation itself. Long-range planning carried out in terms of the federation as a whole was done primarily by French government agencies, which could be influenced only through representation in Paris, or by the offices of the great commercial houses, also based outside the federation.

French West Africa is by no means an area of homogeneous development. Eighty to ninety per cent of the federation's exportable production has come from the littoral zone, extending back about 125 miles from the coast and including less than one third of the population and one eighth of the land area.[15] As Table 6 shows, the coastal territories of Senegal, the Ivory Coast, and Guinea rank highest in most measures of economic and social development, while Dahomey, the "Latin Quarter of West Africa," shows its advantage in educational development, the result more of missionary activity and high population density than of a high general level of development.

15. Benjamin E. Thomas, "Railways and Ports in French West Africa," *Economic Geography, 33* (Jan. 1957), 4.

TABLE 6. Measures of Economic Development of French West Africa, 1956

	African population (millions)	*Non-African population*	*Per cent of population in urban centers of over 2,000*	*Population density per km²*	*African workers in non-agricultural jobs*	*Production of electricity in 1,000 kwh.*	*Number of inhabitants per vehicle*	*Per cent of school age children in school*[b]	*Number of private banks including branches*[c]	*Number of government employees*[d]
Senegal	2.181	48,593	36.5	11.4	52,400	91,567	Dakar 15 Rest 225	23.7	14	15,055
Mauretania	.614	1,627	7.3	.6[a]	1,100	215	620	6.8	1	3,383
Soudan	3.636	7,382	9.2	3.0[a]	16,300	8,238	650	8.0	7	7,855
Guinea	2.498	9,500	9.2	10.2	28,700	14,071	320	9.8	17	6,992
Ivory Coast	2.471	11,638	18.3	7.7	45,000	23,280	120	25.5	17	9,248
Upper Volta	3.322	3,693	8.7	12.1	10,100	2,500	1,050	6.6	2	3,964
Dahomey	1.612	2,767	13.9	13.9	9,700	3,130	350	28.0	5	6,477
Niger	2.333	3,040	5.3	2.0[a]	5,600	2,550	850	3.4	5	3,754
Total AOF	18.667	88,240	11.7	4.0	168,900	145,551	270	13.4	68	56,728

Source: *AOF 1957.*

a. Includes Saharan area.

b. Number of school age estimated as 15 per cent of population.

c. As of 1/1/57.

d. As of 1/1/56, includes employees of territorial, federal, and French governments.

Furthermore, private and public investment since World War II has increased the discrepancy between the richer and poorer territories. The measures of private investment in Table 7 somewhat overstate the economic importance of Senegal, since many of the commercial firms legally incorporated in Dakar conduct operations in other parts of the federation as well, although the simple fact that they do run their operations from Dakar indicates the importance of that city in the federation's economic life.

TABLE 7. Public and Private Investment in French West Africa

	Public investment allotted through FIDES 1947–57 (millions of CFA francs)	*Number of private firms Dec. 31, 1956 (headquarters site)*	*Increase in capitalization of private firms 1947–56 (millions of CFA francs)*
Senegal	22,300	1,267	20,661
Mauretania	2,448		
Soudan	12,586	77	178
Guinea	12,551	245	3,054
Ivory Coast	17,275	597	3,399
Upper Volta	7,137	31	279
Dahomey	7,821	57	486
Niger	4,050	24	122

Source: *AOF 1957*, pp. 316–366.
a. Included in Senegal figure, but very small.

The dominant coastal economies were characterized by the presence of a good deepwater port, a concentration of exportable products, and transportation lines running into the interior from the port. Dahomey's relative economic position within the federation declined rapidly because it lacked a natural harbor, and equally desirable sources of palm oil could be found in more easily accessible locations along the coast. The extent of participation of the interior territories in the modern economy has depended principally on the means of transport linking them with a coastal port. Because of the difficulties and expense of road construction and maintenance in a region with one or two heavy rainy seasons each year, interior transport has depended largely on the railroad. The railroad system was conceived for two primary purposes—support for military operations in the interior, and the removal of export crops. Built initially under the impetus of the Freycinet Plan's enthusiasm for railroad construction in France, the system was designed to link up in the interior along the Niger River and to meet a line running through the Sahara to North Africa. The drain of World War I on French finances and a better appreciation of the difficulties of the terrain in West Africa put an end to such ambitions, and the railway system came to consist of four separate lines running inland from the major ports, connected, if at all, by secondary roads. The failure to link up the railway lines severely handicapped the development of a federation-wide economy, and split the federation into separate trading economies based on individual ports each with a hinterland supplying exportable products and absorbing imported goods.

To analyze the trade pattern within French West Africa, we used the Savage and Deutsch statistical model of transaction flows.[16] Using the 1956 figures of Table 3, we constructed a null or indifference model of trade among the French West African territories and with the outside world, based on each territory's observed overall propensity to import and export. We could then judge the degree to which actual trading patterns diverged from the indifference model and, accordingly, the preferential trading relationships between the different territories. The measure of trading preference is the "Relative Acceptance" of exports from country or trading bloc "i" to country or trading bloc "j" (RA_{ij}).[17]

Table 8 lists in matrix form the Relative Acceptances of trade for the French West African territories for 1956.[18] With respect to

16. I. R. Savage and K. W. Deutsch, "A Statistical Model of the Gross Analysis of Transaction Flows," *Econometrica, 28* (July 1960), 551–72.

17. Statistically, RA_{ij} equals the difference between the actual and the expected trade between i and j divided by the expected trade between them, or $RA_{ij} = \frac{a_{ij} - A_{ij}}{A_{ij}}$. The Relative Acceptance thus measures the degree to which actual trade is greater or less than the amount of trade there would be if i and j traded randomly with all their potential trading partners. If trade were consigned perfectly randomly, (i.e. as predicted by the indifference model), all Relative Acceptances would be 0. Where no trade exists, between i and j, the Relative Acceptance equals −1. If i and j traded exclusively with one another, the Relative Acceptance would equal infinity. The model assumes further that no country trades with itself (i.e. $RA_{ij} = -1$ where $i = j$).

18. I am grateful to Hayward R. Alker, Jr. for his assistance in processing this data.

TABLE 8. Relative Acceptances of Trade of French West African Territories, 1956

	Senegal	*Soudan*	*Sen–Soudan*	*Mauretania*	*Guinea*	*Sen–Soud–Mauret–Guinea*	*Ivory Coast*	*Upper Volta*	*I. Coast–U. Volta*	*Dahomey*	*Niger*	*Dahomey–Niger*	*IC–UV–Dah–Niger*	*Total*	*Rest of world*
Senegal	–1.	2.79	2.79	2.66	– .34	1.88	– .66	–1.	– .74	– .68	– 1.	– .78	– .75	.35	– .21
Soudan	1.73	–1.	1.73	– .21	.40	1.48	– .15	5.21	1.13	–1.	– .04	– .68	.75	1.18	– .99
Sen–Soudan	1.73	2.79	2.46	2.22	– .23	1.78	– .58	– .06	– .46	– .72	– .85	– .77	– .52	.52	– .33
Mauretania	1.13	5.89	2.48	–1.	–1.	2.10	–1.	–1.	–1.	–1.	– 1.	– 1.	–1.	1.01	–1.
Guinea	– .77	– .60	– .72	–1.	–1.	– .73	– .63	–1.	– .72	– .93	– 1.	– .95	– .77	– .74	.70
Sen–Soud–Mauret–Guinea	.81	2.58	1.83	1.94	– .25	1.41	– .60	– .17	– .50	.75	– .87	– .79	– .56	.39	– .26
Ivory Coast	– .95	– .64	– .86	–1.	– .75	– .85	–1.	2.92	2.92	– .90	– 1.	– .94	.89	.55	.44
Upper Volta	–1.	.58	– .55	–1.	–1.	– .61	4.15	–1.	4.15	– .23	– 1.	– .48	2.94	.46	– .43
I. Coast–U. Volta	– .96	– .53	– .84	–1.	– .77	– .83	4.15	2.92	3.21	– .85	– 1.	– .90	1.22	– .45	.36
Dahomey	– .85	–1.	– .89	–1.	– .88	– .89	– .84	–1.	– .88	–1.	18.24	18.24	.68	– .40	.30
Niger	–1.	– .80	– .94	–1.	–1.	– .95	–1.	–1.	–1.	6.96	– 1.	6.96	.20	– .57	.56
Dah–Niger	– .92	– .90	– .92	–1.	– .94	– .92	– .92	–1.	– .94	6.96	18.24	10.82	.44	– .48	.47
IC–UV–Dah–Niger	– .95	– .61	– .85	–1.	– .80	– .85	.37	2.07	1.26	.01	1.19	.41	.95	– .46	.39
Total	– .48	1.17	.18	.72	– .49	.10	– .45	.70	– .10	– .46	– .08	– .33	– .16	– .00	.00
Rest of world	.24	.10	– .11	– .65	.43	– .06	.29	– .63	.07	.41	.07	.30	.12	.00	–1.

Source: Table 3.

trade within the federation, it is apparent that there are three separate sets of intensive trading relationships: Senegal, Mauretania, and Soudan; Ivory Coast and Upper Volta; and Dahomey and Niger. Guinea stands very much alone within the federation—its trading relationships are almost exclusively with the outside world and, except for its food imports from the Soudan, it has significantly negative Relative Acceptances with all members of the federation.[19] These three trading units correspond to the railway routes and all have significantly high positive Relative Acceptances. The Senegal–Mauretania–Soudan region absorbs 244 per cent more of its trade than expected by pure chance, Ivory Coast–Upper Volta absorbs 32 per cent more, and Dahomey–Niger 1,082 per cent more.

If, to simplify matters, we drop Mauretania, the smallest trader, we are left with three tightly bound pairs of countries and Guinea alone, with very little trade going on between the different units. For example, the Relative Acceptance of Senegal–Soudan's exports by Ivory Coast–Upper Volta is –.46 (CR_{ij} = –8.5); the Relative Acceptance of Ivory Coast–Upper Volta's exports by Dahomey–Niger is –.90 (CR_{ij} = –6.1), and so forth. Such trade as there is among these units is carried on along the coast and represents principally a redistribution of imported goods and the sale of locally manufactured goods by Senegal, although, given Senegal's overwhelming commitment to the external market and to Soudan and Mauretania within Africa, this trade is less than might be expected by chance. More important and statistically significant is the interior trade carried on by Soudan with Upper Volta and Ivory Coast (which is probably also somewhat undervalued in the statistics). This trade, most of which is in the hands of Mande-speaking Africans, is a continuation of the traditional Dioula trade which played so great a part in African precolonial history, and gained for Soudan the nickname of "crossroads of French West Africa." More than any other area, Soudan by virtue of its geographic position and commercial traditions, is the single economic link of French West Africa. As the statistics show, it is still a fragile link,

19. Significance is calculated using the Savage-Deutsch formula for the Critical Ratio, pp. 567–69, assuming a consignment size of 25,000,000 CFA francs (about $100,000). In all cases significance is assumed at the .001 level, or when $CR_{ij} = 3.3$. Guinea's imports from Soudan do not deviate significantly from our indifference model; $CR_{ij} = 1.61$ (where i = Soudan and j = Guinea), a figure that would occur randomly about one in ten times.

for it barely touched the easternmost trading unit, Dahomey–Niger, which remains, as in precolonial times, almost totally isolated from the commercial life of the rest of the federation.

By comparing each territory's trade with the rest of the world with its trade with all of French West Africa, we can obtain a crude measure of economic attention for each territory (see Table 9). Leaving Mauretania aside again, we find that three of the coastal territories—Guinea, Ivory Coast, and Dahomey—have significant deficits of trade with the rest of French West Africa. Their economies are turned to the world (or at least the French) market, not to the African market. Just the reverse is true for Soudan and Upper Volta, whose economies are linked with the African rather than the outside market. Niger also appears to fall into this group, but the evidence is inconclusive. Senegal plays a role all its own. It exports significantly more than one would expect by chance to the other African territories, but imports significantly less from them. It imports more from the rest of the world than predicted by chance, but exports significantly less. More than any other of the French West African territories, Senegal is linked with both the African and the French markets, selling to one and buying from the other.

In addition to trade, labor migration represents an important form of economic exchange and one that is extremely difficult to measure precisely. As pointed out in the first chapter, traditional

TABLE 9. Observed Trading Preferences of Some French West African Territories, 1956
(Positive deviations of Relative Acceptances from null model)[a]

	Exports to:	*Imports from:*
Rest of French West Africa	Upper Volta (.70) Soudan (1.17)[b]	Upper Volta (.48) Soudan (1.18) Senegal (.35)
Rest of world	Dahomey (.41) Guinea (.43) Ivory Coast (.29) Senegal (.24)	Dahomey (.38) Guinea (.69) Ivory Coast (.44)

Source: Table 8.
a. Significant at .001 level, assuming consignments of 25,000,000 CFA francs.
b. Somewhat overstated because Soudanese exports to rest of world are included in exports to rest of French West Africa.

Africa allowed a surprising amount of personal movement across tribal political boundaries for traders and certain parts of tribal elites. This movement was greatly accentuated under the colonial regime by the development of cash crops requiring extensive outside labor at specified seasons of the year, by increased interregional trade, and by the growth of cities opening up the possibility of industrial and service employment for large numbers of Africans. Perhaps the greatest amount of migration for economic reasons has taken place within territorial boundaries, notably movements from rural to urban areas, and has served as a means of increasing territorial solidarity.[20] Interterritorial movements have, however, also played a major role in the development of the West African economy and in the patterns of association of the West African peoples.

French West Africa contains two main reservoirs of labor, Upper Volta and Soudan, the two most populous territories. Of these, Upper Volta has been by far the more important, and indeed the present organization of the economies of both the Ivory Coast and Ghana depend heavily on the seasonal influx of about 100,000 Voltaic citizens each.[21] In addition, Upper Volta has supplied much of the labor force for the ambitious rice and cotton project on the Niger River in Soudan.[22] Seasonal migration from Soudan is probably on the order of 30–40,000, two thirds of whom go to Senegal and most of the others to the Ivory Coast, with another 20–25,000 Soudanese traders residing more or less permanently outside of Soudan along the Dioula routes. In addition, Guinea has traditionally sent some laborers to the southwestern section of the Ivory Coast and some to Senegal, while Senegal and Dahomey have ex-

20. For an excellent case study of intraterritorial migration, see Abdoulaye Diop, "L'Immigration Toucouleure à Dakar (enquête 1958–1959)" (Dakar, IFAN, 1960, mimeo.).

21. Estimation of the Office Territorial de la Main d'Oeuvre, Ouagadougou; See also Albert Balima, "La Migration du travailleur en Haute-Volta" (CCTA conference document MIG, February 11–15, 1961), which conservatively estimates the total Voltaic migration at 170,000 per year.

22. See L'Office du Niger, "Note de Présentation Technique" (Ségou, 1960, mimeo.) and "L'Office du Niger en 1960" (Ségou, 1960, mimeo.). There are currently some 6,000 Mossi in the Office du Niger, or about 17 per cent of the total population of the project. On the project's effects on the Mossi, see P. B. Hammond, "Economic Change and Mossi Acculturation" in W. R. Bascom and M. J. Herskovits, eds., *Continuity and Change in African Culture* (Chicago, University of Chicago Press, 1959), pp. 238–56.

ported clerks and government officials throughout French-speaking Africa, including even the former Belgian Congo.

Within French West Africa, the Ivory Coast has been most dependent on foreign labor. Recent studies have shown that about 60 per cent of the Ivory Coast's salaried African labor force was from outside the territory, while some 34 per cent of the population of five major Ivory Coast urban areas was born outside the territory. In Abidjan the figure reaches 38 per cent.[23] By comparison, in Senegal, the next most labor-dependent territory, only about 13 per cent of the salaried African labor force comes from outside the territory. The same percentage of Dakar's inhabitants were born outside of Senegal.[24] In general, the paths of labor migration tend to reinforce the trade linkages between the interior and coastal territories. In addition, the Ivory Coast's dependence on labor from Upper Volta shows a greater degree of integration of the coastal territory in the French West African economic system than is apparent from trade flows alone, although it should be noted that this is an almost exclusive dependence on Upper Volta and not on a wider grouping of West African territories.

While we shall have occasion later to comment on some political consequences of interterritorial labor migration, it should be pointed out here that the interterritorial migrants have not merged their separate identity with that of the people into whose midst they have migrated. Rather, a process that one scholar has called "supertribalization" has taken place, in which the migrants from a given territory have come to consider themselves as belonging to the dominant tribe in their group.[25] Thus migrants from the Soudan in Senegal refer to themselves as "Bambara," since the Bambara are the largest group of Soudanese migrants and since the Bambara language is their *lingua franca*, even though they may be Malinke or Sarakolle. Similarly, Voltaic migrants in the Ivory Coast refer to themselves as "Mossi," although they may actually be

23. *Comptes économiques de l'AOF 1956, 2,* 36; and Côte d'Ivoire, Direction de la Statistique, *Recensement d'Abidjan, 1955* and *Recensement des centres urbains d'Abengourou, Agboville, Dimbokro et Man, 1956–1957.*

24. *Comptes économiques de l'AOF 1956, 2,* 36; and Haut Commissariat de l'AOF, Etudes et coordination statistiques et mécanographiques, *Recensement démographique de Dakar* (*1955*), Résultats définitifs, 1er fascicule.

25. Jean Rouch, "Migrations au Ghana," *Journal des Africanistes, 26* (1956), 33–196. Also, see Immanuel Wallerstein, "Ethnicity and National Integration in West Africa," *Cahiers d'études africaines, 3* (October 1960), 131.

Grunshi or Bobo and barely speak the Mossi language. For the more sophisticated it is an easy step from "Bambara" to "Soudanese," and from "Mossi" to "Voltaic."

While the step from economic preferences to political preferences is a long and hazardous one, the above data do suggest that insofar as economic ties are taken into account by political decision-makers, Upper Volta and Soudan would tend to resolve problems in terms compatible with maintaining close relations with other African territories; while Guinea, the Ivory Coast, and Dahomey would be less constrained by economic links with their immediate neighbors, but would be more likely to consider their relations with the rest of the world. In the Ivory Coast, such a course would depend on its maintaining access to its supply of migrant labor. Senegal, on the other hand, would tend to adopt solutions compatible with maintaining its relations both with its African partners and with its principal supplier abroad. Whether these considerations will be taken into account by political decision-makers cannot be decided by an examination of the economic structure alone. In the following sections we shall look at the activities and interests of French West Africa's political leaders.

4

French West African Political Parties, 1945–1955

IN FRENCH WEST AFRICA under the Fourth Republic the formal governmental organizations remained remote from most people's day-to-day experience. As the main link between the African masses and the governmental structures, the African political parties provided both the major means of popular political education and recruitment, and the primary framework for elite political activity.[1]

TERRITORIAL PARTIES

For analytic purposes we may divide the French West African territorial parties into two main categories on the basis of elite characteristics and party structure. These are generally referred to as "patron parties" and "mass parties."[2] In French West Africa, a patron party was generally organized around a single individual leader or a small group of leaders, who derived preeminence from some factor normally outside the modern political arena. The leaders were often important figures in the traditional system (though not necessarily paramount chiefs), religious figures (particularly among Muslims), economic leaders such as wealthy traders, or African members of the colonial administration. The patron party often had a regional rather than a territory-wide base, if only because its appeal was limited to those likely to be swayed by personal loyalty to the individuals leading the party. The patron party

1. Among the studies on French West African political parties are: André Blanchet, *L'Itinéraire des partis africains depuis Bamako* (Paris, Plon, 1958); Thomas Hodgkin, *African Political Parties* (Baltimore, Penguin, 1962); Ernest Milcent, *L'AOF entre en scène* (Paris, Editions du Témoignage Chrétien, 1958); Ruth Schachter, "Single-Party Systems in West Africa," *American Political Science Review*, 55 (June 1961), 294–307.

2. The distinction is made notably by Thomas Hodgkin in his *Nationalism in Colonial Africa* (London, Muller, 1956) and *African Political Parties*. The term "elite" is sometimes used instead of "patron."

tended to make particularistic appeals and to emphasize rewards to group leaders, not rewards to the group itself. The structure of a patron party was intermittent, functioning mainly around election time. It would typically have few or no permanent members, and membership would carry with it no obligation except to vote for the party's candidates. A patron party generally had a conservative outlook in politics, because any radical change in the status quo might entail a change in the privileged social or economic position on which its leaders depended for success. Because of this conservatism, and because the patron party notables were likely to be known personally to the colonial administration, a patron party usually was looked on with some benevolence by the administration. Among important patron parties in French West Africa under the Fourth Republic were the Parti Progressiste Soudanais (PSP) in the Soudan, based mainly on a few important cantonal chiefs and religious leaders, the Parti Social d'Education des Masses Africaines (PSEMA) supported by the Morho Naba, emperor of the Mossi, in Upper Volta, and the Senegalese branch of the French Socialist Party (SFIO), based on the privileged urban elite of Senegal.

In contrast to a patron party, a mass party was usually led by people whose competence and distinction lay wholly or primarily within the arena of modern politics. Mass parties tended to develop an explicit set of political principles, or ideology, considered valid irrespective of a person's ethnic, social, or economic status. While they made diffuse appeals, they were also somewhat particularistic in their rewards, although the rewards were channeled to members of the group rather than just to group leaders. The mass party was universalistic in its membership rather than exclusive. It usually had permanent, well-articulated structures capable of providing a variety of services for its members. It attempted to integrate people of various groups by means of the party structure and coordinate structures outside the traditional arena, such as labor unions, sports organizations, and social clubs. Membership was commonly associated with certain political duties (e.g. attendance at meetings, propaganda activities, money-raising); the party usually relied on its general membership for most of its finances. The mass party recruited its membership over a fairly wide geographic area, usually the entire territory. Since its leaders and many of its members were drawn from nonprivileged strata of traditional society, it tended to seek radical changes in the political, social, and economic realms and was thus looked upon with less favor than the patron parties by the colonial administration.

Although the mass party sought to induct its adherents from different ethnic groups into loyalty to the larger territorial group, it generally did so by recognition of the existence of ethnic differences and susceptibilities. Accordingly, the party became adept at what Ruth Schachter has termed "ethnic arithmetic,"[3] the conscious balancing of ethnic representation on electoral lists, much the same way that electoral lists in American municipal campaigns traditionally include a member from each major ethnic group. The "ethnic" candidates would not necessarily be men of high traditional prestige. After their dominance was assured some mass parties, notably the Union Soudanaise and the Parti Démocratique de Guinée (PDG), consciously scrambled the candidates and districts, running a Malinke in a Fulani area or vice versa to indicate that the ethnic balance was to be achieved only within the territorial party. Patron parties and those mass parties which faced stiffer electoral competition seldom had such freedom of maneuver. Among the major mass parties of French West Africa in the period under consideration were the Parti Démocratique de la Côte d'Ivoire (PDCI), the Union Soudanaise, the Parti Démocratique de Guinée (PDG), and the dominant Senegalese party known at various times as the Bloc Démocratique Sénégalais (BDS), Bloc Populaire Sénégalais (BPS), and Union Progressiste Sénégalaise (UPS).

By the nature of their activities, structures, and appeals the mass parties particularly tended to reinforce their members' allegiance to the primary formally-constituted political unit, the territory. The mass parties also often focused their members' political attention on larger pan-African problems by stressing the inherent unity of all Black Africa as against their common opponent, the colonial power. On the other hand, the patron parties tended to emphasize ethnic particularism and to induct their supporters more into loyalties toward a common Franco-African community[4] than toward a common territory or a common pan-African movement.

3. Schachter, "Single-Party Systems," p. 301.

4. Compare, for example, the electoral appeals of the PSP in its newspaper *Vérité* (Bamako) and those of the Union Soudanaise in *Essor* (Bamako), January through March, 1959, or Kenneth E. Robinson's contrast between Senegalese SFIO and BPS propaganda in "Senegal: the Elections to the Territorial Assembly, March 1957" in W. J. M. Mackenzie and Kenneth E. Robinson, *Five Elections in Africa* (London, Oxford University Press, 1960), pp. 363–87.

In practice the institutional structure of French West African politics blurred these tendencies. In particular, participation in elections for territorial office obliged the patron parties to deemphasize regional particularism. Since the territory constituted the smallest functioning political unit (except for the few self-governing municipalities), it was advantageous to campaign for office on a territorial base, or, if only successful in a limited region, to combine with other parties within the territorial legislature to implement specific goals and prepare future electoral campaigns. This necessity was increased by the administration's establishment of large electoral districts, cutting across tribal boundaries, from which candidates were elected by proportional representation. A major party was thus obliged to include representatives of different ethnic or local interests to make its list attractive to the widest number of voters. In addition, the elite, if not the entire membership of a patron party, was thrown willy-nilly into politics at the territorial level in order to seek election or nomination to a higher level, be it Dakar or Paris.

The same factors, of course, reinforced the mass parties' inclination to emphasize their territorial base. In addition, without direct control over municipal expenditures, the parties had to rely on control over the territorial legislatures for access to public funds and political patronage. Furthermore, both electoral and financial support were essential if a political leader was to exert influence at the interterritorial or Parisian level of politics, and this support could come only from his territorial base.

Whether the parties involved were mass or patron, territorial politics in each territory inevitably took on a distinctive cast determined by the presence, competition, and need for cooperation in the legislative assembly of the dominant ethnic groups within the territory. Thus, within a state dominated by a mass party, such as Senegal, politics consisted of relations among the dominant Wolof group and the Serer, Tukulor, Diola, Fulani, Lébou, and others, even though they might all function within a single party. Politics in neighboring Guinea would involve balancing the Malinke, Soussou, and Fulani within the PDG. The Union Soudanaise would balance the interests and representation of the Malinke, Bambara, Dogon, Fulani and other smaller groups. Dahomeyan politics would balance the representation and interests of Fon, Egba, and Bargu, not within a single party but within the common legislature. In each case, however, territorial politics involved a unique ethnic mixture which (aside from the Mossi preeminence in Upper Volta) no single group could aspire to dominate and which rendered the political context of each territory different from that of its neighbors. This tradition of balancing interests within the territorial framework in turn reduced the political effectiveness of ethnic overlaps between the territories as a basis for interterritorial political organization, since the different territorial branches of the same ethnic group were involved in political associations with different partners in different territories.

The lack of a single, dominant, core ethnic group in most territories discouraged the sort of counterbalancing of regionalism evident in Nigerian politics. In Nigeria the minorities of Ibo in the West and Yoruba in the East naturally looked for support to the neighboring region where their kinsmen were in the majority.[5] In French West Africa, since groups were more fragmented and no territorial party could build a majority on a single ethnic base, minority ethnic groups could expect significant representation within their own territorial legislature and thus had less need for political alliances based on tribal association across territorial lines.

Interterritorial Parties

Interterritorial associations of territorial political parties grew out of the need to coordinate African political pressure in the Parisian assemblies. At the two constitutional conventions in Paris in 1945–46, the African representatives coordinated parliamentary action through a loose group known as Bloc Africain, under the leadership of Lamine Gueye of Senegal. As Gueye was the leader of the Senegalese section of the French Socialist Party (SFIO) and occupied a position of some importance in that party's metropolitan hierarchy, the Bloc Africain was closely associated with the Socialists. At the beginning of the first National Assembly called under the new constitution, however, the African deputies split up among the three major French parties "for purely tactical reasons of parliamentary effectiveness."[6] The two Senegalese deputies, Lamine

5. See James S. Coleman, *Nigeria, Background to Nationalism* (Berkeley, University of California Press, 1958), pp. 329–31.

6. Le Rolle, "Contribution à l'étude sur l'évolution des partis africains et la création du Parti de Regroupement Africain," Association Française de Science Politique, Table Ronde (March 1959, mimeo.), p. 3.

Gueye and Leopold Senghor, and the one African deputy from Guinea, Yacine Diallo, remained within the Socialist party; Prince Douala Manga Bell of Cameroun joined the Catholic MRP, and Fily Dabo Sissoko of Soudan and Felix Houphouet-Boigny of the Ivory Coast joined the small Mouvement Unifié de la Renaissance Française, linked (*apparenté*) to the Communist party. In the face of a sharp increase in the influence of colonialist groups led by the Etats Généraux de la Colonisation Française, the African deputies called a meeting in 1946 in Bamako in the Soudan, "the center of West Africa," to form a common front against the colonialist "reaction."[7]

The prospect of this meeting provoked an immediate reaction from the French administration. The Minister for Overseas France, Marius Moutet, successfully put pressure on his fellow Socialists, Lamine Gueye and Leopold Senghor, not to attend. Fily Dabo Sissoko, who had meanwhile shifted to the SFIO, did attend but has since denied actually signing the resolutions of the conference circulated under his name.[8] The result of this pressure was to remove the moderating influence of the Socialists and throw the Bamako conference into the arms of the African extremists, led at the time by Gabriel d'Arboussier, and the Communists, the only metropolitan party to send representatives to the conference.

The Bamako Congress resulted in the formation of the Rassemblement Démocratique Africain (RDA). Convinced that the people of West Africa had one overwhelming interest, the fight against imperialism, the RDA sought to form a vast congress-type movement that would be both "the means of expression of the masses and the masses themselves [rather than] an avant-garde political party" and would permit the union of "all ideological conceptions, all ethnic groups, all social levels, all territories around a program of concrete and clearly defined proposals."[9] The RDA quickly went beyond the initial congress-type organization under the tutelage of its French Communist advisors and in response to the success of the RDA's Ivory Coast mass party, the PDCI of Houphouet-Boigny. While the individual territorial parties, or sections, making up the RDA were in principle accorded "great autonomy as to or-

7. "Manifeste du Rassemblement Démocratique Africain," *Le Rassemblement Démocratique Africain dans la lutte anti-impérialiste* (Paris, 1948), pp. 23–24.
8. See his statement in *Le Monde,* September 26, 1957.
9. *Le RDA dans la lutte anti-impérialiste,* p. 48.

ganizational form as well as orientation and direction of their action" on territorial issues, a common model of territorial party, based on the PDCI, was agreed on by the various sections.[10] This structure provided for ward (*quartier*) committees in the towns and village committees in rural areas, grouped together in subsections embracing the town or *cercle*. The subsection in turn provided the basis for the organization of the section at the territorial level. The RDA established sections or acquired the adherence of existing parties in all the French West African territories, in Cameroons, and in parts of French Equatorial Africa.

The RDA established a set of common interterritorial organs to coordinate the activities of the territorial sections. At the head of these was the Coordinating Committee (*Comité de Coordination*), meeting in Paris, which was to assure liaison between territorial sections, elaborate common political positions on matters of common interest, and coordinate parliamentary action in Dakar and Paris. The RDA established a propaganda headquarters in Dakar which published the party newspaper, *Réveil*, and a financial secretariat in Abidjan because most of the RDA's common funds in those early days came from the PDCI. In fact, the role of the Coordinating Committee was a matter of considerable dispute between those who, like Gabriel d'Arboussier and the more communist-influenced younger members of the party, sought to turn the RDA into a single, united interterritorial party and those like Houphouet-Boigny and the more conservative elements, who sought a larger measure of territorial autonomy. Largely because of the preeminence of Houphouet-Boigny's PDCI within the RDA and his great abilities within the French parliamentary arena, the informal caucus of the representatives of the RDA to the French Assemblies rapidly took over the functions of the Coordinating Committee. This caucus was reinforced when, in 1950, Houphouet-Boigny successfully led the RDA to break with the Communists despite the strenuous protests of the left-wing group and several of the smaller territorial sections, like the Union des Populations du Cameroun (UPC) and the Union Démocratique Sénégalaise (UDS). This meant in effect that the primary instrument of RDA unity functioned less within a purely African context than in the context of French Union politics.

Within the African context, the PDCI was unquestionably the

10. Ibid.

dominant RDA section. The Ivory Coast party had been founded by a large group of African cocoa and coffee planters who had protested against discriminatory treatment by the colonial regime. Under the direction of Houphouet-Boigny, an African doctor, traditional chief, and wealthy planter himself, the planters organized into a pressure group, the Syndicat Agricole Africain, which Houphouet-Boigny used to build up a territory-wide mass party that quickly eliminated all serious rivals within the Ivory Coast.[11] The PDCI had access to considerable funds both through territorial patronage and through the party's regularized system of contributions from party members, many of whom benefited greatly from the territory's rapid economic growth following the war. Some of the less successful RDA sections, like those of Dahomey, Niger, and Upper Volta, whose organizations were more like patron than mass parties, were virtual clients of the PDCI and its dynamic leader.

Houphouet-Boigny's personal hold over the RDA, evident in the quarrel with the party's left wing, was considerably increased after the break with the Communists and the full entry of the RDA into the involved game of French parliamentary politics. The PDCI was able to reassure and gain the confidence of the French administration and French commercial interests within the Ivory Coast. This gave Houphouet-Boigny considerable personal prestige in the National Assembly, and alone among the RDA representatives he was able to function effectively in crucial backstage politicking. Houphouet-Boigny's personal position was firmly established when he was made *secrétaire d'état à la présidence du conseil* in the Guy Mollet cabinet of 1956.

Beginning about 1954–55 a secondary locus of power, which might be described as a Conakry-Bamako axis, developed within the RDA as the PDG and Union Soudanaise increased their hold over their respective territories. This was demonstrated when in 1955 a meeting of the Coordinating Committee was called in Conakry, the capital of Guinea. The Guinean and Soudanese parties represented a more radical and autonomist orientation to politics. They were less concerned with maintaining the good will of the local colonial population and of the French parliamentarians than with defending the demands of a purely African constituency.

11. F. J. Amon d'Aby, *La Côte d'Ivoire dans la cité africaine* (Paris, Larose, 1951), pp. 54–67, 110–14, and passim.

Their parties drew their support principally from a nascent proletariat rather than from a nascent middle class. Within the RDA their strength and interests lay primarily at the local or interterritorial levels, and their commitment to the "Franco-African community" was more tactical than a matter of conviction. The common ideological outlook and "proletarian" base of the Guinean and Soudanese parties were reinforced by personal connections amounting in some cases to interchangeability between top leaders. Through their connections with members of the trading community, the Guinean and the Soudanese RDA leaders also maintained contact with Dioula minority elements in other RDA branches, particularly in Upper Volta and in the northern Ivory Coast. Also, through Sékou Touré's leadership of the dominant West African labor movement, they were on close terms with the urban workers' leaders of other territories, some of whom were at the time also leaders of dissident RDA sections expelled when Houphouet-Boigny led the party to break with the Communists. Despite their inefficacy on the French parliamentary level, the Guinean and Soudanese represented an important force in the RDA's African structure, intermittent as it was at this time.

Thus, as the influence of the PDG and Union Soudanaise grew, the RDA shifted from domination by the Ivory Coast to a bipolar structure with, on the one hand, the PDCI and the less well organized or less successful branches and, on the other, the Guinea–Soudan axis with some support from minority groups in other RDA sections and with informal ties to dissident RDA sections, notably the UDS in Senegal and Sawaba in Niger. The new influence of the Guinean and Soudanese parties within the RDA was not as immediately apparent as it might have been had the Coordinating Committee been a regularly functioning body and had the interterritorial level of politics been as important as the French Union level. As it was, the Guinean and Soudanese leaders found themselves obliged to operate in the French assemblies through the person, or under the aegis, of Houphouet-Boigny. The continued dominance of the Ivory Coast leader rested, however, on a continuation of the institutional status quo in which all major decisions would be made at the French Union level.

Whereas the Ivory Coast and its leaders dominated the RDA, Senegal and its two political leaders dominated the two other interterritorial political groups. The first of these was the Socialist party

(SFIO) which established branches in all the West African territories at the end of World War Two. Its Senegalese branch had been founded in the 1930s and in 1945 controlled all the elective offices of Senegal under the leadership of Lamine Gueye and his young assistant, Leopold Senghor. Following in importance were the Soudanese section under the leadership of Fily Dabo Sissoko and the Guinean section under Yacine Diallo. All three sections fall within our definition of patron party. The Senegalese section was based on Lamine Gueye's personal connections among the leaders of the original populations of the Senegalese communes and a few notables in the interior, and the Soudanese and Guinean sections were based on the cantonal chiefs, particularly among the Fulani populations. The Socialists also frequently enjoyed the support of the colonial administration, but none of the branches was in a position to face a prolonged honest fight for electoral support with a mass party. Their greatest advantage, aside from the administration's benevolence, was the direct support they received from their membership within the metropolitan SFIO. Under Lamine Gueye's leadership they scored some notable successes in the early days of the Fourth Republic.[12] This direct connection with metropolitan politics was, however, a weakness in the competition for African votes, for it linked the Socialists with the colonial regime in the minds of the African electors.

The connection with the metropolitan party was deeply felt by most of the African Socialist leaders who participated in the metropolitan councils of the party and who received from time to time minor subministerial appointments in various Socialist cabinets. (Lamine Gueye, Fily Dabo Sissoko, and Hammadoun Dicko were all at one time or another *sous-secrétaires d'état.*) Their political platform stressed cooperation with France and tended "to draw upon past capital so far as ideas are concerned—particularly upon the idea of equality of civil and political rights."[13] Within the French assemblies they followed strict party discipline, voting to

12. Best known are the two so-called "Lamine Gueye laws." The first (law of May 7, 1946) granted immediate citizenship to all peoples of the colonial territories. The second (law of June 30, 1950) extended family allotments and other fringe benefits to African as well as European governmental employees.

13. Thomas Hodgkin, "Background on French West Africa," *West Africa* (February 20, 1954), p. 159. For a good example of the dependence of the African Socialists on the metropolitan party, see the African Socialists' party newspaper, *AOF*, February 14, 1946, "La Vie du Parti."

a man according to the orders of the party's metropolitan hierarchy on votes confirming new councils of ministers in the Fourth Republic.[14] Because of their membership in the metropolitan party and their sometimes vain reliance on the administration for election, the African Socialists, to a far greater degree than other African politicians, made the French Union the focus of their political action and accepted the permanence of Franco–African political ties. Their declining success (from seven deputies elected in 1946 to three in 1956, from control over five territorial legislatures in 1946 to one in 1957) indicates that perhaps their commitment to France exceeded that of African voters.

The Indépendants d'Outre-Mer (IOM), the third major interterritorial formation, was an attempt to coordinate the political action of those representatives in the French assemblies who were not Socialists and who refused to join the RDA because of its initial communist connections. Although not technically its founder (that honor must go to Sourou Migan Apithy of Dahomey, who soon abandoned his creation), Leopold Senghor of Senegal quickly became the leading light of the IOM after he broke with the Socialist party in 1948 over the question of the African deputies' subservience to the SFIO's metropolitan hierarchy. Within Senegal, Senghor and his associate Mamadou Dia built up a mass party, the Bloc Démocratique Sénégalais (BDS) that successfully challenged the Socialists' control of the territory and ousted Lamine Gueye from his seat in the French National Assembly in the elections of 1951. Senghor rapidly assumed a position of considerable importance within the French National Assembly and in African politics in general and, with Lamine Gueye effectively eliminated, he rivaled Houphouet-Boigny for the role of Africa's spokesman in the French assemblies. That the two men's ideas on a wide variety of subjects were fundamentally different, and that Senegal and the Ivory Coast were rivals for economic leadership within the French West African Federation, made their personal rivalry all the more significant and intense.

The IOM, far more explicitly than the RDA, was strictly a parliamentary party, making no pretense of coordinating policy outside of the assemblies or of following a common political program.

14. Phillipe Guillemin, "Les Elus d'Afrique Noire à l'Assemblée Nationale sous la Quatrième République," *Revue Française de Science Politique, 8* (December 1958), 869.

Its cohesion, even as a voting block within the National Assembly, was the lowest of the three African groups.[15] The IOM contained alongside its Senegalese representatives an unimpressive group of patron party representatives, who were in office almost entirely as a result of administration support and who had virtually no political organization to back them up in their own territories. After the elections of 1951 in which the IOM emerged with a majority of the African representatives in the French assemblies, Senghor and Mamadou Dia sought to capitalize on their success to turn the parliamentary party into a genuine interterritorial party somewhat on the RDA model. This, they hoped, would permit the IOM candidates to survive even without administration support and would provide a more effective base for the advancement of Senghor's political program.

Senghor called a congress for this purpose at Bobo-Dioulasso in February, 1953. The keynote speeches and main reports by Senghor, Dia, and a few progressive associates from other African territories spoke out boldly against the lack of progressive reforms in the colonial domain and the congress unanimously passed resolutions calling for major changes in the relationship between France and the African territories and for the constitution of regular IOM sections in all the African territories. The tenor of the congress won it the nickname of the *congrès des audacieux* in the African press, but it soon became evident that the bold resolutions and creation of a permanent secretariat were simply empty forms for most IOM representatives.[16] Since they were dependent on a limited clientele and to a degree on the colonial administration for their election, they were either unwilling or unable to create mass parties capable of supporting a dynamic political program in the individual territories or in the Grand Council, where IOM cohesion was virtually nonexistent on any but procedural matters. The speeches and "the movement thus created touched only the elite and not the Africa of the peasants in the bush and the worker in the cities."[17] Despite this failure Senghor continued to dominate the IOM, which needed just such a persuasive orator and parliamentary operator to head their rather lackluster group and help finance their campaigns at

15. Guillemin, pp. 870–73.
16. The Congress is reported in *Afrique Nouvelle,* March 4, 1953.
17. Le Rolle, "Contribution à l'étude . . . du PRA," p. 6.

home. Senghor in turn needed IOM votes to push through his program and enable him to stand up to Houphouet-Boigny.

During the 1945–55 period, the organization of political parties reflected and reinforced the structure given French West Africa by the formal political institutions of the Fourth Republic. The basic unit of political party activity was the individual territory, and party organization tended to reinforce the distinctiveness of each territorial unit. Representation in the Grand Council and in the Parisian assemblies presupposed control of a territorial base. While effective political organization at the territorial level was thus a precondition of political success, organization at a higher level was possibly desirable but not absolutely necessary. What counted more was the ability to organize a voting bloc in the National Assembly. The initial impetus toward formation of interterritorial political organizations had come in large part from the European parties with which the African politicians were at first allied in the National Assembly. When these ties were broken or weakened, early interest in tight interterritorial organization waned. The RDA alone, in this period, maintained formal organs of interterritorial coordination, but these, too, functioned primarily to assure an effective parliamentary caucus in the Parisian assemblies.

In part the fragility of some of the new political formations was to blame for the lack of structured interterritorial parties. The patron parties, in particular, were much too preoccupied with building up a secure base at home to enmesh themselves in a close interterritorial organization—particularly if their position at home depended on the benevolent neutrality of the French administration.

It is possible that had the Grand Council provided a more dynamic forum for the arguing out of fundamental political issues free from the complications and distractions of the Parisian assemblies, well-structured interterritorial parties might have served a more immediately apparent purpose. As it was, politics in the Dakar Council was dominated by territorial monetary concerns, not by the interests of political parties. Effective crossterritorial coalitions were virtually impossible to maintain except on procedural matters.

Despite their weaknesses, interterritorial political parties did serve the interests of both patron and mass parties. The weaker patron parties saw the interterritorial organizations primarily as a means of assuring moral and financial support for their territorial campaigns. For the major African leaders like Houphouet-Boigny and Senghor, the interterritorial parties provided votes in the National Assembly and a wide range of personal political dependents whose very numbers served to reinforce their prestige, and perhaps ultimately their power.

This approach to interterritorial political organization depended to a great extent, however, on the leaders' willingness to work within the political system as set out in the Fourth Republic's constitution. Were they to desire a more rapid or a different evolution than was provided by French legislative politics, a broad-based political formation would be a needed weapon to force change upon a reluctant administration. To a limited extent, Senghor in the IOM and Touré and Modibo Keita in the RDA were already moving in that direction. The succeeding chapters will show us some of the consequences of this change.

5

"Federalism," "Unity," and "Independence": French West African Politics from the Loi-Cadre to the Referendum

THE FIRST DECADE of the Fourth Republic had established both formal and informal structures for the conduct of politics in French West Africa and had brought into being a modern African political elite capable of dealing both with the masses of its own people and with the involved politics of the National Assembly and the Ministry of Overseas France. As the African elite came to take a greater hand in their own affairs, the great issues of French African politics underwent a major change. The colonial period's quarrel over "assimilation" and "association" was replaced by an Africa-centered conflict over the slogans of "federalism," "unity," and, finally, "independence."

"Federalism" and "Unity" in France and Africa

"Federalism" in the years 1944–58 was one of those highly charged political terms like "republican legality" and "*auto-détermination,*" that have from time to time lent excessive confusion to French legislative politics. As originally propounded, the term "federalism" dealt with establishing relations between the metropolitan country and the overseas territories and associated states. As advanced at the 1944 Brazzaville conference and the First Constituent Assembly, it was given a decidedly liberal aura as the proposal of the Communist and Socialist parties to abandon once and for all any attempt at assimilating the overseas territories into the "Republic one and indivisible." Under the benign guidance of Pierre Cot, the native delegates of the overseas territories inscribed in the Constitution the principle of a French Union based on "the free consent" of its members. This Union would build its institutions from the bottom, starting with the territorial assemblies, until such time as the overseas territories might feel ready to establish a federal parliament and executive with the metropole, or, although it was not stated outright, to break away completely. The idea of "federalism" was opposed by the parties of the right, and particularly by Bidault's MRP, as threatening the dissolution of the French Union. In its place, they vainly held out for a unitary French Union that, the Africans charged, would have perpetuated the colonial system of the Third Republic.

Immediately after the French voters defeated the first proposed constitution, de Gaulle delivered his Bayeux speech in which he for the first time advocated a form of federalism for the French Union.[1] This, however, was quite the reverse of the Communist–Socialist–African proposal, for it concentrated federalism at the top by establishing the Assembly of the French Union and by severely cutting back the powers of the local assemblies. This new form of federalism was taken up by the MRP, who were the largest party in the Second Constituent Assembly and whose Paul Coste-Floret was the chairman of the Constitutional Commission.[2] Their proposal, with some amendments, was accepted as the final version of Title VIII, the section of the Constitution dealing with the French Union.[3] For the militant Africans, federalism thus became a symbol of dark reaction, and it was in this sense that the RDA Manifesto denounced it: "The 'federalism' of the MRP . . . is only a mask for an authoritarian regime. . . . Like assimilation, it can only end up freezing Africa in its present condition of political organization."[4]

As the passions of the constitutional battle died down, and politicians turned their energies toward maneuvering within the system they had created, the term "federalism" faded momentarily from the headlines. It reappeared in 1948 when the newly constituted IOM under Senghor's leadership published its initial statement of purpose. The IOM restored to the term much of the sense it had in the "Pierre Cot" Constitution while avoiding any suspicion of breaking with the French Union. It advocated "the accession of the non-autonomous territories to a statute of their own choosing within the framework of the French Union as it is defined by the

1. Text in *Année Politique, 1946,* pp. 534–39.

2. The MRP's prestige at this time was largely based on its reputation as *"le parti de la fidélité* to de Gaulle." Philip Williams, *Politics in Post-War France* (London, Longmans, 1958), p. 18.

3. *J.O., Documents de l'Assemblée Nationale Constituante II,* Annexes 42 (pp. 33–34), 68 (pp. 61–63), 350 (pp. 291–305).

4. "Manifeste du RDA," *Le RDA dans la lutte anti-impérialiste,* p. 24.

Constitution," and considered that "It is within the spirit of federalism that we must think through and eventually complete the constitutional institutions."[5] The IOM justified a federal union with the metropole in economic terms, arguing that the modern world leaves no place for small economic units. With this and subsequent pronouncements, Senghor made himself, and by extension the BDS in Senegal and the IOM, the new champions of federalism. At this time federalism still referred to relations between the overseas territories and France, not to relations within the West African Federation. The problem of a federal union among the West African territories was not broached directly during the 1947 debates on the Grand Councils. In fact, at the IOM's Bobo-Dioulasso Congress in 1953, where the idea of federalism was much discussed under the Senghoresque slogan "une République une et *divisible*," the final resolution slighted interterritorial political links although it emphasized economic links at this level.

In the following year Senghor took the idea of "federalism" considerably farther than had the IOM as a body by making it the central idea of his own political program.

> *The object of our program, from now on, is not to suppress the inequalities born of class differences, but rather those which result from* [colonial] *conquest,* especially those of ethnic group and of geography. We are federalists by vocation. *For what is "federation," if not the system which establishes equality between countries, and thereby between races?*[6]

Federalism was Senghor's answer to the problems stemming from relations between the Africans and their colonial masters, problems which, in his opinion, the orthodox Marxists had falsely assumed to be class problems. Senghor accordingly wanted a reformed French Union "organized as a flexible federation or a confederation." Each autonomous territory and each group of territories would be a state integated into the French Republic, but with its own local parliament and executive. A federal parliament and a federal executive would be created in Paris. This vision of the future begged one important question: were the West African territories to join a French Federal Republic individually or grouped together in a "primary federation?" A preliminary answer came a few months later. In a

5. "Déclaration du groupe interparlémentaire des Indépendants d'Outre-Mer" (December 24, 1948), text in *Condition Humaine* (January 11, 1949).

6. Statement in *Marchés Coloniaux,* March 27, 1954, p. 814. (Italics in text.)

major article published in October 1954, Senghor proposed that the West African territories be integrated into a French Federal Republic and that they join as two separate groups. French West Africa was to be divided into two territories; one with its capital in Dakar would include Senegal, Mauretania, Soudan, and Guinea; the other with its capital in Abidjan would include the Ivory Coast, Upper Volta, Niger, and Dahomey. Both of these territories would have a local parliament and local executive.[7] Senghor reasoned that this would make good sense both economically and politically: economically, because each bloc would be large enough to form a reasonable productive unit and because considerable trade already existed among the territories of each unit; politically, because each unit, representing some 10,000,000 people, would be large enough to receive substantial autonomy in internal policy and would not be totally lost beside a France of 43,000,000.[8] Equally important, one may assume, was the thought that this would remove much of the rivalry between Senegal and the Ivory Coast for leadership of the French West African territories.

The other major African parties seemed much less interested in the question of federalism. Houphouet-Boigny's RDA, after its break with the Communists, accepted the UDSR's noncommittal views on the subject of transforming the French Union into a federal structure, and continued to oppose any measure which might reinforce the interterritorial governmental, administrative, or economic links. Any devolution of powers from the French National Assembly, they felt, had to be to the profit of the existing territorial units.[9] The Socialists, likewise, held no strong views on the subject, and consonant with Lamine Gueye's general policy, indicated simply that they favored "enlarging the powers of the assemblies of the groups of territories and those of the territorial assemblies of the Overseas Territories, as well as creating [additional] municipalities with elected officials."[10]

7. "L'Avenir de la France dans l'Outre-Mer," *Politique Etrangère, 4* (October 1954), 424.

8. My calculations bear out the argument of existing trade links. On the basis of 1956 figures, the Relative Acceptance of the Dakar group of its own internal trade is 1.41, and that of the Abidjan group is .95. Both are significant at the .001 level.

9. See the motion of the 1951 UDSR congress and other statements in *J.O., AUF, 1955, Documents,* Annex 104, p. 177.

10. Deliberation of the National Council of the Socialist Party, January 1953, text in ibid., p. 174.

The radical wing of African opinion, represented at the time by the dissident RDA parties and especially the African university students, rejected federation between the African territories and France in terms similar to those employed by the RDA 1946 Manifesto, but also emphasized the necessity for the African states to form close political links with one another to present a united front in the anticolonial struggle.[11] From their point of view, independence or, at the very least, full internal autonomy was the overriding goal; federal union among the African territories seemed likely to advance that goal; federal union with France ran counter to that goal. However, they did not often use the word "federalism." The catchword of the radical left was "unity," especially "political unity," which encompassed the idea of a single political movement, the closest possible political links among Africans of all sorts, and by extension, the elimination of all intra-African political barriers, including those established by the division of Africa among the colonial powers. Federal union of French West Africa, for them, was thus a desirable goal but not a final goal.[12] The leaders of the RDA sections in Guinea and Soudan shared a similar intellectual and emotional commitment to the goal of African unity, but they did not at the time publicly advocate immediate independence.[13]

Among the major purely metropolitan parties, only the MRP showed enthusiasm for an increase in federalism, but it understood federalism exclusively in terms of association between individual overseas territories and the metropole and called for weakening the links among the African territories themselves, and for reducing the competence of the Grand Councils and Governments-General of French West and Equatorial Africa.[14] For the MRP, as for most of the French Right, reinforcing federation at the interterritorial

11. See the special issue of *Présence Africaine,* "Les Etudiants noirs parlent," No. 14 (1953), especially the following articles: David Diop, "L'Etudiant Africain devant le fait colonial" (114–17); Maghmout Diop, "L'Unique issue: l'indépendance totale. La seule voie: un large mouvement d'union anti-impérialiste" (145–84); Kader Fall, "Problèmes d'élites en Afrique Noire" (33–39); and Abdoulaye Wade, "Afrique Noire et Union Française" (118–44).

12. See Appendix I.

13. See the "Allocution d'Ouverture" of Mamadou Konaté and the "Rapport Politique" of Modibo Keita in Union Soudanaise, "Les Travaux du 4ème congrès territorial, 22–24 Septembre, 1955" (Bamako, mimeo.), and Sékou Touré, *Expérience guinéenne et unité africaine* (Paris, Présence Africaine, 1961).

14. See the article of Daniel Boisdon, "Préface aux débats sur la réforme constitutionelle," *Marchés Coloniaux,* No. 403 (August 1, 1953).

level was a dangerous game that might give the African territories a strong enough base to break all association with France.[15]

Thus, federalism, when used by the French Right and by the orthodox RDA, referred to a constitutional device for integrating the individual overseas territories more fully into the French Republic. When used by the extreme left wing African politicians and by the students, it referred to a way of uniting the African territories against French colonialism. When used by Senghor, it partook of both these senses, and provided a way of safeguarding African unity and "personality" in close association with France. The connotations of "federalism" could be both radical and conservative and depended on the user and the precise referent, if, as was not often the case, this latter was made clear. As a subject for impassioned political oratory it was ideal; as a means of clearly delineating issues, it left much to be desired. It soon became the dominant theme of French West African politics.

The Background to Reform

By the end of 1955, when the French National Assembly was dissolved and new elections called for January 2, 1956, three important, if subtle, changes had taken place in the French West African political scene. These changes involved both the relations between Africa and France and relations among political groups within West Africa itself.

First came a change in the attitude of the French colonial administration and the major French political leaders in favor of recognizing the legitimacy of African political activity and political demands and of accepting the principle of devolution of increased political authority to the local African institutions. The January 2 elections were therefore virtually free from the administrative pressure that had characterized most earlier elections. In this relatively free climate, the parties with the best mass organization were everywhere victorious at the expense of the patron parties. The RDA territorial sections won great victories at the expense of the Socialists and of the IOM, of which only Senghor's BDS successfully held its own. Of the twenty deputies elected from French

15. For an example of this logic at work, see the discussion of Senghor's ideas by Marc Rucart of the RGR in *J.O., C.R., Débats,* August 11, 1947, p. 1722.

West Africa, twelve were RDA (as opposed to three in the previous election), six were IOM (a loss of eight seats), and two were SFIO (a loss of one seat). The French officials also indicated a willingness to work with the African representatives to plan revisions of Africa's political institutions. In an unusual communiqué following the elections, the Ministry of Overseas France stated: "The results of the elections as well as the declarations made by the various African leaders, confirm the existence of a healthy climate and a general desire for reasonable evolution within the framework of the French Union."[16] Houphouet-Boigny, as head of the RDA, was accordingly made *ministre d'état* (minister without portfolio working directly with the Premier) in the Guy Mollet government and, with Gaston Defferre, the Minister of Overseas France, was charged with preparing the political and administrative reforms for the overseas territories. Although several Africans had held cabinet posts, this was the first instance of one being given a full ministerial position and put to work on African problems.[17]

Several factors may explain this shift on the part of the French. First, the Africans themselves and particularly Houphouet-Boigny and Senghor had by this time fully entered into the game of French politics. In Africa the territorial assemblies and the Grand Councils had managed to conduct their business without bringing on either anarchy or bankruptcy, while in the politically fragmented assemblies of Paris, the African parties' support was frequently necessary for a metropolitan faction to win its point or for a government to stay in power. The UDSR, the most important of the small center groups, in particular owed much of its power to its alliance with the RDA.[18] The importance of African votes in the National Assembly elected in January 1956 was increased by the success of both the Communists and the extreme right (Poujadistes), which threatened the system's stability. Secondly, Great Britain's announcement that the Gold Coast would become independent in 1957 and the United Nations' pressure on France over Togo in-

16. Text in *Le Monde*, January 13, 1956, p. 5.

17. The earlier Africans had been *sous-secrétaires d'état* or *secrétaires d'état*, posts corresponding to an American assistant secretary or undersecretary. Dr. Aujoulat, a white IOM deputy of the Cameroons, had previously held full ministerial portfolios, but these were in the comparatively nonsensitive ministries of Health and Labor.

18. See Philip Williams, *Politics in Post-War France*, pp. 143–46.

creased France's awareness that the winds of change were now blowing, if softly, on Black Africa.[19] Thirdly, and probably most important, France appeared to have learned something from her recent debacle in Indo-China and her growing difficulties in Algeria. A dominant and recurrent theme throughout the parliamentary debates on reform in Black Africa was presented most boldly by Paul Alduy of the National Assembly's committee on Overseas France: "It would be most regrettable that recent or current tragic events should tend to lend credence to the idea that . . . Parliament considers the aspirations of the peoples of the French Union only when they have already lost confidence in the nation. . . . It must not be said . . . that *fellaghisme* pays."[20] In addition to its intrinsic merits, then, reform in Black Africa was intended partially as a reward to loyalty, partially as an attempt to keep ahead of events, and partially to demonstrate to the North Africans that they were going about things the wrong way.

The second important change in the French African political situation was the rise of what might be called the "second generation" of African elites. Within the existing major parties, this meant the rise to positions of top leadership of men like the RDA's Modibo Keita and Sékou Touré, both of whom entered the National Assembly for the first time in 1956. Equally important was the return to West Africa of the first wave of postwar university students from France. To understand the impact of this influx on the intermediate level of the political parties, it suffices to reflect that in 1929–30 there were two French West Africans registered in French universities. Twenty years later there were 165 and by 1954–55, there were 684, with another 200 following university-level courses in Dakar.[21] Among the major African politicians of the immediate postwar generation, only three held university degrees. In an area where the university degree carries inordinate prestige in all phases of life, the recent graduates seemed destined to climb the political ladder rapidly.

The majority of students had been members of the RDA youth group in France, and, not surprisingly, many of them joined the

19. See Praetor Africanus, "Emancipations Africaines II: La Loi-Cadre au banc d'essai," *L'Afrique et l'Asie*, 3 (1957), 14–30.

20. *J.O., A.N., Débats* (March 20, 1956), p. 1065.

21. Institut National de la Statistique et des Etudes Economiques, *Annuaire statistique de la France, 1961*, Table XII, p. 68.

RDA (or in some cases its dissident sections) on their return to Africa. They were particularly attracted to the Soudan and Guinea sections, and within other territorial sections they tended to sympathize with the militant viewpoints of Touré and Modibo Keita. The students' return was particularly felt in Senegal and especially in Dakar which attracted many non-Senegalese graduates as well. There, many of them gravitated to the UDS, the dissident RDA section of Senegal, and in the 1956 elections that party collected a surprising 7,000 votes, almost all from among the young and the urbanized. Others, notably those who had founded the independent Dakar newspaper, *Réalités Africaines,* for the time being stayed clear of the existing parties, waiting for the proper moment to throw their support to one group or another. Without the long association with French governmental authorities that their elders had had, and with the usual ebullience of youth, this second generation of potential leaders was less inclined to accept the existing political situation, and some even let the word "independence" pass their lips in political discussions.

While all the current party leaders saw the necessity of attracting these younger men to their banners, Senghor was particularly concerned. On the interterritorial level, his IOM was greatly in need of new blood and a new image after the January elections. At home in Senegal his BDS had still not reduced the Socialist strongholds of St. Louis and Dakar (the major sources of political patronage), and an alliance between the Senegalese RDA or the UDS and the Socialists might possibly spell disaster for his party. He therefore set out to attract the leaders of the younger generation. His overwhelming electoral victory everywhere in Senegal but in the two coastal cities quite legitimately allowed him to present himself as the spokesman for the Senegalese masses. He was helped also by his party's being excluded from the new Mollet cabinet in Paris, which permitted him considerable latitude in criticizing the French government and administration. On January 24, 1956, the BDS obtained the adherence of an important group of young intellectuals, including Abdoulaye Ly, a young historian, and Amadou Mokhtar M'Bow, a lycée professor and head of the Senegalese Education Extension Service.[22] Senghor quickly advanced them

22. See their letter in *Paris-Dakar,* January 25, 1956. "After the elections whose result . . . is everywhere the flocking of the African masses . . . around men, programs, and slogans challenging more or less openly the structure of the French

to positions of considerable organizational responsibility within the BDS, and with their help soon persuaded most of the UDS to join his party.

The third major change in French West African politics was the growth of interest in a common African political movement uniting all parties and free of all metropolitan ties. This in part was prompted by the young intellectuals who, understandably, had little patience with the personal quarrels of their elders and felt, in the words of the Senegalese intellectuals just mentioned, that "only a solid and broad United Front . . . will assure rapid and decisive victories against the forces of Reaction, Domination and Exploitation."[23] For them, politics was above all a matter of "colonized versus colonizer," and all other considerations were secondary to this struggle. The labor unions, too, were seeking a way to form a common, purely African front. At a meeting in Kaolack in November 1955, the General Committee of the Senegal and Mauretania CGT disaffiliated from the French CGT and the World Federation of Trade Unions and established an independent African union movement, the Conféderation Générale des Travailleurs d'Afrique (CGTA), which they invited all other African unions to join. At the February 1956 meeting of the CGT leadership for all AOF, a major fraction of the federation-wide movement, led by Sékou Touré, broke its French ties and sought alliances with other non-CGT unions.

Unity as a means of bringing combined pressure on both the local administration and on the French Parliament was very much the order of the day, the more so because, in the realm of political parties, one could hark back to the real, if ephemeral, period of unity that had characterized African politics immediately after the war. But unity of all parties was not to be attained easily. Preliminary contacts between the IOM and RDA during the electoral campaign had dissolved in personal recriminations, and more for-

---

Union . . . the African intellectuals are obliged to choose sides or resign from the fight. Senegalese, we have chosen the party of the Senegalese masses, the party which incontestably represents the laboring people, the *real proletariat* of this country, the Bloc Démocratique Sénégalais. . . . If there are contradictions or faults in the party of our choice, honestly we shall attempt, hand in hand not only with our comrades, but also with all Africans of good will, to surmount or to obliterate them." Senghor's response is in *Paris-Dakar*, January 26, 1956.

23. Ibid.

mal talks held in Abidjan on January 17, 1956, had also proved unsuccessful, although it was decided to maintain the dialogue. The Ivory Coast RDA insisted on treating the IOM like errant sheep who had but to return to the fold to bring about unity, while the IOM, and particularly the Senegalese, felt that the movements should amalgamate on equal terms. Obviously, there would be much maneuvering for position and particularly for the loyalties of the uncommitted youth before any final amalgamation of African parties could take place. It is with this background that French West Africa and metropolitan France approached the revision of relations between Africa and France in the spring of 1956.

The Loi-Cadre of 1956 and the Problem of African Unity

The *proposition de loi* sent to the French Parliament by Defferre and Houphouet-Boigny was a double disappointment for the cause of federalism. It did not broach the subject of revising the structure of the French Union in a federal or any other direction. Whatever inclinations the Mollet government may have had toward basic constitutional revision, the government, faced with a strong Communist group on its left and the unforeseen menace of the Poujadistes on its right, wanted at all costs to avoid the subject of constitutional reform, lest it lead to collusion of left and right extremists capable of undermining the shaky structure of the Fourth Republic.[24]

Even more disappointing for the federalists, and particularly for both Senghor and the left-wing Africans, was the refusal of the Loi-Cadre to envisage any sort of "primary federation" at the inter-

24. See the *motion préjudicielle* of M. Cuicci, *J.O., A.N., Débats* (2nd sitting of March 20, 1956), pp. 1068–69, for just such an attempt on the part of the Poujadistes during the debate on the Loi-Cadre. As it was, the form of legislation chosen—the Loi-Cadre or enabling act—was at the time considered a somewhat irregular way to proceed, and its constitutionality was the subject of much pro forma discussion. The general consensus seemed to be that the Loi-Cadre might be stretching the Constitution a bit, but that speed and efficiency dictated the necessity of permitting the government to issue implementing decrees in the name of the National Assembly. See the speech of M. Monichon, *rapporteur pour avis de la commission du suffrage universel, J.O., C.R., Débats* (June 7, 1956), p. 959 ff. Since then, the Loi-Cadre form has been used several times by both the Fourth and Fifth Republics, notably in legislating for Algeria.

territorial level. The Defferre-Houphouet reforms struck the Government-General a death blow.[25] The devolution of powers foreseen in the Loi-Cadre was entirely to the advantage of the territorial assemblies. In the economic realm, the number and amount of obligatory expenditures included in the territorial budgets were substantially reduced, being limited to interest on the public debt, legislators' salaries, and the like. The territorial assemblies were given full legislative power over most internal matters like agriculture, health, customary law, and the territorial civil service, including for the first time the right to institute criminal penalties for non-compliance. In its final version, the Loi-Cadre provided for the establishment of the single electoral college for all future elections in Black Africa. Most important, for the first time the territorial legislatures were permitted to form their own cabinets with executive authority over matters within the assemblies' competence.[26]

No comparable devolution of powers took place at the interterritorial level. The Grand Council remained without executive authority, and the matters under its competence were greatly reduced. Thus, interterritorial services were, for the most part, transformed into *services d'état,* to be paid for out of metropolitan funds and to be administered entirely by the High Commissioner in his capacity of "repository of the powers of the Republic."[27] The interterritorial services left under the authority of the Grand Council were relatively unimportant (such as mineral prospecting and control of epidemics), and its control of financial matters was limited principally to those developmental expenditures common to all territories of the federation (although as has been mentioned before, most of these were in fact bargained out between the territorial representatives and the FIDES governing board in Paris).

25. The text of the Loi-Cadre (Law no. 56–619 of June 23, 1956) can be found in *Année Politique, 1956,* pp. 512–14. For analyses of the law and its decrees see Praetor Africanus, "Emancipations Africaines II: La Loi-Cadre au banc d'essai"; Kenneth E. Robinson, "Constitutional Reform in French Tropical Africa," *Political Studies, 6* (1958), 45–69; F. Borella, "L'Evolution des Territoires d'Outre-Mer et la Loi-Cadre Defferre," *Recueil Penant,* No. 642 (August–September 1956).

26. The chief minister was to bear the title of *Vice-Président du Conseil,* while the territorial governor would be ex officio the cabinet's president with right of veto. In fact this provision was strictly a matter of form, and the vice-president quickly assumed entire leadership of the cabinet.

27. See Robinson, "Constitutional Reform," pp. 56–57, for an enumeration of the *services d'état.*

As a measure of the reduced importance of the Grand Council, its provisional budget for 1958 (the first year after all the Loi-Cadre decrees went into effect) amounted to only 28.6 billion CFA francs, of which 13.8 billion were returned to the territories as rebates and subsidies. In 1956, the federal budget had amounted to 43.7 billion francs of which about 18 billion were returned to the territories. Making allowances for change in the value of the franc, this represented a drop in the monetary value of the crude federal budget of about 45 per cent and of about 51 per cent of the amount left after subsidies and rebates to the territorial budgets.[28]

The Loi-Cadre was a triumph for Houphouet-Boigny personally and for the Ivory Coast, which had so long resented its large contribution to the interterritorial budget. Whereas the Ivory Coast had made a net contribution of 10.2 billion CFA francs to the 1954 budget, its net contribution to the 1958 budget was a mere 2.6 billion. Allowing for a change in the value of the franc, this represented a reduction of 80 per cent.[29]

As one would expect, Senghor, as leader of the federalist forces, objected strenuously. Although as late as January 26, 1956, he had reiterated his proposal to divide French West Africa into two separate states,[30] he now became a passionate defender of the unity of French West Africa and of the prerogatives of the Grand Council. Having failed to change the proposed law in committee, he denounced it bitterly on the Assembly floor for "Balkanizing" the West African territories and betraying a crude policy of divide and rule.[31] His fight was hopeless. The metropolitan French deputies and the colonial administration did not wish to see executive power concentrated in the hands of Africans able to speak for a block of some 20,000,000 compatriots.[32] The IOM itself was badly divided,

28. Sources: *Comptes économiques de L'AOF 1956, 5,* 115–18, and figures supplied by the Direction Générale des Finances of the French West African High Commission.

29. Ibid., and Table 1.

30. See his article, "Création de deux grands territoires en AOF," in *Condition Humaine,* January 26, 1956.

31. *J.O., A.N., Débats* (2nd sitting of March 20, 1956), p. 1070.

32. It is not entirely clear why the French should have been so opposed to reinforcing power at the interterritorial level, although the following factors seem to have played some role. First, the "divide and conquer" argument used by the African radicals against the French was certainly not without a grain of truth. The administration, and particularly the French living and doing business in West Africa, had repeatedly equated "African unity" with "secession" as had the MRP in metropolitan France. Secondly, there is no question but that the federal administration in

with several of its more conservative deputies patently preferring to see power concentrated on the territorial level.[33] On a minor amendment, proposed probably as a test of strength, Senghor collected only six votes, all from among his closest political associates. Houphouet-Boigny, on the other hand, kept the RDA solidly in line, despite the federalist tendencies of its Soudanese and Guinean deputies. Although Senghor and his friends indicated their disapproval by abstaining, the only significant group in the National Assembly voting against the Loi-Cadre was the Poujadistes.

Although defeated in Paris, Senghor determined to make political hay in Africa. Through the BDS newspaper he reiterated his thesis of a West African primary federation joined as part of a Federal French Republic.[34] At the BDS congress at Kaolack in May 1956, Senghor and his lieutenant, Mamadou Dia, denounced "the confusion and difficulties brought about by . . . Balkanization" of the overseas territories that threatened to "cancel out any autonomy that might be acquired."[35] While the theme of federalism provided the backdrop to the congress, Senghor hammered away at the idea of regrouping all the African political forces. The congress heartily approved the initiative of the CGTA labor union in break-

---

Dakar was inefficient, wasteful, and often a roadblock to urgent decisions. Bernard Cornut-Gentille, the High Commissioner in Dakar from 1951 to 1956, had often called for reorganization of the federal services. Thirdly, it has been suggested that certain sectors of French commerce were not averse to "weakening present administrative controls, and hoped to play on the inexperience (or in certain cases the corruption) of the African officials to transform . . . the Overseas Territories into so many new Liberias" (Praetor Africanus, "Emancipations Africaines II," p. 25). Fourthly, the government was at the time concerned with establishing a common organization of the Saharan regions (OCRS) which would have detached parts of Soudan, Niger, and most of Mauretania, something that would have been made additionally complicated by the necessity of gaining the approval of a Dakar assembly. Finally, and perhaps most important of all, Houphouet-Boigny's personal influence and that of the French commercial interests in the Ivory Coast unquestionably counted for much, both within the Mollet government and with the Minister for Overseas France who was also mayor of Marseilles, the seat of much Franco-African commerce. In addition, it has commonly been supposed—and not denied by Lamine Gueye—that the Socialists took particular pleasure in handing Senghor, their former colleague, a defeat on his latest passion. For a good discussion of the problem, see "Un Malentendu sur le fédéralisme," *Marchés Coloniaux* (September 15, 1956), p. 2442.

33. See the speech of Diawadou Barry of the Bloc d'Action Guinéenne (IOM), *J.O., A.N., Débats* (1956), pp. 1070–72.

34. "Confédération et fédération," *Condition Humaine,* April 14, 1956.

35. Mamadou Dia quoted in *Le Monde,* May 29, 1956. The major speeches and resolutions of the congress are in *Condition Humaine,* May 31, 1956.

ing its metropolitan ties and working for a common labor front and called for a similar union of political parties. On the local level this appeal was effective; a substantial UDS delegation to the congress indicated its solidarity with the BDS point of view and opened talks which in August formally fused the dissident section of the RDA with Senghor's party, rebaptised for the occasion the Bloc Populaire Sénégalais. In addition, on June 15, 1956, *Réalités Africaines* agreed to synchronize its editorial policy with the BDS party line. On the interterritorial level, Senghor's appeal had less immediate success. The RDA declined its invitation to the congress, claiming to be in "deep mourning" for the death of one of its founders.

Meanwhile, Houphouet-Boigny, held in France by his cabinet post, paid no apparent heed to the federalist noises in Dakar. On the contrary he hastened to reassure metropolitan opinion that what remained of the Grand Councils would have very little power. "They are not to be organs for decision-making (*de commandement*), but simply of coordination between the territories." He insisted further that he mistrusted any application of a "*fédéralisme prématuré*" and guaranteed that the single college system would not mean the end of European participation in African politics.[36] Despite the Houphouet program's lack of appeal to the intellectuals and African radicals, the RDA in Africa was at least holding its own against Senghor. It acquired a major foothold in Dahomey when part of the governmental party under Justin Ahomadegbe broke away and joined the RDA. In Upper Volta the RDA section fused with the major Mossi party and thereby gained the support of the Morho Naba, and the Union Soudanaise cut its major rivals down to one by absorbing Tidiani Traoré's Bloc Démocratique Soudanais. The municipal elections of November 18, 1956, resulted in another RDA sweep outside of Senegal.[37]

Although the RDA retained its appeal for the West African voters, Senghor, by emphasizing the idea of African political unity, maintained the political initiative in West Africa. The theme with which he chose to identify himself continued to dominate the West African headlines. In January 1957 three major congresses, one led by the IOM, one led by the Socialists, and one by the West African labor unions tried to bring the day of political unity closer. In

36. Speech at Lille, reported in *Le Monde,* June 24–25, 1956.
37. Full election results are given in *Le Monde,* November 18, 1956.

Dakar, Senghor and his chief lieutenants called an "interterritorial congress for regrouping the African political parties" which transformed the amorphous structure of the IOM into a formal "interterritorial unified party," the Convention Africaine, with a structure approximating that of the RDA.[38] Invitations were extended to all the French African political parties, and several sent observers, including the RDA whose prestigious delegation was headed by Ouezzin Coulibaly and included Doudou Gueye, head of the loyal RDA section in Senegal (MPS), and Philippe Yacé, one of Houphouet's chief lieutenants in the Ivory Coast. Senghor's main themes—unity through a common political party, through a primary federation, and through a strengthened Grand Council, and a French Union transformed into a confederation—dominated the congress.

Senghor himself, as if to minimize any conflict his strong personality might provoke, kept out of the limelight. His one welcoming speech was most conciliatory toward all present, and in it he pointedly apologized for having "obeyed orders imposed from the outside" by not attending the RDA's congress in Bamako in 1946. He further disclaimed any desire for Dakar or Senegal to dominate a West African federation.[39] The statutes of the new interterritorial party specifically forbade it to adhere to any metropolitan party (Article 27) and provided that it "could dissolve itself to facilitate a wider regrouping, or affiliate with an 'international' of colonial peoples' parties having the same ideal and the same program" (Article 28). The congress in addition passed two motions sponsoring the grievances of university students and all African youth.[40] By extending the olive branch all around, and by reiterating his appeals to the younger generation, Senghor strengthened both his own position and his new party, and maintained his claim to the role of defender of African unity.

On the same days, the African Socialists were holding a similar, if less publicized, congress in Conakry at which Lamine Gueye brought together under his presidency all the Socialist parties of Black Africa into one purely African movement, the Mouvement Socialiste Africain, which, with Guy Mollet's blessing, broke all

38. Convention Africaine, *Congrès interterritorial de regroupement des partis politiques africains, Dakar le 11, 12, et 13 janvier 1957* (Dakar, 1957).

39. "Discours d'ouverture," Ibid., pp. 4–6.

40. Ibid., pp. 58, 59.

formal ties with the metropolitan SFIO.[41] The MSA was strengthened by the formal adherence of the RDA's dissident Niger section, headed by Djibo Bakary, but it rejected the necessity of forming a single party in West Africa. As Lamine Gueye phrased it after the MSA's Directing Committee's meeting a month later, "That [the parties] by dint of supporting the same positions end up discovering enough affinities to integrate into the same organization, that is the sort of thing that happens as a conclusion, not as a preliminary condition."[42] It should be noted that, on the Senegalese level, any union between Lamine Gueye's party and the BPS could result only in the former's being swallowed up by Senghor's party.

While the MSA opposed the "Balkanization" of Africa, it also supported the Loi-Cadre reforms and the "spirit of liberalism" that inspired them. It refused to be drawn into a discussion of autonomy or independence. As a socialist party, it felt its primary goal to be "the independence of the individual, without which it is vain to speak of the independence of peoples."[43] Thus, if the African Socialists were not yet ready to jump into a common party with the other African politicians, they at least did not consider their reluctance a "fundamental question of principle" and had taken the important step of becoming a purely African organization.[44]

At Cotonou, meanwhile, the theme of unity dominated the labor union congress in which the split between the CGT and Sékou Touré's CGTA was finally healed. The two unions agreed to join in a Union Générale des Travailleurs d'Afrique Noire (UGTAN) headed by Touré which received the allegiance of territorial sections controlling over 80 per cent of French West African organized labor. In its political resolution, the congress denounced the Loi-Cadre as "a mystification, a façade which fools no one; its sole aim is to divide us, to disguise and perpetuate the colonial regime."[45]

Senghor continued to press his initiative, and particularly to seek the support of the African youth and intellectuals and the radical wing of the RDA. In Paris, where the first of the implementing decrees of the Loi-Cadre were under discussion, Senghor seemed

41. The MSA Convention was reported in *Le Monde* of January 14 and 15, 1957.

42. Quoted in *Le Monde*, February 19, 1957.

43. Quoted in *Le Monde*, January 15, 1957.

44. Lamine Gueye's home party, the Senegalese section of the SFIO, adopted the "purely African" title of Parti Sénégalais d'Action Socialiste (PSAS).

45. Text in *Présence Africaine*, Nos. 17–18 (Feb.–May 1958), 124.

purposely to alienate French parliamentary opinion by his impassioned pleas for African autonomy. At the BPS meeting in Dakar, February 22–24, 1957, held under the banner of "The African Community before the Franco-African Community," he called for all parties to join with the BPS in the struggle against colonial reaction, and addressing his followers, proclaimed: "Comrades, I invite you to consider yourselves from now on in a state of legal resistance. From now on, we Senegalese should lead the combat, being ready to sacrifice ourselves on the altar of African unity."[46]

February and March 1957 brought elections again, this time for the territorial assemblies and the prize of constituting the first territorial executives. Serious attempts at political unity yielded for the time being to campaign oratory. The RDA's local organizations again proved their worth, and RDA sections won virtually all the seats in Ivory Coast, Guinea, and Soudan, with slight majorities in Upper Volta and Niger. In Senegal the BPS reinforced its supremacy over the Socialists and token RDA resistance.[47]

Houphouet-Boigny's victory speech exuded confidence and Franco-African good will: "It is . . . comforting to state that the masses have shown confidence in those who have agreed to follow the road of cooperation. . . . *The raw truth is that there are no extremists in Africa.*"[48] Perhaps he spoke overhastily. Word leaked out of bickering and restlessness among the younger RDA members who were increasingly attracted to Senghor's mode of thought.[49] Sékou Touré found it necessary to issue a statement affirming that "there is only one RDA grouped around one course of action, and which maintains its full and entire confidence in Felix Houphouet-Boigny."[50] His actions belied his words. Touré's inaugural speech as head of the Guinea government[51] was a scathing attack against the French commercial interests that Houphouet-Boigny had been so assiduously cultivating, the same interests that Senghor had at-

46. Quoted in *Le Monde,* February 26, 1957. The main congress documents appear in *Unité* (the BPS newspaper) of March 5 and May 25, 1957.

47. Election results for French West Africa can be found in *Afrique Nouvelle,* April 2, 1957, and *Le Monde,* April 3, 1957. The Senegalese election is thoroughly analysed in Kenneth E. Robinson, "Senegal."

48. *Le Monde,* April 3, 1957. The italics are Houphouet-Boigny's. See also his "Black Africa and the French Union," *Foreign Affairs, 35* (July 1957), 593–99.

49. Léo Hamon, "La Mise en place des pouvoirs politiques en Afrique Noire," *Cahiers de la République,* No. 7 (May–June 1957), 57–59.

50. Quoted in *Le Monde,* April 21–22, 1957.

51. *Le Monde,* June 18, 1957.

tacked for seeking to divide and rule French West Africa. The full congress of the RDA, the first since its establishment in 1946, which was to have been held in July 1957, was postponed until September in the hope of first settling internal differences quietly.

The Grand Council, meeting for the first time since the March elections, elected a homogeneous RDA slate of officers: Houphouet-Boigny was president (a largely honorary office); d'Arboussier first vice-president; and Doudou Gueye head of the permanent commission charged with preparing bills for debate. Then came the greatest blow to Houphouet's position. As soon as Houphouet-Boigny had left for Paris (to consolidate his position in the new Bourgès-Manoury cabinet), the Grand Council, on a motion by Touré supported by d'Arboussier, passed a unanimous resolution denouncing those provisions of the Loi-Cadre limiting the Grand Council's power. To the cheers of the Convention Africaine, the RDA delegates formally demanded that steps be taken toward the creation of a federal executive for all of French West Africa.[52] When questioned in Paris on the Grand Council's action, Houphouet-Boigny had no comment.[53]

Houphouet returned to Africa only for the RDA conference in Bamako which opened on September 25, 1957. The question of federalism dominated the agenda. Both the Guinea and Soudan sections had previously received mandates from their members to press for the creation of federal executives, and the younger members of the other parties favored the policy repeatedly advocated by Senghor. The reception accorded the Ivory Coast delegation was decidedly "cool," as one of its leaders later complained,[54] and even Houphouet-Boigny, who had announced to the French press on boarding his plane at Orly that the purpose of the conference was "the study of the proper methods for reinforcing the Franco-African community," was unable to draw his usual enthusiastic response from the rank and file membership.[55] Houphouet's opening speech was carefully calculated to cut some of the ground out from under the radical "federalists." He implicitly adopted half of Senghor's program and demanded that the French Union be revised by "the creation of a great federal egalitarian State with a federal par-

52. See the reports in *Afrique Nouvelle,* September 3, 1957.
53. *Le Monde,* September 5, 1957.
54. Auguste Denise quoted in *Afrique Nouvelle,* October 29, 1957.
55. Houphouet-Boigny quoted in *Le Monde,* September 26, 1957.

liament and federal government, composed of federated autonomous States including the metropole itself." He concluded dramatically with the threat to the colonial power, "This federalism will be based on equality, or just will not be at all."[56] But if this was one form of federalism, it was the wrong form as far as most of the conference was concerned. The vision of federation directly between the individual territories and the metropole was much too close to the old MRP proposal that the founding congress of the RDA had denounced so vehemently in this same town some eleven years earlier. To many it seemed that Houphouet-Boigny had sold out, and the outspoken student delegation to the conference denounced the RDA leadership for having "renounced the combat and turned Black Africa away from the struggle for its independence."[57]

More fighting went on behind the scenes. The congress was prolonged from three to six days without explanation, and as the fifth day drew to a close with still no decision as to political line or who would lead the party, d'Arboussier announced that discussions would continue all night. On the final day it was learned that Houphouet-Boigny had yielded and accepted most of the theses of the younger wing of the party. On a motion by Sékou Touré, Houphouet was unanimously reelected president. The congress voted a resolution calling on the RDA deputies in Paris to propose a law "for the democratization of the existing federal executive organs" to be followed by a law "for the constitution of a Federal State, composed of autonomous States with a federal government, a federal Parliament, and supreme organs of a unified State."[58]

With Houphouet-Boigny away somewhere else "in conference," Touré pronounced the closing speech in which he extolled the RDA president as a great political leader, although subject to the "natural fallibility of mankind." He summed up what was agreed to be the new balance of power in the RDA: "Felix Houphouet remains our president, but he will support in the government not his own ideas, but those defended by the RDA."[59]

The young Turks quickly learned that they and their resolutions were no match for a determined and wily parliamentarian like Houphouet-Boigny. The proposed bills were duly submitted to the

56. Extracts from the speech in *Le Monde,* September 27, 1957.
57. *Le Monde,* September 27, 1957.
58. The text of the resolutions is given in *Afrique Nouvelle,* October 8, 1957.
59. *Le Monde,* October 2, 1957.

French Parliament whence they were referred to committee where they died of old age without reaching the floor. Back in Africa, a spokesman for the Ivory Coast branch of the RDA announced blandly that the Bamako congress could not possibly have decided to back the concept of a French West African primary federation. As proof he stated: "The delegation of the Ivory Coast RDA would have refused to let M. Houphouet-Boigny assume the presidency of the movement if the work of the Bamako congress had led to the creation of a federal executive in Dakar, a sort of super-cabinet opening the way to secession."[60]

During the winter and spring of 1958 the attempts to unify the French West African parties continued and had some success on the territorial level. In Senegal, talks between the BPS and the Socialists led in February to a tentative agreement on a common "minimum political program" and the splitting off of some of the younger Socialists who demanded integration of the Senegalese Socialist movement into the party of Senghor. This, too, was finally accomplished in April 1958. The new party took the name of Union Progressiste Sénégalaise (UPS). The only Senegalese parties now opposing Senghor were the MPS (Senegalese section of the RDA), and the Parti Africain de l'Indépendance (PAI), a small party heavily influenced by Marxism-Leninism, animated by the extreme left wing of university students and graduates who demanded immediate, unconditional independence.[61] Neither party had a significant popular following. In Guinea, Sékou Touré invited the opposition Socialists to join his PDG during its January 23 congress, and attracted a few of its lesser lights with the possibility that the rest of the Guinean Socialists might soon join. In Soudan, four of the minority party members of the territorial assembly rallied to Modibo Keita's Union Soudanaise, giving that party 67 out of the 70 seats.

On the interterritorial level, the trend toward unity was even more impressive. At the invitation of the RDA, all of the major West African parties met in Paris on February 15, 1958, to elaborate a common program of action and to investigate the possibili-

60. Auguste Denise, statement reproduced in *Afrique Nouvelle,* October 29, 1957.

61. On the PAI, see its newspapers, *La Lutte* and *Momsarev,* and Majhmout Diop, *Contribution à l'étude des problèmes politiques en Afrique Noire* (Paris, Présence Africaine, 1958).

ties of uniting in a single political party. On the RDA side, particularly notable was the prominence of the younger elements, led by Sékou Touré and Modibo Keita, and the effacement of Houphouet-Boigny and the Ivory Coast section, as well as the rapport between these younger men and the younger elements in the Senegalese UPS. When the PAI demanded intransigently that the conference enshrine the principle of immediate and unconditional independence at the head of its political program, it was Modibo Keita and Abdoulaye Ly of the UPS who jointly engineered the PAI's expulsion from the conference.[62] The meeting was unable to agree on a formula for party unity, the sticky point being the RDA's and particularly the PDCI's insistence that any united party maintain the initials RDA, which was taken by the other parties to be simply an invitation to total absorption. The conferees, on the other hand, did agree on a common goal for their political action, "federation and autonomy with the right to independence," and to meet again a month later in Africa.[63]

The conference was reconvened in Dakar on March 26, after an intensive correspondence among the delegates and a meeting of the RDA Coordination Committee failed to break the deadlock on the conditions for fusion. Both sides remained intransigent on the question of the name, and it was apparent that the RDA would remain outside any new regroupment of parties.[64] No high level RDA delegation was present at the conference's reopening, and Houphouet-Boigny and Touré showed up only at the last minute. As a result, the non-RDA parties of West Africa, including those previously in the Convention Africaine, the MSA, and most of the unaffiliated, formed a new interterritorial party, the Parti de Regroupement Africain (PRA). The PRA thus included all the significant non-RDA parties except the PAI and the Union des Peuples Mauritaniens (UPM), the government party of Mauretania, which did not wish to get involved in purely Black African quarrels. The PRA held undivided governmental power only in Senegal, but participated in government coalitions in Upper Volta,

62. See *La Lutte,* April 3, 1958, for a partial transcript of the incident and the PAI's comments.

63. See the reports on the conference and resolutions in *Afrique Nouvelle,* February 21, 1958, and the articles by Lamine Gueye, Sékou Touré, and Mamadou Dia in the issue of February 28, 1958.

64. See the exchange of letters between conference members and Houphouet-Boigny in *La Semaine Sénégalaise,* No. 9 (April 1958).

Niger, and Dahomey. Like the Convention Africaine and the IOM before it, it was dominated by its Senegalese section. With the West African parties now split into two formal blocs, once again politics took on the allure of a contest between Senghor and Houphouet-Boigny.

The neatness of the split between the RDA and the PRA was apparent at the opening of the Grand Council session. In the absence of Houphouet-Boigny, the Councillors lined up seventeen RDA, seventeen PRA, with the balance held by the five Mauretanians who announced that they were going to play the role of "arbiter and reconciler [*trait d'union*, literally, "hyphen"] between the RDA and the PRA."[65] The election of officers took a whole day's wrangling before the Councillors agreed on Gabriel d'Arboussier of the MPS (RDA) for president and Souleymane Ould Cheikh Sidya of Mauretania as first vice-president.[66]

The issue of federalism soon appeared at the Grand Council's session. On April 5, 1958, the Grand Council passed a resolution demanding internal autonomy for French West Africa and the creation of a federal executive. This resolution immediately split the ranks of the RDA. The Ivory Coast Territorial Assembly opposed the motion, which was nevertheless reiterated in the name of the RDA by Sékou Touré and Tidiani Traoré of Soudan. A meeting of the RDA Coordination Committee called in Paris on April 24 arrived at a compromise between Houphouet-Boigny and Touré which, however, only papered over the dissension by asking that the question of primary federation be left to the individual territories.[67]

In retrospect one cannot but be impressed with the cohesiveness of the RDA, which succeeded in containing men as strong-willed and as different in political ideology and training as Felix Houphouet-Boigny and Sékou Touré. In the absence of strong central

65. Quoted in *Afrique Nouvelle*, April 4, 1958.

66. D'Arboussier was a logical compromise choice. A man of wide experience in West African politics, he had been Secretary-General of the RDA at its founding, then leader of the RDA dissidents before rallying to Houphouet-Boigny in 1955. At the time he represented Niger in the Grand Council and was on good terms with Djibo Bakary, the Niger PRA leader who, like d'Arboussier had once been a dissident RDA. D'Arboussier made his home in Dakar where he headed the MPS, and had connections in UPS circles. Furthermore, his half-sister was married to the Grand Marabout of French West Africa, Seydou Nourou Tall, a staunch supporter of Senghor and Mamadou Dia.

67. Report in *Afrique Nouvelle*, April 25, 1958.

directive organs, the interterritorial party nevertheless managed to find a temporary compromise between conflicting forces and to maintain its unity before the outside world. This can partially be explained by the structure of the party, which permitted each territorial section to solve its local problems in its own way without outside interference. In part it was because the territorial leaders needed one another's skills and votes for success at the interterritorial and Parisian levels of political activity. Touré needed the help of a good parliamentarian in Paris, just as Houphouet needed a good organizer and dynamic spokesman in West Africa. Furthermore, personal ties built up in the earliest days of student and political activity linked the RDA leaders in overlapping circles of common experience and friendship. These were symbolized in the person of Ouezzin Coulibaly, the RDA's perennial organization secretary who, with his strategic background of Dioula origin and experience as prewar director of studies at William-Ponty, cemented the personal bonds linking the RDA leadership. But even beyond this, there was a strong emotional attachment to the RDA, the symbol of common African political action. This attachment brought party unity on any crucial vote in the Grand Council or the National Assembly and led each territorial section to affix with pride the suffix "section territoriale du RDA" to its name and, except during the great crisis of 1950, prevented any dissatisfied section from leaving the fold.

In these last days of the Fourth Republic, French West Africa was closer to a practical form of political unity than it had been since the days of the colonial regime of the Third Republic. While the political parties had not been able to fuse into a single movement, they had formed two competitive parties which, in their action within the individual territories and within the Grand Council, behaved according to the rules of a loose two-party system. Both the RDA and the PRA were composites of local and territorial sections without a strong common program at the interterritorial level. In ideology, there were sections of the generally conservative PRA that were notably more radical than most sections of the RDA; while the ideological center of gravity in the RDA was probably to the "left" of the PRA, it contained also a very conservative (indeed "states rights") section in the Ivory Coast. While some territories were one-party states, politics in others were highly competitive, as they were at the interterritorial level.

Once the new two-party system began functioning, the minority parties seemed to take a new lease on life as they received support and encouragement from their more successful partners. Thus, the MPS (RDA) of Senegal, which had been quiescent since its founding, began a series of public meetings in May and June 1958 to win supporters and to lambaste the PRA, and the newly consolidated PRA sections in Guinea, Soudan, and even, tentatively, the Ivory Coast did likewise. Behind all the political oratory, both parties agreed on the basic problems facing West Africa and on the range of acceptable solutions. If the problem of primary federation set the Ivory Coast RDA against its neighbors, the PDCI at least was willing to accept a coordinating role for the Government-General. While there was considerable disagreement over what precise forms of association there should be with France, all were publicly agreed on the basic principle of internal autonomy and, most important, the only party to raise the explosive cry of "immediate independence," the PAI, had been ruled outside the system. Finally, this loose, compromise-ridden, two-party system was held together by the universally recognized necessity of presenting some semblance of a united front in Paris to achieve the reforms that all desired. While for the moment it took an incomplete, bargaining form, African unity for the purpose of wresting concessions from the colonizing power had been achieved.

Unfortunately, the weaknesses in the structure were soon to outweigh the strengths. Personality conflicts between leaders assumed enormous proportions and promoted polarization rather than bargaining. The duel between the RDA and the PRA was still, to a great extent, a personal battle between Houphouet-Boigny and Senghor. Within the RDA, the differences of opinion between the old guard and the new were seen by their followers as involving the personal reputations and ultimately the qualifications for leadership of Houphouet-Boigny and Sékou Touré. Within the UPS, Abdoulaye Ly and Mamadou Dia were engaged in a subtle personal struggle for the number two spot. Secondly, violence occasionally erupted between two parties competing within a single territory, particularly when ethnic divisions played a role as they did in Upper Volta, Niger, and Guinea. Thirdly, this party system had little legitimacy in the eyes of most West African politicians. This was not the "unity," the great consecrated solidarity of all Black Africans, that so many had hoped for. "Unity" meant *one* party, not two—especially not two competitive parties. Imbued with the concept of ideological parties, as were most of the younger politicians, they could not accept the "contradictions" inherent in the newly evolved system. Finally, although the phrase was not used in polite public discourse, the idea of "total independence" from France had a great attraction for the younger elements of all parties, while it threatened the political habits and careers of their elders. Were total, immediate independence suddenly to become a burning political issue, the existing alliances would be seriously affected.

One can only hypothesize how well this loose two-party system might have continued to function had it been left to its own devices. It was not given a chance. On May 13, 1958, less than two months after the PRA's formation, the French Army in Algeria revolted, and the Fourth Republic collapsed. With it collapsed the political unity of French West Africa.

From the 13 Mai to the Referendum

West African political leaders viewed the return of de Gaulle to power with mixed emotions. The older politicians were impressed with the liberalism of his initial utterances on Black African problems and delighted with the prospect of finally revising the structure of the French Union. In particular, federalists of all stripes were cheered by the General's radio speech of July 13 addressed to the problems of the overseas territories, in which he declared: "We are going toward a vast and free [*libre*] community. In 1958 we must construct new institutions, establish according to federal principles the links of our union, organize a great political, economic, and cultural ensemble that fits modern conditions of life and progress."[68] The younger and radical politicians, more concerned with the General's right-wing associations and visions of French grandeur, adopted a more reserved attitude, and in Senegal, the young Turks in the UPS led by Abdoulaye Ly kept Senghor from accepting de Gaulle's offer of a cabinet position, an offer accepted by Houphouet-Boigny.

While the PAI and the student organizations seized the opportunity to renew their demands for immediate and complete independence for the African territories, the leaders of the RDA and

68. *Année Politique, 1958,* p. 90.

PRA territorial sections tried to limit the demands that their more impatient members put forth. Sékou Touré's action was typical of most. He asked that Africa be given the right to determine freely its form of association with France, but upheld the necessity of maintaining close links with the metropole.

> *We shall not renounce our Independence; we shall not renounce our Liberty.* Using our independence, we want to yield the exercise of certain attributes of this independence to a vaster ensemble, so that our state of freely consented interdependence confers on our actions a value and extent conforming to our interests. *We have already affirmed that France remains the Nation with which we intend to link our destiny.*[69]

The PDG demanded that the new constitution set up a federal executive, transform the Grand Council into a legislative assembly with full powers, establish a federal parliament and executive for the whole French Community, and recognize the African territories' right to internal autonomy. Similar resolutions were passed by the Union Soudanaise and most of the major PRA sections.

The word "independence" thus entered common political discourse, but in a qualified form. What the African leaders demanded was the right to an independent choice, to express freely their desire to join a "community of free and equal peoples." In this period of French West African politics, however, words sometimes seemed to have a life and will of their own. As "federalism" and "unity" earlier had seized the imaginations of African politicians without ever being precisely defined, so "independence" now became a rallying cry and was exploited by those who first had associated themselves with it. Perhaps because it had so long remained unspoken, perhaps because it is such a powerful concept in its own right, and perhaps simply because the freedom to say yes implies the freedom to say no, "independence" did not long remain so qualified. It burst its bonds with startling effect at the interterritorial PRA conference in Cotonou on July 25–27.

As if conscious of its dangers, Senghor's opening political report played down the idea of independence and emphasized the great need of the African territories for economic and social development. As he phrased it, "The new Constitution will probably affirm

69. Speech to the Fourth Congress of the PDG, Conakry, June 5, 1958, in *Expérience guinéenne et unité africaine,* p. 50. (Italics in text.)

our right to independence, but independence is a victory gained not so much over others as over ourselves."[70] This was not what the conference wanted to hear. The Senegalese delegation, which had not seen the speech in advance, repudiated Senghor's statement. In a generally feverish atmosphere the conference fell into the hands of Abdoulaye Ly of the Senegalese UPS and Djibo Bakary of the Niger Sawaba, who whipped up general enthusiasm behind the demand for "immediate independence." Lamine Gueye, arriving late, quickly sized up the mood of the conference, and to wild applause announced that he was for "unconditional independence." From there on in it became a contest to see who could find the most felicitous phrase using the word "independence." Even Senghor ended up declaring: "We must be independent before the month of September." Other issues, even federalism, were secondary. The final political resolution stated: "The Congress adopts the slogan of immediate independence and decides to take all necessary measures to mobilize the African masses behind this slogan and to make a reality of this will to independence."

The desire for immediate independence was by no means an unequivocal desire to break with France. For most of the delegates it was simply a stronger and more impassioned way of stating what Sékou Touré had stated at the PDG congress. It represented a desire to keep the possibility of total independence open, should events, and particularly the constitution which had not yet been written, turn out badly. As Lamine Gueye said on the last day of the conference, "When one is a *grande dame* like France, one must not quibble over details. Paris should say, like London, 'You are free to remain or to leave the French family.' "[71] The younger and minority elements used independence as an issue with which to take over direction of the party, both on the territorial and interterritorial levels. In particular Abdoulaye Ly and his close associates had increasingly been eased out of control of the UPS party apparatus by Senghor, Mamadou Dia, and their old comrades from BDS days.[72] The issue of independence was a good one on which to recoup their fortunes in local politics. This is not to say that Ly

70. For quotations from and detailed résumés of the major speeches and texts of resolutions, see *La Semaine en AOF*, August 2, 1958. A good eyewitness account of the proceedings which captures the feverish atmosphere is in Gil Dugué, *Vers les Etats-Unis d'Afrique* (Dakar, Lettres Africaines, 1960), pp. 94–104.

71. Quoted in *Combat*, July 28, 1958.

72. Ly had resigned his cabinet post in Mamadou Dia's government in June.

did not also seek independence as a goal in itself, but local politics made this dramatic means of capturing the issue much more attractive. On the interterritorial level, Ly teamed up with Djibo Bakary of Niger, a man with whom he shared a common ideological outlook, to shake the old guard's hold over the PRA executive bureau. Thus the issue of independence accentuated a regrouping of forces within the PRA on the basis of ideology.

Two days after the close of the Cotonou conference, de Gaulle convened the first meeting of the Constitutional Consultative Committee. The Committee included three Africans, Gabriel Lisette of the Tchad RDA, Senghor, and Lamine Gueye of the Senegal PRA. Houphouet-Boigny participated ex officio in his capacity of minister of state. At the Committee's first meeting it became apparent that the word "consultative" in its name was to define the limits of its powers. The working draft of the constitution elaborated by the cabinet under Michel Debré and presented to the Committee was extremely detailed and, in the matter of Franco-African relations, represented a clear triumph for the theses of Houphouet-Boigny. No mention was made of a federal executive. Senghor stated, "My impression is catastrophic. This text is worse than that of the Constitution of October 27, 1946."[73] Whether Senghor's presence in the cabinet alongside Houphouet-Boigny would have modified the constitution on this point is problematic. As it was, the African federalists lost all hope of turning French West Africa into a strong primary federation.

The argument in the Committee then revolved around the question of how close were to be the links between France and the African territories. Houphouet-Boigny backed a tight federation between the individual territories and France, while the PRA delegates sought, in keeping with the resolutions of their Cotonou congress, a modified commonwealth form of association. The final compromise—the Community—combined features of both a federation (such as a common nationality, Senate, and Presidency) and a commonwealth (such as periodic conferences of prime ministers and treaties between the different parts of the Community for common decisions and actions). But the Senghor forces lost the main battle. West Africa was to accept or reject the constitution by individual territory although later these territories might be allowed

73. Quoted in *Année Politique, 1958,* p. 96.

to form larger primary groups. Explicit recognition of the right to independence was nowhere mentioned.[74]

Just before publishing the final version of the constitution, de Gaulle undertook a selling trip to Africa. Although his first two stops, Brazzaville and Abidjan, received him and his constitution with open arms, the situation was quite different elsewhere. Guinea, Senegal, and Soudan were in similar dilemmas. Most of the party leaders and particularly the lesser party elites were dissatisfied with the constitution's refusal to provide for a federal executive and for the right to independence, but, as the final text of the constitution had not yet appeared, they were hopeful of receiving at least oral assurance from de Gaulle that their right to opt freely for independence at any time would be guaranteed. Such was not the way of de Gaulle.

The encounter between de Gaulle and Sékou Touré at Conakry resulted in a complete misunderstanding between two strong and proud political leaders, each thoroughly in control of his forces and each unwilling to see his personal position lessened by yielding to the other. Touré demanded the right to choose independence; de Gaulle replied that independence could be had only if Guinea were to refuse the Community at the time of the referendum. Touré demanded the substitution for French West and French Equatorial Africa of "two powerful States fraternally linked with France;" de Gaulle stated that his offer stood as is, take it or leave it. Touré left it.[75] There was no doubt Sékou Touré could make his option stick. He controlled the PDG, and the PDG controlled the countryside. Most of the administrative posts in the interior of Guinea were in the hands of Guineans—all loyal to the PDG—and the traditional chiefs had been suppressed completely the year before.[76]

In Dakar, where rallies for and against the Community had filled the streets and the sports arenas during the preceding week, de

74. Article 72: "The territorial collectivities of the Republic are the communes, the departments, the Overseas Territories. Any other territorial collectivity is to be created by law." Article 76: "The Overseas Territories may maintain their [present] status within the Republic. If they so manifest their will through deliberation of their territorial assembly . . . they become either Overseas departments of the Republic, or, individually or in groups, States members of the Community."

75. The texts of Touré's and de Gaulle's statements are in *Expérience guinéenne et unité africaine*, pp. 77–109.

76. See the documents in *Guinée: Prélude à l'indépendance* (Paris, Présence Africaine, 1958).

Gaulle's public reception was actually more hostile than it had been in Conakry. As both Senghor and Dia were out of the country, the French President was received by Valdiodio N'Diaye, the young Minister of the Interior, and Lamine Gueye. These two men outlined their party's demands of the right to independence and of a primary federation.[77] But Senegal was not Guinea, and de Gaulle appeared more conciliatory than he had with Touré, avoiding any definitive split on the spot. The UPS upper echelons seemed to favor a negative vote on the constitution; the young Turks of the party saw no reason to give in to de Gaulle, and Senghor himself was disappointed enough with the constitutional proposal to have considered a "no" vote.

However, powerful forces opposed such a course of action. The Muslim religious leaders who had prospered under French rule and who feared any change in the social and political order were united in support of de Gaulle. Their ability to command the votes of the mass of Senegalese peasants was undoubted. The original populations of the old communes and particularly the powerful leaders of the Lébou people in Dakar demanded the right to secede from Senegal if the rest of the territory voted against the constitution. Some local party bosses with large commercial interests, like Ibrahima Seydou N'Dao, threatened to bolt the party if it campaigned against the constitution.

Finally, the French authorities and commercial interests were busy on their own account. The French army garrisons in Senegal were reinforced and engaged in ostentatious maneuvers. The High Commissioner in Dakar, Pierre Messmer, was exceptionally active in pressing home the "full consequences" of a negative vote, while French commercial interests spoke of calling in all outstanding loans. The top UPS leaders were in a most dangerous position. If they tried for a negative vote and were unsuccessful, the French and conservative interests within the country would see to it that they were definitively eliminated from Senegalese politics. Even if they were successful, they risked being put in a delicate position by having been forced to accept the more radical theses of the

77. Valdiodio N'Diaye, "We say 'independence,' and then we say 'African Unity.'" Lamine Gueye, "A OUI has value only to the extent that he from whom it comes is free to reply NON." Text of speeches in *La Semaine Sénégalaise,* No. 17 (September 1958). Senghor and Dia were criticized for having avoided the confrontation, and both issued sharp statements denying any thought of having ducked their duty. See *Afrique Nouvelle,* September 5, 1958.

younger wing. In two tumultuous meetings in Rufisque on September 11 and 20, Senghor and Dia obtained a majority vote in the UPS executive committee in favor of the constitution and then demanded that party discipline be enforced to back up the decision. At this, the young Turks behind Abdoulaye Ly broke with the UPS and formed the PRA-Sénégal, which, "faithful to the slogan of 'immediate independence' adopted at Cotonou," led the campaign for a negative vote.[78]

The Union Soudanaise leaders in Bamako shared the UPS's problems. They, too, would have preferred a solution of association with France, with their right to independence officially recognized and with the establishment of a primary federation. Like the Senegalese leaders, those in Bamako feared the consequences of attempting a campaign for a negative vote and then failing.[79] Unlike Touré, they still had potentially serious trouble with conservative chiefs and religious leaders in the interior, particularly in the Saharan north where the Muslim leader of Timbuktu was both powerful and strongly attached to France. Like Senegal, they were faced with large and very active French garrisons whose officers exercised considerable sway over the votes of Soudan's numerous veterans of the colonial troops. After much argument, and a near revolt by the junior cadres of the party, the Union Soudanaise leadership decided definitely to vote "yes."[80]

In Niger, the PRA section (Sawaba) led by Djibo Bakary was faced with the same dilemma, but with one difference. While to all intents and purposes Senegal and Soudan, like Guinea, were single-party states, Niger had a strong RDA opposition closely attached to Houphouet-Boigny. If after first announcing its option for "independence in union with France" and insisting on a federal executive the PRA were to back down, it would hand the initiative and probably territorial leadership over to the RDA. The Sawaba de-

78. On the position of the PRA-Sénégal, see their newspaper, *Indépendance Africaine*, No. 1 (January 10, 1959).

79. In its "Résolution Générale," of August 17, 1958, the Union Soudanaise "requests that the Constitution mention explicitly the right to *self-determination* and to *independence* of the *Overseas Territories*, recalls that the Federation with France will be effective if it is based on African Solidarity and Unity, requests that the vote of the overseas territories in the *Referendum* be uniquely on the nature of their links with France." (Typescript of proceedings. Emphasis in text.)

80. For an explanation of the Union Soudanaise's decision, see "Intervention du Camarade Modibo Keita," *Troisième Conférence de l'Union Soudanaise RDA* (Koulouba, Imprimerie du Gouvernement, n.d.), pp. 21–24.

cided to take the chance of voting "no." The results were brutal. The French administration and army combined with the conservative Hausa chiefs to defeat the Sawaba, a successful effort which ended only several months after the referendum with the constitution of a homogeneous RDA government closely allied with Houphouet-Boigny and the flight of Djibo Bakary into exile. The Niger affair showed that the decisions of the UPS and the Union Soudanaise were based on realistic assessments of the situation.[81]

The referendum choice posed little problem elsewhere. In Dahomey and Upper Volta, the local political parties were too divided, and French and traditional interests too strong to make a negative vote a realistic choice even if the political leaders had so desired. Mauretania was far too dependent on French money and French support against Morocco to say no to de Gaulle. A hurried interterritorial conference of the PRA leaders met in Niamey and decided that each territorial section should have the freedom to make its own decision. The RDA Coordinating Committee despaired of harmonizing the conflicting positions of Houphouet-Boigny and Sékou Touré and did not even meet. French West Africa thus went to the polls on September 28, with six territories determined to vote "yes," one, Guinea, determined to vote "no," and Niger split. The student organizations, UGTAN, and minority parties like the PAI and the newly constituted PRA-Sénégal campaigned for a negative vote, but their efforts were not taken seriously in the face of concerted action among the French, the dominant political parties, and traditional interests in the six territories who had firmly decided on the "yes." The constitution was approved by 99 per cent of the voters in the Ivory Coast and Upper Volta, 98 per cent in Dahomey, 97 per cent in Senegal and Soudan, 94 per cent in Mauretania, and 78 per cent in Niger. Ninety-five per cent of the voters in Guinea followed Sékou Touré in saying "no" to de Gaulle.

The referendum and the new constitution destroyed the colonial federation of French West Africa. France disdainfully refused Guinea's attempts to associate itself "of its own free will" with the Community and cast "Sékou, the traitor" into outer darkness. The interterritorial political parties were shaken, but held on. The RDA Coordinating Committee emulated France and under pressure

81. See the "Conférence de presse sur la situation politique au Niger" by Leopold Senghor on December 16, 1958 (mimeo.).

from Houphouet expelled the PDG "for having deviated seriously from the fundamental principles of the RDA in choosing independence and secession."[82] The split within the interterritorial party remained, however, and Modibo Keita and the Union Soudanaise took over Guinea's role of opposition to Houphouet-Boigny and the PDCI. The PRA leadership vigorously supported its vanquished Niger section, but was considerably weakened by the Sawaba's crushing defeat. The strain of the campaign inflamed social relations throughout West Africa. Street fighting between the partisans of a negative vote and UPS militants broke out in Dakar, while in the Ivory Coast violent riots led to the expulsion of some 18,000 "foreign" Africans, mostly Dahomeyans and Togolese, from Abidjan. West African unity seemed further away than at any previous time.

Although the referendum put an end to effective political and administrative union of the French West African territories, it did not end the desire of many African leaders to see a new union come about. The terms of the new French constitution and even more the attitude of the French government and administration made it perfectly clear, however, that any union would now have to be strictly the work of the Africans themselves. Here at last was a chance for Africa to mold its own political future, to create its own institutions without Europe's direct supervision.

82. Text in *Afrique Nouvelle*, October 17, 1958.

6

Founding the Mali Federation

PRELIMINARY POLITICAL MANEUVERING

THE REFERENDUM of September 28, 1958, broke up the existing political alliances, which had been determined by the struggle for territorial political power and by the need to exert political influence in the governmental councils of Dakar and Paris. The months following the referendum led to new alignments based initially on attitudes toward a primary federation, but also reflecting the African leaders' need to maintain territorial control, exert influence in the interterritorial political arena, and draw what advantages could be had from the alliance with France. The political habits of the Fourth Republic still exerted a substantial influence on the activities and plans of West African political leaders.

The opening move in the renewed battle over federation was made by the PRA, as Senghor and his lieutenants sought to hold the initiative in interterritorial politics. At a meeting of the UPS Executive Committee, Mamadou Dia presented the drive for a primary federation as an action "conforming to the dominant idea of the Cotonou Congress"[1] (thereby cutting the ground out from under the UPS's newly-formed domestic opposition, the PRA–Sénégal). On October 14 the Directing Committee of the PRA laid before the other parties "a proposal for a federal constitution."[2]

The RDA, torn between its strongly federalist Soudan section and the adamantly anti-federalist Ivory Coast section, was obliged to yield the initiative to the PRA. With Houphouet-Boigny in the chair, the RDA Coordinating Committee met in Paris and declared itself unanimously in favor of joining the Community "at the level of the [individual] territories."[3] It is not entirely clear how unanim-

1. *Déclaration faite par M. Mamadou Dia . . . devant le Comité Executif de l'Union Progressiste Sénégalaise, Section Sénégalaise, du P.R.A., à Rufisque le 4 octobre 1958* (Dakar, 1958), pp. 16, 18.

2. Text in *Afrique Nouvelle,* October 17, 1958.

3. Communiqué in ibid.

ity was attained, but it apparently did not reflect the thinking of all the RDA leaders. A subsequent meeting of the RDA Political Bureau decided to investigate the idea of federating the three core RDA territories still remaining in the Community, Soudan, Upper Volta, and Ivory Coast. This idea was referred to the party's Constitutional Committee where it was buried with the explanation that to be economically effective, it would have to include territories without an RDA majority (presumably Senegal).[4] This proposal, had it been adopted, could have led to the creation of a political unit based on the traditional Dioula trading infrastructure that had been important in giving coherence to West African economic life for so many centuries and in spreading support for the RDA in its earliest days. Although the proposal appears to have received serious support from many of the older, middle-level RDA politicians in Upper Volta and Soudan and from the Dioulas themselves, the play of political interests at the party's summit and Ivory Coast intransigence prevented the idea from being followed up.

The split within the RDA broke into the open on November 12, when Gabriel d'Arboussier, then head of the orthodox RDA Senegalese section (MPS), circulated a proposal for a primary federation to all the French West African heads of government. Most embarrassing, his proposal was virtually identical in principle with that offered earlier by the PRA leaders.[5] Three days later Houphouet-Boigny called a second meeting of the RDA Coordinating Committee in Abidjan, to which d'Arboussier did not come. The federalist position was ably represented by Modibo Keita of Soudan and d'Arboussier's fellow Senegalese MPS leader, Doudou Gueye. The Ivory Coast leader was backed up by Niger's Hamani Diori, who had profited from the PRA's discomfiture in that territory after the referendum. Both sides proved intransigent, and the meeting, it was announced, never took place "officially."[6] Official or not, it was the last meeting the RDA Coordinating Committee ever held.

4. Dugué, *Vers les Etats-Unis d'Afrique,* pp. 166–67; Modibo Keita, "Compte-rendu des travaux du comité de coordination du R.D.A.," 2ème Conférence de l'Union Soudanaise RDA (October 1958, typescript), and personal information.

5. I am grateful to M. d'Arboussier for making the texts of this and other of his proposals and reports on a primary federation available to me. See also the reports in *Afrique Nouvelle,* November 14, 1958.

6. See the unofficial report in *Afrique Nouvelle,* November 21, 1958.

Following the decisions taken by the party leaders and congresses in October, the assemblies of four territories—Senegal, Soudan, Dahomey, and Upper Volta—in quick succession chose formally the status of "state member of the Community empowered to join in a federation (*pouvant se fédérer*)." The decisions of the latter pair of territories, however, were somewhat less enthusiastic than those of Senegal and Soudan. In Dahomey, the vote was strictly along party lines, with the PRA majority of the assembly carrying the day by a slim margin. In Upper Volta, nominally united in a "*groupe d'union*" behind RDA leadership, the non-Mossi PRA representatives of the western areas were decidedly more enthusiastic than were the representatives of the country's dominant tribe, which so long had sent its younger sons to work the Ivory Coast plantations.[7] Mauretania, faithful to its policy of remaining above the quarrels of its black brethren, decided to listen attentively to the arguments of both federalists and antifederalists without taking sides. Its assembly chose membership in the Community without a declaration either for or against the primary federation.

Thus began a period of intense activity in which federalists and their opponents multiplied formal missions to coordinate activity and informal attempts to persuade the hesitant. At first the federalists seemed to carry the day. The Senegalese and Soudanese transcended party differences to call jointly a meeting of all West African federalists at Bamako on December 29 and 30.[8] The four territories that had formally chosen to federate sent representatives, and Mauretania sent observers. The status of the Voltaic delegates was unclear, however, since they had been obliged to pay their own fares and accordingly, some argued, could not represent the territory "officially." Despite such inconsistencies the proceedings conveyed a surprising impression of unity of purpose and resolution in which party, sectional, and personal differences were muted, if not totally buried. True, the Dahomeyan Premier, Sourou Migan Apithy, did insist that the federation permit his territory to continue to enjoy "flexible relations" with its neighbors who might

7. Although the motion was finally carried unanimously, the crucial decision on its wording was carried by only 34 to 32. See the interview with Ali Barraud, representative of Bobo-Dioulasso, in *Paris-Dakar,* December 13, 1958.

8. The following account is drawn principally from personal interviews. The major resolutions can be found in *Afrique Nouvelle,* January 2, 1959, and a good description of the proceedings is in Dugué, pp. 185–92.

not join the federation, but his signature was nonetheless appended to the final resolution, while the rest of the Dahomeyan delegates accepted the primary federation unconditionally.

Perhaps most significant was the conference's decision to appeal to political leaders of all parties and groups "to unite their efforts to bring about political unity within each State, as a guarantee of the Federation's cohesion and development."[9] The motion's significance lay first in its author, Doudou Gueye, leader with d'Arboussier of the Senegalese MPS-RDA. Here was a minority group asking to be absorbed in the territory's dominant party, a loyal RDA man putting himself at Senghor's service. Secondly, this motion formally broke with the pattern of bi-party interlocking politics that had given French West Africa its pluralistic cohesion since 1956. No longer was the fight to be PRA against RDA; now it was to be federalists against anti-federalists, each solidly organized in exclusive territorial parties.

The conference concluded with a resolution to meet in a Federal Constituent Congress at Dakar two weeks later, and despatched official delegates to explain its position to the Ivory Coast and to Mauretania, in an attempt to bring all of French West Africa (save Guinea, now ruled out of the system) into the primary federation. Neither mission met with success. Houphouet-Boigny maintained his intransigence, and the Mauretanians maintained their noncommittal attitude which, in this case, amounted to a de facto rejection of the federation.[10]

The focus of attention shifted rapidly from Bamako to Dakar, where the AOF Grand Council met in special session on January 8, 1959, to put an end to its functions. Once again, the federalists maintained the initiative. At the first meeting Doudou Thiam of the Senegalese UPS proposed Modibo Keita as a candidate for president of the Council session. This move caught the RDA anti-federalists completely by surprise, and their response was a measure of what had happened to the pattern of French West African politics since the referendum. Houphouet-Boigny's lieutenant, Phillippe Yacé observed:

> It is for me a great surprise to see the candidacy of our friend Modibo Keita presented today by M. Thiam. . . . I should however raise the point that we have up to now worked in this As-

9. See Dugué, p. 189.

10. On the failure of these missions, see the interview with André Guillabert in *Paris-Dakar*, January 7, 1959.

> sembly in two officially recognized blocs . . . the RDA on one hand, and the PRA on the other, with our Mauretanian friends always observing a position of neutrality. . . . I do not contest Modibo's worth, even less his candidacy . . . but I do claim that among friends we could, at a time when certain dissensions are developing, have . . . solved our problems within the RDA before contracting certain alliances which do not seem sufficiently urgent to me.[11]

Modibo Keita's response left no doubt as to the finality of the break:

> Personally, I have no complexes about seeing my candidacy presented today by our colleague Thiam. If certain men, at a particular moment, found themselves together in the same political formation, it was by reason of the fundamental political options that they had made; but as soon as there is a divorce and the flux of opinions brings other options to the fore, well, the men who take account of these opinions will shoulder their responsibilities and have the duty of joining forces, even if yesterday they fought one another.[12]

With the old political order formally buried and the new alliances announced, the Grand Council elected Modibo to its presidency; the Ivory Coast, its political dependency, Niger, and the ever-prudent Mauretania abstained from the vote. Now, completely in the hands of the federalist forces, the Grand Council suspended its session on January 10, and gave over its hall to the body consciously designed to be its successor, the Federal Constituent Assembly, which was to translate the political options of the Bamako conference into a binding West African federal constitution. As prime symbol of this continuity, Modibo Keita himself was promptly elected president of the Federal Constituent Assembly.[13]

Although the Constituent Assembly had to be hastily arranged,

11. *Grand Conseil de l'AOF: Procès-verbaux de la session extra-ordinaire de janvier 1959*, No. 28 (January 8, 1959), 16.

12. Ibid., p. 17.

13. The federalists took great pains to present the Constituent Assembly as a natural continuation and enlargement of the Grand Council's federal powers. Thus Modibo, in thanking well-wishers for his election to the Grand Council's presidency, stated: "I cannot dissociate your kind wishes from those I formulate for the future of our young States, for the Federation of West Africa born . . . in the early hours of the year 1959." Ibid. (January 10, 1959), p. 28.

the two dominant delegations from Senegal and Soudan worked smoothly together, and events proceeded not only according to schedule, but indeed with considerable éclat. Although Apithy, the Dahomeyan Premier, had refused to come, the Dahomeyan delegation seemed firmly under the control of Alexandre Adandé and Emile Zinsou, both convinced federalists. The Voltaic delegation, this time, arrived with full official powers, and its hitherto hesitant leader, Maurice Yameogo, veritably bristled with protestations of federalist faith.[14] Both the Senegalese and Soudanese delegations, of eleven men each, had carefully included opposition members who accepted the idea of federation. The Senegalese UPS leaders, particularly, took pride in presenting Gabriel d'Arboussier of the MPS-RDA as one of their own, while the Soudanese included two second-ranking members of the Socialist, PRA-affiliated opposition. Thus domestic political unity was enhanced by the campaign for interterritorial unity. Even within the Voltaic delegation the cooperative spirit held forth; the non-Mossi RDA leader from Bobo-Dioulasso, Ali Barraud, yielded his vice-presidency of the Constituent Assembly to the Mossi RDA leader, Maurice Yameogo.

The actual work of the assembly took only three days, with the main drafting being done by d'Arboussier and the Senegalese legal expert, Doudou Thiam. The draft constitution for the Federation of Mali was approved without public discussion and by acclamation of the assembled delegates. Whatever bargaining had gone on behind the scenes seemed to be of only minor moment compared to the simple political fact that this was, as one orator put it, "*l'Afriqué retrouvée.*" The most memorable aspect of the assembly was its conclusion in which the majestic figure of Modibo Keita led the delegates in swearing three times "to defend everywhere the Mali Federation, to become tireless pilgrims and preachers of political unity, and to accept the ultimate sacrifice for the realization of African unity."[15]

The document that emerged from this extraordinary session went considerably beyond the initial proposals for granting executive power to a federal government, and even farther beyond the

14. "Upper Volta . . . gives its total and unrestricted adherence to [the Federation]." Quoted in *Le Monde,* January 20, 1959.

15. *Agence France Presse, Bulletin,* January 18–19, 1959. The emotional content of the moment has been stressed by numerous participants. Even the public gallery, including some pickets protesting the Senegalese government's repression of trade unions, joined in the oath.

feeble powers of the colonial Grand Council. Whereas d'Arboussier's original proposal had bent over backward to subordinate the federal executive to the component territorial executives by providing that the federal cabinet would include all the territorial prime ministers, the new constitution specifically excluded territorial ministers and officers of the territorial legislatures from cabinet status at the federal level.[16] The territories' only formal control over the selection of the federal executives came from the requirement that the nomination of a man to the federal cabinet had to be approved by the parliamentary delegation of the territory from which he came.[17] The federal premier would himself be chosen by majority vote of the Federal Assembly, without formal reference to the territorial delegations.[18] Although everyone expected much informal consultation to take place off the assembly's floor to permit the individual territories to voice objections privately, the principle of a strong federal executive, independent of formal territorial control, was accepted without question.

The powers of the federal government were to extend to all the domains controlled by the Government-General in both its legislative and administrative capacities before the Loi-Cadre decentralization decrees. Furthermore, it would have charge of foreign representation, within the limits laid down by the Federation's membership in the French Community and with the proviso that foreign treaties must be ratified by the individual territories. Finally, the federal government would enjoy the full taxation power originally possessed by the Government-General, would lay down conditions for each territory's internal taxes, and would decide itself the basis on which any subsidies would be reallocated to the budgets of the territories.[19]

The individual territories were to be represented equally in each governmental branch, each territorial assembly was to choose twelve deputies to the unicameral Federal Assembly, and each territory was to contribute two men to the federal cabinet.[20]

Perhaps most encouraging for the future of the new federation was the easy spirit of compromise that animated the different terri-

16. Article 4.
17. Article 7.
18. Article 6.
19. Article 43 and Title II.
20. Articles 26 and 7.

torial delegations. Soudan, the most populous territory, had originally wanted representation proportional to population, but raised no objection to continuing the strict territorial parity of the Grand Council. Similarly, the question of locating the capital, which was expected to prove the most difficult issue, was resolved in favor of continuing in Dakar (which had, of course, the best facilities). In response to Soudan's graciously yielding its preference to see Bamako the capital,[21] the Senegalese accepted that Dakar be only the provisional capital and that a simple federal law be sufficient to change the seat of government.[22]

In another gesture of great symbolic importance, Senghor himself proposed the name, Mali Federation, thus reviving Soudanese memories of their exalted past, memories kept alive in the folklore and songs of the extended Mande linguistic family.[23] More concretely, Senegal agreed that federal revenues should be derived principally from customs and excise duties, that is to say, from the operations of the port of Dakar.

Aside from their efforts to establish a strong federal authority, the Constituent Assembly's overriding concern seems to have been to leave the door open to the other West African states of the French Community. This was the prevailing reason for the desire to make the Constituent Assembly appear as the logical continuation of the Grand Council. The preamble of the constitution states: "This Federation remains open to all autonomous states of West Africa who desire to join. . . . It affirms its determination to maintain friendly relations with the autonomous states who have not opted for the Federation." The only conditions for joining "at any time" were that the state so desiring be a "democratic Republic" and respect "the separation of legislative, executive, and judicial powers." No vote of previous members would be needed to ratify a new member. This insistence on maintaining "*une Fédération ouverte*" was underlined in all the major speeches concluding the

21. On this and other Soudanese preferences, see Idrissa Diarra's "Rapport Politique," Deuxième Conférence Territoriale de l'Union Soudanaise RDA (typescript).

22. Senghor reinforced this by public statements declaring himself willing to see the capital moved elsewhere, if that seemed necessary. He in particular suggested Bobo-Dioulasso in Upper Volta as a likely spot.

23. In one sense this was a major personal sacrifice for the Senegalese leader, for it gave added personal prestige to Modibo Keita, who has some claim to be a lineal descendant of Soundiata Keita, the founder of the Mali Empire, and who has adopted Soundiata's personal motto, "Death rather than Dishonor," as his own.

session. Senghor, using an expression dear to his new Soudanese associates, stated "Our four-partner Federation is naturally only a beginning. I am convinced that the other states will join the Federation because it 'goes in the sense of history.'"[24] Part of this open invitation to other members was just good politics in the sense that it built up the promise of the new federation and reassured waverers in Dahomey and Upper Volta that they were riding the wave of the future. Of at least equal importance, as Senegalese and Soudanese leaders subsequently stressed in interviews, was the feeling that the Mali Federation was to be the nucleus for the recreation of the French West African primary federation destroyed by the referendum. The four-party federation was just the beginning; if it maintained its promise and dynamism, the federalists confidently expected that the other territories would be obliged to recognize the error of their ways and return to the fold under the leadership of the federalists of Senegal and Soudan. In this sense, the founding of the Mali Federation was a continuation and extension of the struggle for French West African leadership that had been going on throughout the days of the Fourth Republic.

The Reaction

While the federalists were winning all the headlines, their opposition, both in Paris and Africa, was not asleep. The African opposition, led by Houphouet-Boigny and the Ivory Coast RDA, was well known, but also among the French many tended to assume that "federation equals secession," much as, on the other side, many African nationalists linked federation, or unity, with eventual independence. This tendency in France was reinforced by the close identification of Houphouet-Boigny with a variety of policies supported by the new de Gaulle regime and by the opposition of some original proponents of federation, most notably Sékou Touré, to many de Gaulle policies. Although the African federalists quickly jumped to the conclusion that reactionary forces in France were deeply opposed to any federal arrangements in Africa out of a simple desire to divide and rule, it is not necessary, for the purpose of explaining France's actions, to adopt such a sweeping hypothesis.

24. Speech quoted in *Agence France Presse, Bulletin,* January 18–19, 1959, p. A–21. Inner quotation marks added. See also speeches of Adandé, Yameogo, Modibo Keita, and Mahamane Haidara, passim.

Until conclusive evidence is available, this writer would prefer to emphasize three more limited, but sufficient, reasons for France's actions.

Because Houphouet-Boigny had cooperated closely with Michel Debré in drawing up the new constitution for the Community and because his fidelity to France and the new regime was unquestioned, the French government was inclined to follow the Ivory Coast leader's advice in matters affecting the Community as a whole, particularly in cases where Houphouet-Boigny's personal prestige and interests were involved. Simply out of a desire to maintain a friend of France in power in a wealthy territory, it was a logical strategy not to permit his personal opponents, which Senghor and Modibo Keita certainly were at the time, to dominate the West African political scene.

Secondly, the French administration was accustomed to direct, if sub rosa, intervention in the affairs of African territorial governments, and to continue this practice after formal independence was not a surprising response from a colonial administration not inhibited by too many scruples.

Finally, the example of Guinea's open hostility to the de Gaulle regime, however well justified, was seen as a very real danger to the implementation of good economic and political relations between France and the other West African territories. Indeed, a cardinal element of French African policy during the fall of 1958 and throughout 1959 was to establish some sort of *cordon sanitaire* around Touré's regime, something that was particularly evident in France's refusal to vote for Guinea's admission to the United Nations. Here, chance seems to have taken a hand against the federalists. The formation of a political union between Guinea and Ghana on November 21, 1958, appeared to many French politicians and to the French press as a blow directed specifically against France, possibly with the connivance of that all-purpose villain, "le Foreign Office" of perfidious Albion.[25] This event cast the question of interterritorial political regrouping in a particularly bad light in the eyes of those already inclined to see dangers inherent in the idea of federalism. Even the influential *Le Monde,* which had traditionally taken a sympathetic view of African aspirations, hinted darkly that there was a close connection between the

25. See especially *Le Monde* of November 23 and 24, 1958.

Ghana–Guinea union and the activities of the federalists in Bamako and Dakar.[26]

In a period when France herself was undergoing substantial change, and one in which the new regime was searching for an acceptable way out of its difficulties in Algeria, the French government was understandably apprehensive about any radical political changes in Black Africa. To the extent that African politics could be viewed as a choice between the "moderate" policies of Houphouet-Boigny, and the "adventurous" policies of Senghor and Modibo Keita, both equally "African" in origin and content, France tended to support the theses of the former, particularly if the cost did not appear too great.

Nor was the Ivory Coast leader caught without a policy to support. On December 5, following his return from Paris, Houphouet-Boigny had announced his preference for maintaining direct political links between the individual territories and France while establishing a loose *"conseil d'entente"* consultative arrangement for "economic harmonization" among the West African territories members of the Community.[27] This arrangement seemed to find support within the French government, and was closely akin to the loose customs union agreement worked out the next month in Paris for the Equatorial African states. In meetings with influential Africans and Frenchmen in Abidjan, Paris, and Ouagadougou, Houphouet-Boigny had opportunity to present his views fully. In this he had the backing not only of the French government but of his own Ivory Coast political party, the PDCI, and of the major Ivory Coast commercial interests as well. In particular, the Abidjan Chamber of Commerce voted a special contribution from its members to assist the Ivory Coast leader in attaining his political goals.

The combined political weight of the Ivory Coast leader and the French administration was brought to bear first against Upper Volta, the country which supplied most of the labor for the Ivory Coast's plantations.[28] Upper Volta was in no position to withstand

26. See the article of Philippe Decraene in *Le Monde,* January 1, 1959, and especially his front page article of January 20, 1959.

27. The press conference is reported in *Le Monde,* December 6, 1958. See also the radio broadcast of Philippe Yacé, reported in *Afrique Nouvelle,* January 23, 1959.

28. Information for the following discussion of Upper Volta and Dahomey is derived primarily from personal interviews. A very lively and generally accurate account of these complex maneuvers is in Dugué, pp. 172–246.

strong outside pressure. It was divided by regional and ethnic differences, principally between Mossi and non-Mossi, and the RDA-led government, although in principle backed by a coalition, was in fact maintained in office only by its two-man majority in the legislative assembly. Furthermore, this slim majority was not a solid one. The strength of the RDA depended on unofficial backing of the Morho Naba, emperor of the Mossi, who had a year earlier fused his own personal party, the PSEMA, with the RDA. In part because of the Mossi hegemony in the new RDA councils, the RDA leaders from the non-Mossi area adjacent to Soudan, who were friendly with the Union Soudanaise leaders, frequently differed from the party's official hierarchy on matters of importance.

At first, federalist sentiment seems to have been fairly widespread among the Voltaic leaders. The country was, as we saw in Chapter 3, very much on the receiving end of the redistribution of money from the Grand Council; furthermore Upper Volta had a substantial interest in maintaining internal African trade. This was particularly important to the Dioula communities of the western Bobo-Dioulasso region. Even the Morho Naba, whose conservative orientation was unquestioned, declared himself, on December 6, firmly in favor of a primary federation as the best means of preserving "the work of France" in Africa.[29] The PRA leaders were even more pleased with the prospect, since a rapprochement with Bamako and Dakar might strengthen their position while it almost certainly would undermine that of the Voltaic RDA once it was cut off from direct political contact with the PDCI. The instability of these positions soon became evident.

Following the visit of an Ivory Coast delegation, the Morho Naba started hedging and warned about "going blindly into a Federation which could become a dangerous weapon in the hands of subversive elements."[30] France quickly gave a concrete indication that it was supporting the anti-federalist policy of the Ivory Coast. When the Voltaic delegation arrived in Dakar for the Constituent Assembly, it was greeted with the news that France, without consulting the Voltaics, had appointed a new High Commissioner in Ouagadougou, M. Masson. Masson, who had been the last Secretary-General to the Governor of Guinea before the referendum,

29. Statement in *Paris-Dakar,* December 7, 1958.
30. Cited in *Le Monde,* December 30, 1958.

was well and not favorably known to the African politicians. Anger at this move is assumed to have played a considerable role in Maurice Yameogo's enthusiastic participation in the Dakar Assembly. Masson stayed on despite Yameogo's protest to Paris, and he seems to have impressed the Voltaic Premier with the force of his arguments against the Mali Federation. At about the same time considerable anti-federalist activity was noted among Upper Volta's 17,500 African veterans of the French army, who were extremely loyal both to their European Voltaic leader and to France.[31] Since their number and their leader's influence were particularly concentrated in the PRA regions, the veterans' activities suggested second thoughts to the PRA leaders who could count on no effective internal support from their political comrades outside the territory.

On January 28, 1959, the Voltaic Assembly approved the Mali federal constitution without a dissenting voice, but with several important individuals absent. Since this vote did not oblige Upper Volta to join the Federation, its significance was not entirely clear. In the month following this action, pressure from the Ivory Coast increased. A PDCI delegation visited the major Voltaic trading centers stressing the importance of Abidjan as a commercial outlet and reminding the Voltaic leaders of how important the Ivory Coast was as a place of employment for Voltaic labor. A delegation of chiefs from Niger paid a formal call on the Morho Naba and reportedly warned him of the dangers to the *chefferie* implicit in the activities of the radicals in Dakar and Bamako. It is commonly assumed that during this period considerable Ivory Coast funds found their way into Voltaic pockets.

Precisely which of these pressures was decisive is not certain, but the cumulative effect was overwhelming. On February 28 at a hastily called midnight meeting of the Voltaic Assembly, the bare quorum (39 of 70) present approved Yameogo's draft constitution which made no mention of the Federation.[32] The constitutional referendum, held two weeks later, approved the Assembly's draft, and Upper Volta by that action ceased to belong to the Mali Fed-

31. See C. Charpentier: "Les Anciens combattants dans les états africains d'expression française," *L'Afrique et l'Asie,* 53 (1er trimestre, 1961), 16–19.

32. The federalists charged that in fact only 22 were present and that the vote was therefore illegal. See *Le Drame de la Haute Volta* (Paris, Documents Africains, 1960), p. 12.

eration.[33] Yameogo's speech to the Assembly, for all that it may have glossed over some of the more immediate determinants of his and his country's decision, did present well the dilemma in which Upper Volta found itself. After invoking at length his country's economic and geographical position, Yameogo concluded:

> The Government of Upper Volta wants African unity and will fight to bring it about. But just as one bloc unites, so two blocs divide. Upper Volta . . . does not want to choose between Dakar and Abidjan. It says that both Dakar and Abidjan are necessary. . . . It will lend its active support to all efforts at a rapprochement coming from those . . . who are aware of the need for uniting the former AOF in its entirety.[34]

Had in fact the federalists in Dakar been able to hold out a real promise of recreating French West Africa "in its entirety," their task might have been much easier. As it was, Upper Volta's geographic position and the weakness and division of her political structures left the country open to the group most able to bring effective pressures to bear on the political leaders. The pressures that Houphouet-Boigny and France brought to bear were not simply verbal arguments, but effective, if implied, threats of eliminating a specific group or leader from participation in Voltaic political life. Once the Morho Naba was decided on his course, Yameogo was in no position to go against his will. Once the veterans had been convinced of the evil nature of the Federation, the PRA leaders were obliged to give priority to the problem of staying in politics over the opportunities of weakening RDA control. With no means of bringing direct pressure to bear, the federalists in Dakar and Bamako had no effective riposte. As one of the Voltaic politicians who shifted from a strong federalist to an anti-federalist position put it in an interview, "Frankly, at that time we were just trying to hold on; we were in no position to take chances." Dakar offered a chance at unspecified long-term gains; Abidjan (and Paris) guaranteed continued existence. For Upper Volta's politicians, the latter was the better offer.

33. With the cooperation of the French authorities, the constitution was approved by a vote of 1,018,936 to 254,243. Of the dissenting votes, 90 per cent came from the region bordering on Soudan. Detailed results in *Afrique Nouvelle*, March 20, 1959.

34. *Agence France Presse, Bulletin*, March 13, 1959, p. A1.

The situation in Dahomey offered many of the same possibilities for maneuver as were evident in Upper Volta: the Dahomeyan economy too, was dependent on outside aid, and no strong single political party dominated the scene. In this case, however, open outside intervention was kept to a minimum. The local section of the PRA, representing primarily the southern part of the territory, held a slim majority of the territorial legislature (35 of 60 seats) but its leadership was divided between the old-line Premier, Sourou Migan Apithy, and the younger intellectuals led by Alexandre Adandé and Emile Zinsou. Since party discipline was close to nonexistent, it was to each faction's advantage to seek alliances outside the party and assistance from whatever source possible. The other parties within the country were the Dahomeyan section of the RDA whose control was exercised in the central region, site of the ancient Dahomeyan Fon kingdom, and two parties of the North which, although bitterly opposed, together threw their support to the PRA or the RDA as best served the interests of their comparatively backward and traditionally oriented region.

The issue of federation provided a chance for an ambitious leader like Apithy to build a more stable political base than that provided by the PRA. Since both Adandé and Zinsou had been among the earliest federalists, and both were associated closely with Senghor, Apithy's strategy was to adopt an anti-federalist stance, thereby making possible a rapprochement with the local RDA. Dahomey's peculiar economic and geographic position opened up even more interesting possibilities. As we saw in Chapters 2 and 3, Dahomey's economic situation had steadily declined since the 1920s because the country lacked a good deep-water port. Extensive lobbying in Paris had brought a tentative French agreement in 1958 to build such a port at Cotonou, the Dahomeyan capital, as part of a general plan (Opération Hirondelle) to reinforce trade links between Dahomey and its interior neighbor, Niger.[35] This plan was of great interest to the northern Dahomeyan politicians whose hitherto isolated constituency would now be favored by a major commercial route, ultimately an extension of the Cotonou–Parakou railway to the Niger border.

After a quick trip to Paris Apithy refused to join the Dahomeyan delegation to the Dakar Constituent Assembly, and opened quiet

35. The French were particularly concerned to stop the extensive trade across the Niger-Nigerian border.

talks with leaders of the Dahomeyan RDA and northern parties. At these talks he pointed out, as he later put it, "how necessary the good will of France was to us at this stage of our economic development."[36] On January 29, 1959, Apithy resigned from the PRA and formed a common front with the parties of the North and with the RDA. His letter of resignation and subsequent statements stressed two themes, his "profound conviction that the proposed Federal Constitution would harm the free development of the Republic of Dahomey's economy," and his belief that Dahomey needed to reinforce its economic ties with the Benin region.[37] This placated both the Northerners and the Ivory Coast oriented RDA.

The Dahomeyan Constituent Assembly met the following month under the control of the new alignment of interests and, despite riots in the streets outside the building, refused a motion to inscribe in the constitution "the intention of the Republic of Dahomey to bring about African unity."[38] By accepting the new constitution on February 14, 1959, Dahomey officially refused entry into the Mali Federation. The loyal PRA leaders resigned from Apithy's cabinet; the total collapse of the federalist position was assured when they felt unable to present candidates at the April 2 elections, which were won by Apithy.[39]

The Federation Survives

In neither Soudan nor Senegal were the opponents of Mali able to bring effective pressure to bear against the determined and committed leadership of the two territories' respective mass parties. The triumph of the federalist option in Soudan and Senegal was reinforced by the decisive victories of the Union Soudanaise and the UPS in the March 1959 elections for new territorial legislatures.

In waging their campaign, the Union Soudanaise leaders seized upon the issue of federalism to split the opposition. The Union Soudanaise government had included two opposition members of the legislature in the Soudanese delegation to the Federal Constituent

36. Interview, July 23, 1961.

37. Text of the letter and statements in *Semaine en Afrique Occidentale*, February 7, 1959.

38. See the report in *Semaine en Afrique Occidentale*, February 21, 1959.

39. For the justification of their refusal to run, see their statement in *Semaine en Afrique Occidentale*, March 28, 1959.

Assembly in Dakar. Being assured of continued jobs at the federal level, these two, and several of their followers, announced on February 14 that they would join the Union Soudanaise. The position of the socialist opposition, now called Parti de Regroupement Soudanais (PRS), was particularly vulnerable on the federalist issue since, as the Soudanese section of the PRA, it had formerly supported Senghor's and Lamine Gueye's attacks against the "Balkanizing RDA."[40] Speaking in the name of federalist orthodoxy, Modibo Keita put the opposition on the spot: "Militants of the PRS (Soudanese section of the PRA), we who have remained faithful to the exalting program which has climaxed in the [Mali] Federation, invite you to join with us for the great victory of all Africa."[41]

The new PRS leader, Hammadoun Dicko, a former *sous-secrétaire d'état* in the Debré government who returned to Soudan only at the campaign's opening, replied with the comparatively sophisticated argument that while he, too, was interested in federation, he would stick by his old party slogan, *"Faire le Soudan d'abord, l'Afrique ensuite."* He argued that the Mali Federation was really just a divisive maneuver that would cut Soudan off from its neighbors to the south and east.[42] Whatever the intrinsic value of his arguments, they were weakened notably by the widespread suspicion that his new-found interest in Upper Volta and the Ivory Coast was motivated either by pure political opportunism or by orders from France. Unlike the cases of Upper Volta and Dahomey, where Houphouet-Boigny had ready access to important political figures, the Senegalese this time had several trump cards they could play. Lamine Gueye, in particular, was able to play up his role of leader of West Africa's Socialists to prevail upon many of the PRS, including Fily Dabo Sissoko, the party's elder statesman, to moderate their opposition.

Nor did the Union Soudanaise neglect to use its absolute majority within the Soudanese government to decrease the opposition's freedom of maneuver. Since the referendum in September, most of the European *commandants de cercle* had been replaced by loyal

40. See their newspaper, *Vérité,* of September 13 and 16, 1957, and especially the article "L'Union Française sera fédérale ou ne sera pas" in the issue of September 30, 1957.

41. Radio broadcast, February 16, 1959, cited in *Semaine en Afrique Occidentale,* February 21, 1959.

42. See his statement in *Semaine en Afrique Occidentale,* February 28, 1959.

Union Soudanaise men; and numerous cantonal chiefs, the traditional basis of PRS rural strength, were deposed or obliged to leave their home districts. Among the conservative traditional leaders, only the Cadi of Timbuktu came out flatly against the Union Soudanaise and the Federation in a public pronouncement made from the relative safety of Abidjan.[43] The Union Soudanaise majority passed a law enlarging the electoral districts, requiring all parties participating to present lists in all districts (thereby eliminating the PRS's regionally-based patron party allies), and awarding all seats from a district to the list receiving the highest number of votes. With these precautions the Union Soudanaise received 76 per cent of the total vote and all the seats.[44] Soudan had thus voted conclusively for the Federation. In the weeks following the election, the PRS leaders, some under a certain amount of pressure, accepted the offer of the Union Soudanaise to dissolve their party and join the victor. Thus, the Union Soudanaise achieved its long-term goal of internal political unity at the same time it was leading the way to African unity.

The situation in Senegal was more complicated, and the UPS federalists had a more difficult battle to wage than had their Soudanese colleagues. Once the UPS had firmly captured federalism as a campaign issue, the opposition party, the PRA-Sénégal, felt obliged to campaign on an anti-federalist platform.[45] Since prior to the split the PRA-Sénégal leaders had been among the most ardent defenders of the West African primary federation, it was not difficult for the UPS to pin an opportunist label on their campaign. Because the PRA-Sénégal could count on help from neither Houphouet-Boigny nor the French, they were not by themselves much of a threat.

Much more serious was the opposition from Senegalese conservative interests, in particular the Muslim marabouts who had prospered and been accorded great honor under the French administration. Since Senegal is 80 per cent Muslim, and since many of the Senegalese Muslims, especially the 600,000 members of the

43. See his announcement in *Abidjan-Matin,* February 25, 1959.

44. Complete results are in *Semaine en Afrique Occidentale,* March 14, 1959.

45. See the PRA-Sénégal paper, *Indépendance Africaine.* Their argument was based on the premise that the Ghana–Guinea Union was the only true path to African unity, and the Mali Federation was only a disguised imperialist maneuver. This was understandably a difficult position to argue.

Mouride sect, believe that their entry into paradise depends on following the wishes of their religious leaders, the great marabouts could wield considerable political power.[46] The marabouts' attachment to France had been one of the major factors causing the UPS leaders to conclude that a negative vote in the referendum would be politically unwise; but by March the UPS was in a better position to handle this opposition.

Senghor, who had originally received support from many marabouts in his defeat of the Senegalese Socialists in 1951, had since then paid particular attention to the religious leaders, and his government had to a large extent supplanted the French administration as the major prop for the marabouts' financial manipulations. Many of the marabouts were accordingly not in a position to oppose the UPS openly, lest some of their financial aid be cut off. Since Senegal had acquired autonomous control over its budget after the referendum, this could involve considerable sums of money. Furthermore, the marabouts were divided among themselves over questions of personal prestige and by disputes over succession, a matter which had often been influenced by the temporal powers in Dakar.[47] Since the referendum, the marabouts had banded together in a Conseil Supérieur des Chefs Religieux du Sénégal with the intention of influencing the country's political evolution in harmony with the precepts of Islam.[48] The marabouts proved unable to work together, however, largely out of jealousy over who was to dominate the Conseil. When in early February the most outspoken of the marabouts, Ibrahima Niasse of Kaolack, sent a telegram to President de Gaulle protesting the constitution that the UPS government was "forcing on the country," the other

46. On the importance of the marabouts, see Gouilly, *L'Islam en AOF,* pp. 90–95, 108–25; Abel Bourlon, "Actualité des Mourides et du Mouridisme," *L'Afrique et l'Asie, 46* (1959), 10–30; and Fernand Quesnot, "Les Cadres maraboutiques de l'Islam sénégalais" in Centre des Hautes Etudes Administratives sur l'Afrique et l'Asie Moderne, *Notes et études sur l'Islam en Afrique Noire* (Paris, J. Peyronnet, 1963), pp. 127–93. I have discussed the role of the marabouts in Senegalese politics at greater length in "Senegal," in J. S. Coleman and C. G. Rosberg, Jr., eds., *Political Parties and National Integration in Tropical Africa* (Berkeley, University of California Press, 1964), pp. 47–49.

47. See, for example, Governor Maestracci's delicate allusions to his role in settling the Mouride succession, in AOF, *Conseil de Gouvernement, Session de décembre 1945* (St. Louis, 1946), p. 59.

48. The Conseil's statutes are in *Paris-Dakar,* February 3, 1959.

religious chiefs either through governmental pressure or out of a desire to discredit Niasse, hastily disavowed his initiative.[49] This destroyed the Conseil as an effective political weapon.

The most politically and economically dissatisfied religious leaders along with a few secular conservative leaders did, however, form a new political party, the Parti de la Solidarité Sénégalaise (PSS) to fight the March elections. Although the PSS received financial support from some elements of Senegal's French population and from the PDCI, it did not enjoy the backing of the French administration. In part this may have been because, either out of naiveté or desperation, the PSS contracted an electoral alliance with the PRA-Sénégal, thus raising the possibility that if the UPS were defeated, the country would be ruled by a coalition of politically conservative religious leaders and bright young radicals, with every assurance that the religious leaders would not last long.

This sort of opposition, while possibly effective in Upper Volta or Niger, was no match for politicians as skillful as Senghor, Mamadou Dia, and Lamine Gueye, particularly since they were in control of the government apparatus and wrote an electoral law like that of Soudan to maximize their party's chances. The UPS was even spared the opposition of the MPS–RDA, which, since its leaders had chosen to back the Federation, integrated its candidates into the UPS lists. The final result gave the UPS 81 per cent of the vote and all the seats in the new legislature.[50] Following a riot on election day the PSS leader, Cheikh Tidjane Sy, was arrested and remained in jail until he was persuaded to rejoin the UPS a year later. His party subsequently announced it would join the RDA, and then quietly disappeared.

Although credit for their victories must first go to the leaders of the UPS and the Union Soudanaise, it is apparent that things might not have gone so easily for them if the French had been truly determined to stop the Mali Federation. While neither the French government nor the administration in Senegal and Soudan can be said to have ardently supported the efforts of the federalists, they appear to have appreciated the costs of trying to unseat the mass parties of Senegal and Soudan. In neither country was there a convenient and effective indigenous force to manipulate, nor a sufficient reason to commit France to the direct political and military

49. See *Paris-Dakar,* February 3 and 4, 1959, for the various communications.
50. Complete results are in *Afrique Nouvelle,* March 27, 1959.

intervention necessary to carry on without such a force. Certainly, France was not about to take such risks just to please Houphouet-Boigny or the few local *petits blancs* who saw secession from the French Community in every move of the African politicians. Nor, as one administrator put it, "could one exactly mount a crusade against Senghor and Lamine Gueye" who had for so long been part and parcel of the French political scene. If the Soudanese leaders seemed somewhat less certain in their intentions toward France, this still hardly justified the military operation it would have taken to unseat them.

The French business interests in Dakar, unlike the planters of the Ivory Coast, had no economic reasons to fear federation. Indeed, for those involved in Dakar's small manufacturing sector, close ties with other territories would assure continued access to a large African market. While there is no indication that the Dakar businessmen were especially enthusiastic supporters of the Mali Federation at this time, they at least did not actively oppose it. Finally, both Senegalese and Soudanese leaders went out of their way to offer public and private reassurances to France that they had no intention of leaving the Community. As Senghor observed with pointed reference to Guinea, "It is in fact balkanization that would lead to secession."[51]

Although the prime issue at stake in Soudan and Senegal as in Upper Volta and Dahomey was that of federation, the crucial battles were fought out in terms of intraterritorial politics. In Upper Volta, Yameogo was faced with elimination as a political force in his country. In Dahomey, the federal question opened up possibilities for each contending faction within the dominant party to increase its power at the expense of the others. Apithy chose to make his alignments with domestic political forces, while the Dahomeyan federalists in vain sought to triumph by the prestige of their activities in Dakar. In this situation, the interterritorial alignment could not prevail against a solid domestic coalition.

The Union Soudanaise, on the other hand, was firmly committed to federation and for reasons discussed in the next chapter could not easily have changed its course even if its leaders had so desired. Still, the Soudanese mass party skillfully used the Mali Federation as an issue with which to divide and weaken its domestic opposition. The case of Senegal was slightly different, for the Senegalese

51. Interview in *Le Monde,* January 3, 1959.

leaders did run some risks in opposing the conservative forces in the country. However, Senghor, the UPS leader, had made federalism the central issue of his political career since 1950. Had he backed down at that particular point, his influence within his own territorial party would have been seriously weakened. In addition, the UPS as a whole profited by absorbing d'Arboussier's and Doudou Gueye's MPS–RDA, something made possible only by their common commitment to federalism. In this way Senegal, too, used the emotional issue of African interterritorial unity to promote internal political unity and reinforce the position of the dominant mass party.

This preoccupation with territorial politics, and in particular with maintaining one's domestic political base, is a perfectly understandable and rational approach for politicians operating in a rapidly changing political environment, which has no established patterns of peaceful replacement of a ruling group. In such a situation every political leader has to be aware that a false step in his home territory could eliminate him permanently from political life. The case of Niger's Djibo Bakary, who guessed wrong on the referendum, stood as an object lesson of this homely truth. Since any major political issue was likely to be interpreted by the political decision-makers largely in terms of their own domestic political experiences and positions, we shall turn next to a consideration of what federalism meant in the domestic politics of Soudan and Senegal.

7

The Political Meaning of "Federalism": Soudan

ALTHOUGH the colonial history of the French Soudan dates from the last quarter of the nineteenth century, effective occupation of the territory was not completed until the eve of World War One. Compared with its coastal neighbor, Senegal, Soudan was a political, economic, and cultural backwater throughout most of the Third Republic era. During this time its main claims to renown in the outside world were the story-book mystery of Timbuktu, the thousands of its soldiers who under the misnomer, Tirailleurs Sénégalais, died at the Marne, and the inefficient and expensive Office du Niger rice and cotton growing scheme. Although Soudan was a great producer of food crops, fish, and livestock, and although its Dioula merchants carried on trade throughout West Africa, it produced little for international commerce. Although by geography and history it was the "crossroads of West Africa," the commerce and communications lines of the colonial power treated it more as a dead end than a crossroads. Here French civilization was at its least radiant. Under the Third Republic a maximum of three per cent of school-age children attended school, and although several of these went on to William-Ponty in Senegal, none was sent to France for advanced training.

Native administration in Soudan had combined several approaches. In the major cities and along the main communication lines, particularly in the case of Muslim populations, the tribal chiefs went through the same process of abject subordination to the European administration that effectively destroyed their political influence in the coastal territories. These areas were also affected by contact with Africans from other areas, notably Dioula traders, and Senegalese traders, soldiers, and functionaries. In the bush, however, particularly in the case of nomadic populations and sedentary animist groups, the chiefs were left considerably more power and leeway in making decisions on local matters, although here, too, they were often reminded that their continued existence depended on the good will of the colonial administration. French willingness to use this unsystematic expedient was increased by the fragmentation and dispersion of Soudanese ethnic groups (in part the result of the disruptive wars of Samory and El Hadj Omar) which meant that none of the more than seven hundred cantonal or tribal chiefs was likely to mount a significant opposition to governmental authority.[1] By the end of the Third Republic, a perceptible difference had arisen between those populations completely under the control of their chiefs and those who had closer contact with the central administration and with "foreign" Africans.

The best known of the chiefs, and one of the few educated, was Fily Dabo Sissoko who represented the interests of the West African chiefs at the 1944 Brazzaville Conference. As head of the official, but powerless, Union of Native Chiefs, Fily Dabo seemed the logical choice to lead his territory through the new postwar political institutions. Early in 1946, he became associated with the French Socialist party, a choice made all the more logical by his friendship with Lamine Gueye of Senegal and by the fact that the Soudanese administration was largely in the hands of the French Socialists. Along with most of the other leaders of French West Africa, disgusted with the defeat of the first Fourth Republic Constitution, he attended the founding meeting of the RDA held in Bamako in October 1946. When the French Socialist party invoked party discipline against its members participating in the RDA, Fily Dabo, along with most of the others, dropped his connection with the new movement.

The Soudanese Socialist party was a typical patron party. A high proportion of its nominees were chiefs, members of great families or those closely associated with them, and the cantonal and village chiefs were the primary electoral agents. The party was more or less openly supported and, in the beginning at least, more or less supervised by the French administration. Its strength lay in the areas completely under the thumb of the local chief and also among the older African civil servants who gave their loyalty to the administration. The Socialists were also allied to a multiplicity

1. Soudan had one third of all cantonal chiefs in French West Africa in 1939. By comparison to Soudan's 700 chiefs, Senegal had 136 and Guinea 262. Cf. Delavignette, *Freedom and Authority*, p. 73.

of small ethnic or regional parties, most of them short-lived, who supported the candidacy of a local patron.

The Union Soudanaise, the territorial section of the RDA, was quite another matter. The party was led by young products of William-Ponty, many of whom had participated in the Groupes d'Etudes Communistes after the fall of the Vichy authorities. It found its audience among the non-tribally oriented masses of the urban centers, many of the traders, and those villages where the chiefs' authority was weakest. The Union Soudanaise had to battle not only against the Socialists, but also against the colonial authorities. Of its 1959 political bureau at least three, including Modibo Keita, had spent time in French prisons, and many others, as government functionaries or teachers, had been banished to the least desirable posts in the desert or in the farthest bush. The political intervention of the colonial authorities and particularly of the French army, which manipulated the votes of the many Soudanese veterans, was seldom subtle. Despite such handicaps, the Union Soudanaise steadily increased its audience, thanks to its superb mass-party organization and defense of the interests of broad categories of the population across tribal lines, and thanks in particular to the support of many of the African Dioula traders who provided the party with funds and used their contacts—and credit—in bush areas to spread the party from its urban base into the interior. By late 1956 when the French finally made peace with the Soudanese and Guinea RDA sections, the ascendancy of the Union Soudanaise was apparent. It won two of the three Soudanese seats in the French National Assembly in the January 1956 election and, with a local ally, all but six of the seats in the Soudanese Assembly a year later. By the time of the September 1958 referendum, the party of Modibo Keita was assured of general popular support, although it still encountered opposition from many local chiefs and from certain regions and ethnic groups.

The strength of the Union Soudanaise derived from its tight and all-encompassing organization and its strictly enforced discipline. In part this resulted from the lessons learned from the communist contacts of the early years of the RDA, but equally important is the character of the party's leadership and of the Soudanese people themselves. While we have no scholarly analyses of the Soudanese "national character," comments by careful observers of the core

Bambara and other Mande-speaking peoples of Soudan center on the traits of stubbornness, patience, passivity, and perhaps even dullness.[2] This perception, for all it may be unfairly influenced by the observers' personal biases, is echoed with slightly different emotional overtones by the Africans themselves. When asked to describe themselves, the Soudanese use the words "honest," "frank," "simple," "constant," "loyal" or sometimes "outspoken" (*ayant la parole directe*), "stubborn." Searching for words in which to praise his compatriots, a Soudanese leader declared: "The world recognizes that the Soudanese do not change their opinions from one day to the next."[3] The Soudanese also sees himself as a "son of the land," a *bon paysan,* disdaining fripperies, with all the virtues and faults that go with such estate. Above all, he is a "true African."

The Union Soudanaise considers itself the "guide and organizer of the Soudanese people, so as to lead it as rapidly as possible in the path of liberation and well-being."[4] As this statement implies, initiative and directives come from the party and are applied to the masses, who are seen as passive in the decision-making process. This does not mean, however, that the party leaders have complete liberty of choice as to the directives they will send out. "Since the party holds in its hands the destiny of the country and has absolute power, the danger consists . . . in believing that all problems can be resolved at the summit, at the level of party *responsables* of whatever echelon, without surrounding itself with guarantees of popular agreement."[5] The party realizes that it cannot be successful if the masses do not go along with its chosen course of action. But more than this, the masses are for the party an ultimate judge of the correctness of its political program. Party leaders speak constantly of the *bon sens paysan* of the masses which must not be challenged. The masses thus are the repository of a fundamental virtue which the party must recognize and interpret: "We must

2. Thus, Charles Monteil wrote in 1924: "The Bambara is a bumpkin; he is dull and slow to understand, but he clings to his ideas, doubtless rare, and has an insurmountable stubbornness. He is patient; he endures every tyranny . . . but when he has resolved to exact vengeance . . . nothing can stop him." A more recent writer protests this and other such judgments, but concludes, "The Bambara is, in fact, intelligent, patient, and stubborn." Viviana Paques, *Les Bambaras* (Paris, Presses Universitaires de France, 1954), p. 110.

3. Idrissa Diarra, "Rapport Politique," Deuxième Conférence Territoriale de l'Union Soudanaise-RDA (October 2, 1958, typescript).

4. Statuts de l'Union Soudanaise-RDA, Article 2.

5. *Essor* editorial, December 11, 1959.

never forget this eternal truth, *that the people is always revolutionary in its aspirations and that the revolution will be effective if the Party never ceases to identify itself with the masses, to blend into them, to refer without ceasing and forever to their possibilities and to their desires.*"[6] The judgment of the masses is likely to be swiftly felt by the party, for it recognizes that it is only through popular action that its program can be carried out. It must find "directives [*mots d'ordre*] likely not only to be approved by the masses but to be carried out [*portés*] by them."[7]

Finding such directives is recognized as a difficult problem by the political leaders who, after all, are *not* the masses. The distinction between party and mass is clearly maintained and is most apparent in exhortations that the party leaders must "melt into" the masses. Generally, this operation is fairly self-conscious. What is required is "a close analysis of the political conditions and the eventual reactions of the masses. There must be a concordance in time between the thoughts of those who make the choice and those who . . . permit its realization: the people."[8]

Unfortunately, the French schooling, which alone makes it possible for the party leaders to lead the masses, threatens to cut them off from this fundamental source of wisdom. The problem can become a tormenting one:

> How many comrades would agree to enter the dark, smoky hut, to sit on the mat that by its color and age blends into the earth, to dip his hand—without the least repugnance—into the dubious dish of *tô* or rice, to carry to his lips and without apprehension drink milk on which swims a thick layer of dust? . . . So long as we have not accomplished this evolution towards Africa, we will only brush by the problems that confront the masses.[9]

Apparently the Soudanese political leader was somewhat unsure that he had not been corrupted by the ways of the colonialists and lost the prized character of a good, honest, African peasant.

6. Ibid.
7. *Essor* editorial, March 27, 1959.
8. Ibid. The words for "make the choice" are *dégager l'option,* which carry the nuance of selecting a course of action out of a mass of unstructured possibilities, or possibly of interpreting the real though unrecognized preference of the masses.
9. Modibo Keita, "Rapport Politique," Les Travaux du Quatrième Congrès Territorial de l'Union Soudanaise-RDA, 22–24 Septembre 1955 (mimeo.).

With all this emphasis on securing the support of or following the fundamental will of the masses, there is no question of letting the masses participate in a direct and unstructured way in making decisions. This is the province of the party. Decision-making is a one-way operation, although eventually the decision must be ratified by the people. Even as the party tailors its program to fit the aspirations of the masses, so it must condition the masses to make the program work.

> We must create a national consciousness within the peasant masses. . . . Subsequently, we must use this national sentiment, to extract from it its constructive content and orient it toward collective tasks. . . . What must first be created is an atmosphere (*ambiance*). Within this atmosphere we must progressively inculcate the sense of responsibility demanded by our new objectives and proceed to the rational organization of the rural masses.[10]

Perhaps the most sophisticated appreciation of the Union Soudanaise's relations with the masses is in the statement of a sympathetic Senegalese party (the PRA–Sénégal), which described the Union Soudanaise as the party "which truly and democratically controls the Soudanese masses."[11] Although control is a one-way process, it is "democratic" and effective because it is accepted by the masses and is in the masses' interest.

The strength of the party, which permits it to make an accurate choice of a political position and to control the masses, resides in three related factors: collective leadership, organization, and discipline. Collective decision-making is defended most simply on the theory that two heads are better than one. "Whatever may be the intrinsic value of our leaders, taken individually, the decisions that they might be brought to take alone are likely to be marred by errors. We can thus never emphasize sufficiently the necessity and efficacy of working as a team."[12] Not only does collective decision-making help prevent "errors," it is the only sure way to "choke off the politics of personality and to insure the continuity of the Party."[13] By drawing many people into the decision-making process, one stands a better chance of representing the view of the

10. *Essor* editorial, May 22, 1959.
11. *Indépendance Africaine*, July 11, 1959.
12. Idrissa Diarra, "Rapport sur l'Organisation," Quatrième Congrès Territorial.
13. Ibid.

masses. By surpressing the cult of personality, the party can more easily "depersonalize itself," and at the same time insure its own immortality by not being linked to one person, as were the opposition parties. The emphasis on anonymity, one may hypothesize, brings the party more into line with its own appreciation of the faceless masses. Decisions are always taken in the name of the whole party, or of the Soudanese people, or of the party's political bureau, never in the name of an individual leader.

The political bureau's decisions are carried out through the party organization.

> Comrades, the dynamism of any organization's political and economic action is a function of the quality of its organization. If the organization does not reach the smallest cells of human groups, the directives are not disseminated and mobilization of the masses proves difficult.[14]

But a pervasive organization is not enough to assure success. Strict discipline must be enforced. "The strength of a party is measured by the discipline shown by all of its organizations."[15] This means strict application of the principle of democratic centralism. Once a decision is reached, everyone "must bend to the decision of the majority, whatever may be his appreciation of the worth of that decision, he must make that decision his very own and work for its success."[16]

Collective decision-making, organization, and discipline are all means to assure that the party always acts as a united front, without fissure, and without second thoughts. Once a program is launched, all criticism becomes "divisive activity," one of the worst —if not the worst—crimes a party member can commit. "Any attempt at demoralization, any divisive work or attack against the Party's candidates or leaders must be vigorously denounced to the Party's directing body."[17] Or, in the words of the party's first president, "Any fractional enterprise likely to amputate or weaken this vast movement . . . is ferociously criminal."[18] From the violence of

14. Modibo Keita, "Rapport Moral et Politique," Cinquième Congrès de l'Union Soudanaise-RDA (August 13–17, 1958, typescript).

15. Idrissa Diarra, "Rapport Politique," Deuxième Conférence Territoriale.

16. Union Soudanaise, *Règlement Intérieur,* Conclusion number 2.

17. Ibid.

18. Mamadou Konaté, "Allocution d'Ouverture," Quatrième Conférence Territoriale. The French, *férocément criminelle,* is as unusual and forceful as its English equivalent.

the language employed it is apparent that this point is crucial for the party leaders. Not only must they "surround themselves with the guarantee of popular support," they must also have a guarantee of unquestioned allegiance from their own associates in the party. The solidarity of the movement must be preserved at all costs. This insistence on anonymity and popular acquiescence may have further implications. Were a man to feel himself personally responsible for a wrong decision, he might also fear loss of the essential contact with the masses, with his own African heritage of the *bon sens paysan.* He might even judge himself forever corrupted by the siren call of European ways.

The Union Soudanaise upholds the ideal of unity of the people with great determination. This unity is seen as a reflection of the classlessness of traditional African society, now threatened by the introduction of European economic and social forms—and even more, paradoxically, by the prospect of European withdrawal which will remove the outside threat against which unity could be achieved.

> Everyone . . . is agreed in recognizing that the traditional solidarity which plunges its roots deep in the African soul, is in danger of crumbling slowly, but surely. The departure of the colonizer is likely to accentuate this in some degree, for the presence of its dominating force (*force dominatrice*), despite the famous "divide and rule," had permitted the reinforcement of that solidarity.[19]

After independence the party will have to be doubly careful to break down the divisive and individualistic structures that colonialism has implanted on African soil. Thus, if only to maintain the desired relationship between the party and the masses and within the party itself, independence can bring no relaxation of discipline. Indeed, once the party is in complete control of the government, any fractional activity becomes subversive activity, for it now attacks the state as a whole.[20]

The fundamental tenet of the Union Soudanaise's doctrine is the supremacy of the political in all things. *"Priorité au 'Politique'"* its newspaper proclaims.[21] The belief in the supremacy of politics may

19. *Essor* editorial, April 24, 1959.

20. See the speech of Jean-Marie Koné, *Troisième Conférence de l'Union Soudanaise-RDA, Section du PFA* (Koulouba, n.d.), p. 48.

21. *Essor* editorial, October 23, 1959.

be traced directly to the colonial state's insistence on retaining "political" power for itself, even when according other concessions to the Africans. The early African legislative assemblies were permitted to handle economic questions only. Politics thus acquired the aura of forbidden fruit—and of Aladdin's lamp. Possession of the secret would bring unlimited power. This seems confirmed by their conviction that: "All those who have minimized the role of politics, have always opposed all social progress, and have always been in the camp of the enemies of democracy."[22]

Politics is something that is "rational," "logical," "constant," and, like the party and the masses, it can be organized and controlled. It is also all-encompassing, for every action, every organization has its political dimension. A good political program must be "rooted in reality," must be "dynamic" and "comprehensive." It must "go in the sense of history and the interests of Africa."[23] The leaders of the Union Soudanaise, unlike their erstwhile communist mentors, waste little breath discussing the "sense of history," probably because they feel its sense is sufficiently clear for a country nearing the last stages of colonial rule. After a particularly dramatic turning point in the party's fortunes, a leader declares: "The essential thing is to study the past to draw the practical conclusions from it. . . . With the total support of our peoples (*des populations*), we shall point out (*dégager*) the new political orientation that imposes itself."[24] The political orientation is thus manifest to the party leaders, it "imposes itself" on them. Their only worry is to assure themselves of popular support, which, despite the surface optimism of the statement, may not be automatic, for the speaker finds it necessary to speak of "peoples," not of an automatically responding and united "mass."

If politics is omnipresent and all-encompassing, it also has a fundamental unity. No political problem exists by itself, but implies a host of related problems. What many others would consider to be discrete problems are in fact but epiphenomena of a single, fundamental problem, sometimes called "the political content of the nation."

22. Ibid.

23. Mahamane Alassane Haidara, in "Assemblée Législative Soudanaise" (March 31, 1959, typescript).

24. Idrissa Diarra, in *Congrès Extraordinaire de l'Union Soudanaise-RDA, le 22 septembre 1960* (Koulouba, 1960), pp. 8–9.

> We of the Union Soudanaise affirm that the problem of Federalism, the problem of Chiefs, etc., are but particular aspects of the single and same problem: the problem of the very conception of the structures of the Nation and of its framework, the problem of the general political orientation in function of the economic and social organization of the State.[25]

Politics has an essential unity, just as the party and the nation each must have its unity and indeed just as their opposition has its unity.

All the opposition to the party and to the party's program somehow relates to "the fact of colonialism," which destroyed the natural collective unity of traditional African society; "all our misfortunes are the result of colonization, of the loss of our total sovereignty." For what is colonialism, but that which has introduced "divisive structures" into Africa, which has supported the chiefs against the party, which has robbed Africa of its natural resources? "We affirm that without colonization we would at this moment be busy finishing off the construction of African nations. . . ." The solution is "to conquer the cause to stop the effects and the prolongations of the effects."[26] For this battle, unity is more than ever necessary because the opposition's strength, too, lies in its unity. "It is not with dispersed troops that one effectively combats colonialism which forms a single front."[27] When colonization and its effects are eliminated, then Africa will have renewed the continuity of its great history.

As politics is accorded all honors, so economics falls to the level of the minor arts. "If the political line is correct, the economic side will take care of itself [*ira tout seul*]."[28] However, economics, like the masses, may prove dangerously undisciplined if it is not brought under political control. "We do not underestimate the importance of economics; on the contrary, because we know its reverse effects on 'politics' we try to domesticate it, to fit it into a political perspective, by removing its empirical and anarchical character."[29] This is more than just the reaction of a group of men with little experience in the intricacies of high finance. Economics is also

25. *Essor* editorial, March 13, 1959.
26. *Essor,* August 14, 1959.
27. Modibo Keita, "Rapport Politique," Quatrième Congrès Territoriale.
28. Interview with Ousmane Ba, a Soudanese cabinet minister.
29. *Essor* editorial, October 23, 1959.

the province of the capitalists and the French trading companies who never take Africans into administrative positions.

For all the straightforward dynamism of the Union Soudanaise's language in discussing itself and its view of the world, it is evident that it leaves some room for internal contradiction and even a bit of hedging when necessary. Such was the case when the Union Soudanaise had to take a position on the September 1958 referendum. On the one hand, all that was implicit in their outlook on the political world would lead them to emulate Guinea by voting against de Gaulle's Community. On the other hand, the party's sense of "local realities" told it that the dangers of a negative vote might outweigh the advantages. If the French administration remained neutral, the Union Soudanaise was sure of obtaining a majority of votes for whatever course of action it chose, but the French made it quite clear that the administrators in the countryside would use all their influence on the chiefs, religious leaders, and people to obtain a positive vote. In particular, the northern area of Soudan, bordering on Algeria, was directly under the influence of the French administration and army which, the Union Soudanaise charged, had inspired "a certain opposition between white nomadic elements and black sedentary elements." Thus, with Soudanese unity in danger:

> If under these conditions we had adopted an attitude which might have put us in opposition with the solidly implanted colonizing element, the Soudan incontestably would have had its northern part amputated.
>
> It is to avoid this that, after an objective, sincere, and honest analysis . . . the *Direction* of the Union Soudanaise thought it should not choose an adventurous course [*aller à l'aventure*].[30]

The decision to accept de Gaulle's Community was motivated by the desire to maintain Soudanese unity as well as by the fear of being eliminated totally once this unity were broken. It was also motivated by a desire to maintain the unity of French-speaking West Africa:

> We have first preferred to pass through the stage of unity before taking up the stage of independence, because it is difficult

30. Modibo Keita, in *Troisième Conférence de l'Union Soudanaise-RDA*, pp. 21–22.

> for countries who have won their independence by their own efforts to renounce this independence . . . to disappear in order to constitute a federal ensemble, a single nation. It is in taking into account these realities that we have thought first to bring about . . . a great ensemble which, politically and economically viable, would accede to its independence.[31]

Independence is to be achieved once an overpowering unity of African states has been formed, which alone will provide the political power to counteract the divisive forces of colonialism and lead West Africa to real independence.

In this sense, general African unity is the guarantor of internal unity. It is true in another sense, too. "Only the realization of organic Unity [between territories] will permit the former territories of French West Africa to avoid . . . these sharp minority problems that could not but compromise their close understanding."[32] The vexing problem of ethnic minorities, which threaten Soudanese and party unity, is to be solved by submerging these minorities in a vast federation.

Soudan's geographic position at the "crossroads of West Africa," her flourishing commerce with neighboring states, and her dependence on a port in a neighboring country continued to play a role in her advocacy of federalism, but these factors would not have been enough had not the whole political vision of her leaders so concentrated on the problem of reinforcing unity as a precondition to success and even survival. The leaders of the Union Soudanaise saw federalism not only as a matter of economic convenience, but as something closely related to their very political survival. Such an approach to the problem of federation carried with it a vision of what should be the "political content" of the Mali Federation, which in turn influenced the comportment of the Soudanese leaders in their relations with their Senegalese partners.

The federation would be dominated by a single "general political outlook." It would group "political organizations favorable to federalism and which, as a function of this choice, must logically have the same general political outlook."[33] This is not simply a preference on the part of the Soudanese. For them, this is a basic

31. Ibid.

32. Mahamane Alassane Haidara, in "Assemblée Législative Soudanaise" (March 31, 1959, typescript).

33. *Essor* editorial, March 20, 1959.

law of politics: "To be for Federation is to be for political progress. . . . To be against Federation is to be for political stagnation [*immobilisme*]."[34] Just as internal Soudanese politics demanded a common political point of view, so, "for us it can only be a question of union of similar [*semblables*] elements. How can you build an association with governments that would not have the same perspectives on the future?"[35]

In this perspective, the defections of Upper Volta and Dahomey, while deplorable, were seen as having the beneficial effect of removing politically unsure elements from the new federation. As Modibo Keita expressed it:

> Mali is ready to go; it has thrown its ballast overboard. This lightening of the load brings Mali back to the limits of Senegal and Soudan in which our consecrated political unity and the action of our Governments will permit an acceleration of the process of evolution of our Federation towards the affirmation of its personality and its national sovereignty.[36]

Since the Soudanese considered the future federation to be constructed in their own image, it "will be constructed with States and peoples united and organized."[37] There was no question of leaving the federation to agreements between leaders, much less to individual initiative. The populations were to be organized, united, and mobilized behind their political parties which then must unite to lead the federation.

The Soudanese saw the federation as a modern expression of traditional African unity. It was to continue the heritage of the great Sudanic empires of the Middle Ages and of Samory and El Hadj Omar by taking as its "primary preoccupation the affirmation of the African personality."[38]

Since the federation was "to go in the sense of history" and represent political progress, it must inevitably lead to "eventual inde-

34. Ibid.

35. Jean-Marie Koné, in "Assemblée Territoriale Soudanaise, Session Extraordinaire" (November 24, 1958, typescript).

36. Mali, *J.O., Débats,* No. 2 (Meeting of April 6, 1959). The term for "throw the ballast overboard" is *jeter du lest.* This carries connotations both of making a sacrifice to preserve the essential, and of getting rid of excess baggage.

37. Madeira Keita in *Essor,* May 6, 1960.

38. Jean-Marie Koné, in "Assemblée Territoriale Soudanaise, Session Extraordinaire" (November 24, 1958, typescript).

pendence."[39] It must "lead . . . still-dependent African territories to national sovereignty," just as it will eventually "guarantee and consolidate newly acquired independence."[40] Independence was more than a doctrinal issue for the Soudanese. In deciding to approve the de Gaulle constitution, the party leaders faced a near revolt from many of the lower-level party workers who felt "a certain disappointment" at not being allowed to vote for immediate independence.[41] To maintain party unity at that time, the leaders had to explain that "real" independence required special preparations and safeguards, and that "*only* [*federal*] *UNITY is the safeguard for INDEPENDENCE.*"[42] The party leaders, thus, had to achieve real independence once the federation was established, lest they betray their word (and accordingly their self-image as good Soudanese) to their own people.

Other practical considerations demanded that independence follow federation. As long as the country was still associated with France, the colonial power would be able to intervene against it. As one leader said delicately: "If we remain in the Community . . . and one day we have trouble with it, they (*on*) will bring forces against us, and we might experience the saddening events that Algeria is experiencing even now as we are speaking."[43] Not only does unity guarantee independence, independence may well guarantee unity.

Federation, then, was not to be the end of the line, for the Soudanese saw a complete "inter-penetration of the two notions of Unity and Independence."[44] They could not conceive of one without the other.

39. *Essor* editorial, March 20, 1959.

40. Madeira Keita in *Essor*, May 6, 1960.

41. See the discussion by Seydou Traoré, secretary-general of the Sikasso section in the *Troisième Conférence de l'Union Soudanaise-RDA*, p. 77.

42. Idrissa Diarra, "Rapport Politique," Deuxième Conférence Territoriale. (Emphasis in text.)

43. Jean-Marie Koné, in *Troisième Conférence de l'Union Soudanaise-RDA*, p. 45.

44. *Essor* editorial, April 3, 1959.

8

The Political Meaning of "Federalism": Senegal

DURING the precolonial period, present-day Senegal was generally not part of the large-scale political units of the Sudanic regions and their ramifying commercial routes. The colonial period greatly accentuated the separation. In the words of Leopold Senghor:

> A different face on Colonization, a different treatment by the Colonizer . . . have augmented our differences. Without mentioning that our political education . . . has been different for fifteen years. All these differences have created divergent sociological conditions: habits, mentalities, and psychological reactions.[1]

Nowhere in West Africa has French influence been more thoroughly implanted than in Senegal, and nowhere has it been more thoroughly combined with the predispositions of the native population.[2] In part this has been the result of the long period of French occupation. The first permanent French settlement, St. Louis, was established on an island in the Senegal River in 1659, and French traders plied the coast and the lower reaches of the river throughout the seventeenth and eighteenth centuries. Senegal subsequently provided the base—and much of the manpower—for French conquest of the Sudanic interior. Senegal was the one colony in which the policy of assimilation was seriously employed under the Third Republic. By the end of the nineteenth century French citizenship and extensive political and civil rights were extended to all inhabitants of the four communes, St. Louis, Rufisque, Gorée, and Dakar. The African inhabitants of these towns and their descendants, together with the local European population, elected munici-

1. "Rapport sur la Politique Générale," Deuxième Congrès de l'UPS-PFA (St. Louis, 1960, mimeo.), p. 45.

2. For an excellent short study of the interpenetration of French and African culture in Senegal, see Michael Crowder, *Senegal, A Study in French Assimilation Policy* (London, Oxford University Press, 1962).

pal authorities, sent representatives to a Colonial Council and a deputy to the French National Assembly. Although political assimilation was limited to the privileged few of the communes, the interior regions were brought under a system of direct administration that completely subsumed the cantonal chiefs under the administrative hierarchy and almost everywhere destroyed traditional political institutions.

Along with its political privileges, Senegal ranked consistently first among the French West African territories on all indicators of economic and social progress. By the end of the Third Republic, Senegal's rate of school attendance had passed 10 per cent; it had three secondary schools and the federal normal school. Before World War II Senegalese were almost the only French West Africans to be educated in France, and Leopold Senghor was the only African to receive the *agrégation* degree. Because of their education, Senegalese frequently occupied administrative posts in other territories, or worked in minor capacities as agents of the European commercial houses.

Although the French did not succeed in creating a nation of black Frenchmen in Senegal, relations between the two races did not have the clear master–servant aspect that characterized other colonies in Africa.

> The Senegalese are naturally an immensely proud people and have little feeling of racial inferiority. Close contact with a French community that ranges from the Olympian civil servant to a taxi driver and a clerk without work, has left them under no illusion about the equal fallibility of the European. . . . The Senegalese on the whole do not have any complex about the European as a person although he does about the technical superiority of the European and about France's insistence on the superiority of its culture.[3]

Nor is this a recent product of political evolution. In the 1920s Buell noted with some dismay that a European had no special claim on a seat even in a first class railway carriage and that African Councillors "unmercifully criticized European officials."[4]

If direct familiarity with things French did not penetrate the in-

3. Ibid., pp. 67–68. See also Paul Mercier, "Le Groupement européen de Dakar," *Cahiers Internationaux de Sociologie, 19* (1955), 130–46.

4. R. L. Buell, *The Native Problem in Africa* (New York, Macmillan, 1928), *1*, 980.

terior of Senegal, the prestige of Senegal's urban centers, themselves heavily influenced by French culture, has been more widely spread. At the present time over one quarter of Senegal's population lives in a city or in one of the trading centers of the interior. Rare indeed is the individual without a relative or close friend in Dakar, Thiès, Kaolack, or St. Louis, and while the elders may lament, few can deny the prestige and advantages of urban life. With the exception of Western Nigeria (already urbanized before colonial times) Senegal is the most heavily urbanized region of West Africa, with 36.5 per cent of the population living in towns of more than 2,000 people.

Because of the weak position of the chiefs, and the prevalence of a monetary economy in the interior, the prestigious leaders of the Senegalese bush areas were men with much greater contact with the urban world. These men, most of whom also had some traditional social rank, might be peanut-traders, truck-owners, civil servants, or—and most important—Muslim religious leaders who generally were heavily involved in modern economic dealings with Dakar commercial interests. While many of these leaders could not be considered as representatives of modern Africa, they were not simply brushed-up versions of traditional leaders; they owed their positions of leadership uniquely to qualities which distinguished them from tribal society. Because of these elites' competence in various aspects of modern life, they were better able to act as leaders for their people in the complex new world of modern politics. The general discrediting of rural elites that led to their elimination in Soudanese politics did not take place in Senegal, where they have been able to function within the confines of a modern mass party. In addition, the rural elites provided a natural and convenient link between the masses and the modern urban politicians.

The dominant ethnic group of Senegal, and that which most sets the tone of Senegalese life, is the Wolof. Although the Wolof represent only about 35 per cent of the Senegalese population, they are closely allied with the Serer (16 per cent) and the Lébou, the old and wealthy inhabitants of the Dakar area. The Wolof language is the lingua franca for most of Senegal, and is understood by an estimated 80 per cent of the population. As one non-Wolof respondent stated, "The Senegalese is he who speaks Wolof." The preeminent position of the Wolof is due not only to their numbers but to their great facility for absorbing individuals into their group. Also, as one anthropologist has pointed out: "One of the characteristics of the Wolof is that from earliest times they have shown themselves extremely adaptable and taken over from those with whom they were in contact . . . new skills and ideas which enabled them to occupy and hold leading positions in relation to neighbouring peoples."[5] Largely because of this adaptive characteristic, the Wolof have been able to mediate between and integrate the traditional cultures of Africa and the conquering culture of France. They have also reaped the benefits associated with this role.

Social structure and history have combined to eliminate many of the divisive effects of tribalism in Senegal. The major tribes of Senegal have a closely interlocking relationship. Aside from the alliance of the Wolof with the Serer and Lébou already mentioned, the Tukulor are a mixture of Fulani and Serer, while the Diola claim to be descended from the same ancestor as the Serer. Only the Malinke of southeastern Senegal lie outside this interlocking net. The Muslim religion is adhered to by all but some of the Serer and Diola, and all tribes except the Diola share a common caste structure. This last is an extremely strong social and political factor. Whereas marriage between different tribal groups may reach as high as 29 per cent of all marriages in an urban setting, marriage between members of different castes is virtually unknown, even among those most touched by Western culture.[6]

While ethnic differences are still noted, and ethnic conflicts are not unknown, Senegalese society is, by African standards, remarkably homogeneous. Senegalese who have entered into modern life refer to themselves simply as Senegalese, not Wolof, Tukulor, or whatever. This has been particularly true for those who have ventured outside Senegal. As Delavignette noted when he was serving as an administrator in Upper Volta before World War II:

> The case of the one and only Senegalese is interesting. There you have a man no longer designated by his tribe, but by his colony. We are not told what tribe he belongs to. . . . That he comes from the Colony of Senegal is enough to give him some sort of status, and for native policy to know whom it is deal-

5. David P. Gamble, *The Wolof of Senegambia* (London, International African Institute, 1957), p. 53.

6. Paul Mercier, "Etude du mariage et enquête urbaine," *Cahiers d'Etudes Africaines, 1* (January 1960), 36 and Thiam Bodiel, "Hiérarchie de la société ouolove," *Notes Africaines,* No. 41 (January 1949), 12.

> ing with. He is not a *déraciné* from a small, isolated Africa; in Bobo *Cercle* he is a son of the mother colony of all the colonies of the Federation. He is settled in Bobo as he might be elsewhere, as a man of the new African world that has got beyond race, where natives of all races give life to the colonial structure and break it open from within.[7]

This experience of being apart from the other Africans they met when outside their own territory served to reinforce the Senegalese feeling of territorial identity and superiority, particularly since most Senegalese outside of Senegal under the Third Republic were able to pass for citizens, even if they were not in fact from the privileged communes.

Because of Senegal's special position under the French, and because of the closer integration of the urban and rural components of Senegalese life, the idealized image of the Senegalese has been quite different from the *bon paysan* of Soudan. The ideal Senegalese is the *samba-linguère*, the "first among the nobles," a proud, aristocratic individual who by personal strength of character and unstinting generosity stands out from even his nominal peers, and whose praises are recognized and sung by all.[8] He is a man who combines traditional attributes of virtue with a mastery of modern urban life. The worth of the *samba-linguère* is not demonstrated by any quiet self-assurance on his part, but rather by the ostentation and amount of his expenditures and the number and quality of praise-singers (*griots*) and other hangers-on he supports to make his worth known. The Senegalese accordingly affect gladly a bombastic turn of phrase, a delight in dance and public show and a seemingly irresponsible insouciance that have earned them the nickname of the "Latins of Africa." These traits have been carried over into politics where they have reinforced the position of dominant individual leaders able to command a coterie of personal clients, placed a premium on fine political oratory, and lent a carnival atmosphere to political meetings and demonstrations.[9]

The Senegalese political outlook can be understood better in

7. Robert Delavignette, *Freedom and Authority*, p. 53.

8. This characteristic is best portrayed in Ousmane Socé Diop's fine novel about the Senegalese, *Karim*, first published in 1936 (Paris, Nouvelles Editions Latines, 1948).

9. See the discussion of the opposition party's *khawarés* (political celebrations) in *Condition Humaine*, March 24 and May 8, 1951.

terms of its historical evolution than in terms of any coherent doctrine. Senegalese politics grew out of the four communes and their tradition of self-government and representation in France. When political life was reborn in French West Africa after World War II, the coastal communes continued their political preeminence under the leadership of Lamine Gueye's Senegalese branch of the French Socialist Party (SFIO). His protégé, Leopold Senghor, broke from the SFIO in 1948 to form an opposition party, the Bloc Démocratique Sénégalais, based primarily on the newly-enfranchised bush electors and on the new populations flooding the urban areas. To obtain their allegiance Senghor first sought the support of the notables of the interior and the various regional, ethnic, religious, cultural, and occupational protective societies that had grown up since the war.[10] In particular he sought, and obtained, the backing of the Muslim leaders. The new party was organized as "an organic federation" of the participating groups, and although three years later all were required to take membership directly in the parent party, the traditions of local responsibility and of intra-party bargaining among local leaders were well established.

The continued prevalence of political interest groups dominated by a local personality, called *clans* in Senegal, is attested to by the frequency and vehemence with which they are denounced by party leaders.[11] The territorial party leaders have found it politic not to challenge directly these habits so deeply ingrained in Senegalese political traditions. They have allowed *clan* groups considerable control over local party activities and patronage and have concentrated on reducing the *clans'* influence, and in asserting the primacy of the party's executive bureau in the making of territorial policy. Thus, the leaders ostentatiously pay homage to the wisdom of the Muslim marabouts, and have continued the French administration's habit of according them considerable financial assistance, but have determinedly resisted their demands for a direct say in party and governmental affairs. Although they are denied much power of initiative, these local interests continue to exercise a negative influence on the party. They often set policy limits beyond

10. On the importance of these, see Thomas L. Hodgkin, *Nationalism in Colonial Africa*, Chapter 3.

11. For recent denunciations see Senghor's "Rapport sur la Politique Générale" at the July 1960 UPS congress, pp. 48–49, and Thiam Mame Ciré's "Rapport sur l'Organisation" at the July 1961 UPS Youth Movement Congress (mimeo.). Robinson, "Senegal," gives an example of *clan* infighting, pp. 344–45.

which the territorial leaders cannot go without risk of having their plans sabotaged on the local level. This was notably the case when the pro-French and Islamic interests obliged the party leaders to vote for the de Gaulle constitution. Keeping *clan* leaders in line behind the party's territorial policies has demanded considerable skill on the part of the party's top leadership in bargaining, peacemaking, and occasionally knocking local heads together to maintain party solidarity.[12]

The BDS of Senghor and Dia grew in influence over the years by incorporating other political parties until in 1958, with the accession of the Socialists, under the name UPS it attained a position of electoral preeminence comparable to that enjoyed by the Union Soudanaise. While the party hierarchy was able greatly to strengthen its hold over the local *clans*—particularly once it gained access to territorial patronage and coercive resources—the incorporation of new groups increased the number of cleavages within the party structure. The fight for influence between old Socialists and ex-BDS members has been particularly sharp in the towns where once the party of Lamine Gueye held sway.

Unlike the Union Soudanaise, which in the early days suffered greatly from the administration's open opposition and repression, the party of Senghor and Dia was accepted, if not always graciously, as a legitimate competitor for political positions and as pursuing political goals with reasonable limits. The influential personal contacts of Senghor in Paris as in Dakar furthermore permitted a much wider area of mutual comprehension to exist between the dominant Senegalese party and French administration and commercial interests. This did not mean that all Senegalese nationalist politicians basked in the glow of benign French approval; indeed, as we have seen, Senegal produced also a crop of decidedly radical (in African terms) anti-imperialist politicians associated particularly with the youth movements, trade unions, and the PAI. To the extent that these elements were incorporated within the structure of the party they constituted a bargaining group on a par with other bargaining groups. When they were outside the party, their effective power was greatly reduced.

12. The tolerance of divergent points of view and interests within the party so long as a façade of unity can be presented to the outside can perhaps be traced to the Senegalese party's evolution out of the French SFIO. On this same effect in the SFIO, see Constantin Melnick and Nathan Leites, *The House without Windows: France Elects a President* (Evanston, Row, Peterson, 1958), pp. 93, 101, passim.

Despite frequent appeals for "party solidarity" or "union behind our leaders," the goal of total unity, so ardently desired by the Union Soudanaise, was not actively sought by the UPS. The open expression of diversity was accepted as a normal aspect of party life, so long as the electoral aims of the party were not compromised. Thus Mamadou Dia, speaking at a party congress: "all those assembled here, each and every one, [have] the right, precisely because we share common objectives, to come here and express the most diverse, the most varied opinions so that there will be no confusion [over points of view]."[13] Structurally, the informal division of the party into competing *clans* and the formal power and independent initiative enjoyed by the local party committees made a monolithic façade impossible to attain. Also, the tendency to personalize issues, programs, and party units is deeply ingrained both in Senegalese habits and in the traditions of the UPS. The name of the party, which has undergone two changes since its inception, carries little of the emotional appeal for the masses that "Union Soudanaise" does further inland. For much of the population of the Senegalese bush, the UPS is simply "the party of Senghor," and one party official in Eastern Senegal expressed doubts that many people in his area would recognize the party under any other name.

This personalization is evident in formal publications of the party. Editorials in the UPS newspaper are habitually signed by the author, and while they nominally reflect the position of the party's political bureau, they are generally considered to reflect primarily the author's personal viewpoint—which may, indeed, conflict with that formally espoused by the party's hierarchy.[14] Whereas the names of individual party leaders appear rarely in Union Soudanaise writing, they recur constantly in that of the UPS. In a comparable sample of party newspaper editorials over a two year period, the names of individual party leaders were cited 9 times in the Union Soudanaise's *Essor* and 35 times in the UPS's *Unité Africaine.*[15] Within the UPS, an idea is judged not only on the basis of its intrinsic worth, but also on the basis of whose idea

13. "Congrès Constitutif du PFA, Débats" (Dakar, July 2, 1959, mimeo.), p. 93.

14. See, for example, the editorial by Ousmane Socé Diop in *Unité Africaine*, September 19, 1959, which contradicts almost point for point the economic program of the UPS Executive Bureau and the Premier.

15. See Appendix II.

it is. This is doubtless true to a certain extent even for a party as resolutely anonymous as the Union Soudanaise, but in the UPS this is accepted as a normal procedure and one that simply reflects the "diversity of the party's audience" and the preeminent right of an individual leader to have a specific point of view.

The UPS formally rejects the idea of the single monolithic party. "We are against the *parti unique*. We are in favor of a unified party [*parti unifié*]."[16] The formula "unified party" is nowhere extensively defined in the writings of the UPS leaders, although its distinctiveness is habitually defended with great force. The formula contains two notions. First, the party is constituted of units having at least a modicum of autonomy. It permits "integration of different populations and regions without suppressing their particular characteristics."[17] The second notion implicit in the idea of the unified party is that it is not necessarily the only political formation permitted. Indeed, the UPS leaders specifically recognize the right of opposition, though subject to certain conditions: "The rights of the opposition will be safeguarded on condition that it be a *national*, and constructive opposition. Rights to found a party; rights for the members of this party to exercise all the liberties inscribed in the constitution."[18] The emphasis on a national opposition is to exclude "any action, any propaganda in favor of a foreign power."[19] This tolerance may not be extended to the point of permitting an opposition party to become a major electoral threat, but the Senegalese leaders believe it important to maintain the form of a competitive democracy.

But just as the opposition outside the party has its limits, so diversity within the party must not degenerate into perpetual discussion to the point where it inhibits effective action. The emphasis, however, is slightly different from that employed by the Union Soudanaise when its leaders demand the extirpation of fractionalism. The UPS is not worried by the fact of discussion or even disputation except to the extent that it hinders the carrying out of a program. The Senegalese are asked "to construct their unity around a national program," not to rally around the monolithic *parti*

16. Senghor, "Exposé devant le Groupe Fraternel d'Etudes Socialistes," text reproduced in *France Observateur,* February 2, 1958.

17. Interview with Valdiodio N'Diaye.

18. Senghor, "Rapport sur la Politique Générale," Deuxième Congrès de l'UPS-PFA, p. 52. Emphasis in text.

19. Ibid.

unique.[20] Divergences are dangerous only in that they may make the action of the party and of the government less effective; they are not the "ferociously criminal" acts threatening the very existence of the party and the cohesion of the nation that so worry the Soudanese.

Particularly in the thought of Senghor, diversity is considered a natural and even advantageous quality. In calling for some limitation on intra-party quarreling he uses expressions like "quarrels under the baobab," referring to the distinctive tree that dominates most Senegalese villages and is now the official symbol of the country, or "quarrels of N'diongolor and N'dialakhar," an image drawn from Wolof tradition.[21] These are perfectly legitimate African tendencies which, given the need for national progress, must be subordinated to more pressing matters. Senghor recognizes the usefulness of limited diversity by arguing, with indirect reference to Father Teilhard de Chardin, who has greatly influenced Senghor's thought, that "diversity . . . is a good thing to the extent that it provides *complementarity.*"[22] In the context of the party, this extends the two-heads-are-better-than-one approach by recognizing that this is true precisely to the degree that the two heads have different, but compatible, approaches.

If the Union Soudanaise doctrine trumpets the priority of politics over economics, the UPS comes close to reversing the order. Mamadou Dia, speaking before the Senegalese Constituent Assembly, stated: "I have not yet spoken of the essential, of the key to our future: I mean our *economic problems.* In fact, all our problems can be brought down to this: Senegal is an under-developed country. Under pain of catastrophe, we must face up to this situation. . . . This is reality. Anything else is just literature."[23] The question of economic development is crucial even in domains usually reserved for politics. "[Economic] development signifies for us true independence, liberty, and human dignity also, for *we believe that there is no independence without development.*"[24]

20. Mamadou Dia, *Déclaration faite . . . à l'ouverture de la session ordinaire de l'Assemblée Constituante du Sénégal* (St. Louis, 1958), p. 26.

21. "Rapport sur la Politique Générale," Deuxième Congrès de l'UPS-PFA, pp. 27 and 51.

22. *Unité Africaine* editorial, June 1, 1959. Emphasis in text.

23. Dia, *Déclaration faite . . . l'Assemblée Constituante du Sénégal,* p. 10. Emphasis in text.

24. Dia, *Déclaration d'investiture . . . 4 avril 1959* (Dakar, 1959), p. 9. Emphasis in text.

Politics, instead of being the essential force for guiding and controlling economics, as it is for the Union Soudanaise, is frequently a danger for economics, bringing the very anarchic factor into a well-ordered realm that the Union Soudanaise feared economics would bring to politics. In speaking of the village cooperatives, a long-time source of political power in Senegal, Dia proclaimed, "We must renovate the institution, to make it the instrument *par excellence* of development in a rural milieu. This supposes that we take away from it all its political traits."[25] While for the Union Soudanaise economics is a dangerous and confused realm and politics is the great organizing principle, for the UPS politics means primarily the *clan* quarrels and fights for influence inherited from the politics of the four communes, while economics means the clarity and purity of a principle and guide to action.

For the UPS, politics may have two other and more positive senses, too. It may touch the realm of pure philosophy, of fundamental cultural options, as it does in Senghor's disquisitions on *négritude.* In this sense it provides a distant guide for governmental policy that is made concrete through the application of economics.

> Politics, we are accustomed to say, is "the art of governing the city." It is an orientation in the sense of a general option. *Man* [is] our general option. This black man, our closest neighbor, must be promoted in all domains in order to make of him, not only a consumer, but above all a *producer* of *culture.*[26]

When used in this sense it is even safe, as Senghor here does, to affirm the "primacy of politics." In the second sense, politics becomes identified with administration, that is to say it becomes the servant of economics. "We put the emphasis on economic and social development; but we shall see . . . that political, that is to say 'administrative,' ways and means are not lost sight of for all that."[27] In this sense politics is a technical matter, to be handed over to the best technicians, be they members of the UPS, political agnostics, or even foreigners. The UPS leaders accordingly insist on going slowly on the touchy question of Africanization of administrative

25. Ibid.

26. Senghor, "Rapport sur la doctrine et le programme du parti," *Congrès Constitutif du Parti de la Fédération Africaine* (Dakar, 1959), p. 57. Emphasis in text.

27. Senghor, "Rapport sur la Politique Générale," Deuxième Congrès de l'UPS-PFA, p. 4.

posts, for, "The question of Africanization is . . . not political; it is technical."[28]

While adopting the economic and technical outlook of the colonizing power, the UPS refuses to see the forces of colonialism as responsible for the wide variety of evils with which they are charged in Soudan. Although they may ritually denounce colonialism or the colonialist spirit in the abstract, the UPS leaders are quite generous when it comes to referring to the French and their influence in Africa.[29] Whereas the Soudanese see France as interrupting the normal flow of African history, the UPS sees French occupation as a necessary and normal step in the continent's development. "[France] has realized in part the dream of the old African Emperors. It has done more; it has organized and structured. It has realized their dream of creating a federation out of individual countries and building a common spirit through the French language."[30]

The Senegalese precisely reverse the Soudanese view of who is responsible for divisions among Africans. Against the Soudanese belief that the colonialists were uniquely responsible for dividing Africa, the Senegalese see the French as unifiers who went beyond "this precolonial fact of territorialism."[31] It makes sense in terms of precolonial history for the Senegalese to see their territory as forming a distinct territorial unit, and for the Soudanese to see their region as part of a general West African empire. Whereas the Soudanese leaders define their task as one of taking up directly where the precolonial heroes like Samory left off, the Senegalese leaders envisage their role as continuing what the French started: "It is up to us . . . to take up where the French left off, to give a soul to the spirit created, a little despite itself, by the colonial administration."[32] The UPS leaders thus see no immutable difference between their own interests and goals and those of France. There may be friction with individual Frenchmen, and certainly the UPS disapproves of the subordination of African interests to French interests implied in the colonial system, but in the long run, they believe, cooperation

28. Senghor, "Rapport sur la doctrine et le programme du parti," *Congrès Constitutif du PFA*, p. 66.

29. In a comparable sample of editorials, whereas *Essor* mentioned France as facilitating Soudanese goals just once and as blocking them seventeen times, *Unité Africaine* mentioned France as facilitating Senegalese goals fourteen times and blocking them only twice. Cf. Appendix II.

30. Editorial by Senghor in *Unité Africaine*, June 1, 1959.

31. Mamadou Dia, *Nations Africaines et Solidarité Mondiale* (Paris, Presses Universitaires de France, 1960), p. 140.

32. Editorial by Senghor in *Unité Africaine*, June 1, 1959.

with France is not only tactically right, but a perfectly natural and unobjectionable way of achieving their goals. Although they may seek independence, this is not to take them totally out of the French orbit. "If we intend to realize our national independence, it is not against France but with France, in a great Franco–African ensemble. . . . Above and beyond constitutional independence, what we want to bring about is effective independence and the guaranteed cooperation that [France] offers."[33] Caught between its African past and its French training, Senegal sees no reason not to enjoy the best of both worlds.

The issue of federation can be understood only in terms of Senegalese political experience and attitudes. The Senegalese interest in federation was originally a question of external Senegalese politics. For Senghor particularly, it was a useful issue in the fight for influence in Parisian politics, and was closely linked with a general redefinition of Africa's relations with France. At a second stage, the issue also proved useful as a means of rallying support from younger Senegalese elements to Senghor's party. Federalism was, however, an issue personal to Senghor and those elements of his party who chose to champion it. Mamadou Dia, for instance, repeatedly emphasized that federation in and of itself was of little intrinsic importance, and was simply a useful aid to his economic development plans. The issue was not in any sense intimately bound up with the total life of the party as was the case in Soudan. "Federalism," unlike "unity" for the Soudanese, was primarily an instrumental goal, leading to increased political power or more efficient economic development.

Secondly, federation did not mean for the Senegalese absolute unity and total elimination of internal differences, but the close cooperation of distinct but complementary units. "Local diversities, by virtue of their complementarity, will enrich the Federation."[34] Senghor declared as early as 1951 that a federation would have to guarantee "autonomy of the Senegalese soul."

> From this point on the BDS declares itself ready to aid the poor territories that nature and history have slighted. . . . But if the Federation requires economic solidarity, it no less supposes moral autonomy and political autonomy. It is not the business of representatives of other territories to indicate to

33. Senghor, speech of December 13, 1959. Partial text in *Le Monde,* December 15, 1959.

34. Senghor, "Rapport sur la doctrine," p. 57.

> the Senegalese people whom it should choose to represent them.[35]

Federation was not to include interference with the delicate inner workings of the Senegalese political system. It was not to be something that would be "pushed into a unitary state."[36]

Thirdly, and closely related to the previous point, the main cement of the federation would be the coordinated action of top political leaders, not of a united, politically homogeneous population. As Senghor put it, "The primary condition for effective action at the base is a reciprocal esteem and confidence between Mali's leaders, between those of Senegal and those of Soudan."[37]

The formal justification for federation was that it made sense economically. For reasons of internal markets and diversification of production, "dwarf states" of four or five million people are uneconomic.[38] If it is to make sense economically, however, it must "come out of isolation to link up with more developed economies."[39] The federation must forge links that are "both vertical and horizontal," for the economy must be both "a continental and a transcontinental economy."[40] In particular it must maintain its economic links with France. But to fulfill its vision of a continental economy, the federation must be an "open" one that will be ready to cooperate for mutual advantage with its neighbors in the hopes of attracting them into its political links.

Although the Senegalese party, like the Soudanese, accepted the formula of "independence and federation," they were careful to note that this would be independence in cooperation with France. Federation for the Senegalese leaders was a means of strengthening their country so that they could cooperate with France on as nearly equal a basis as possible. If, for the Soudanese, African unity was a way of guaranteeing independence, federation, for the Senegalese, was a way of making true interdependence possible.

35. Senghor, "Fédération aofienne, mais autonomie de l'âme sénégalaise," *Condition Humaine*, November 29, 1951.

36. See Senghor, "Rapport sur la doctrine," p. 15.

37. Editorial in *Unité Africaine*, August 22, 1959.

38. This idea, a feature of Senghor's first program for the IOM in 1951, is developed most systematically by Mamadou Dia in his *Nations Africaines et Solidarité Mondiale*, esp. pp. 106–32.

39. Ibid., p. 97.

40. Ibid., p. 107.

9

The Mali Federation

> Je ne crois ni à la durée ni à l'efficacité du Mali.
>
> FÉLIX HOUPHOUET-BOIGNY
> (*Paris-Dakar*, MARCH 25, 1959)

FROM the foregoing analysis of the differing political experiences, perceptions, and goals of the Senegalese and Soudanese, one would perhaps, in 1959, have been tempted to accept the dismal prediction of the Ivory Coast political leader. But these differences by themselves do not tell the whole story. Whether they would in fact cause the Mali Federation to fail would depend on:

(1) the degree of social integration and compatibility of the populations at large

(2) the personal connections and relations between the Senegalese and Soudanese political elites

(3) the balance between the costs and gains of continued cooperation compared to the costs and gains of breaking up the Federation as perceived by the political leaders of each side

(4) the flexibility of the federal political institutions, whether they tended to reconcile or exacerbate differences

(5) the willingness of each side to modify its goals for the sake of preserving the Federation

We shall investigate in turn each of these factors, before proceeding to an analysis of why the Mali Federation failed.

SOCIAL RELATIONS BETWEEN SOUDANESE AND SENEGALESE

As we have seen in Chapters 7 and 8, the Soudanese and Senegalese perceived themselves as having distinctly different group characteristics. On the level of the popular stereotype, these were the proud, stubborn, true African Soudanese and the ebullient, Westernized, sophisticated Senegalese. For our purposes here, the mere fact of their perception by the populations involved is more important than how closely these stereotypes corresponded to reality. While it was impossible to pursue the matter systematically, it was apparent that each territory's people agreed on a common stereotype of the other's. When put in a position of contrasting their own good qualities with their opposite numbers' bad qualities, the Senegalese spoke of themselves as being *évolués*, friendly, and intelligent, and considered the Soudanese to be primarily stupid, cliquish peasants.[1] The Soudanese, on the other hand, recalled their days of medieval glory and usually described themselves as "sons of kings," possessing a noble, honest soul, and characterized the Senegalese as crafty and devious "slaves" who had sold out to the French. The fact that these stereotypes were frequently expressed to the writer in terms of traditional status distinctions indicates that this was something that went close to the heart of the social preferences of the people involved.

The social distinctiveness of these stereotypes was reinforced by the fact that each territory used a different lingua franca, Wolof for the Senegalese and Bambara for the Soudanese. There were thus few individuals from each territory able to communicate freely and easily in the vernacular with people from the other territory. While even low-ranking politicians and government employees could when necessary communicate in French, they used African languages in everyday life for anything except formal communications. A common complaint among the Senegalese employees of the Federal Government in Dakar was that, as one put it, "All of a sudden you had to speak Bambara to get anything done in the Administrative Building."

These cultural and linguistic differences might be minimized on a society-wide scale if there were a substantial overlap of populations between Senegal and Soudan. In fact, Senegal's native population did include about seven per cent Malinke, Bambara, and related "Soudanese" ethnic groups, but these were localized in Eastern Senegal and the Casamance, the two most isolated and politically underrepresented regions of the country. At the time, only three of 80 members of the Senegalese Territorial Assembly were of Malinke–Bambara origin, and there were none from these

1. The term most frequently used was *badolo,* a word with derisive overtones that a Wolof noble would use to describe a country bumpkin.

groups on the UPS executive bureau.[2] On the Soudanese side, only 4 to 5 per cent of the population could be considered members of distinctively "Senegalese" ethnic groups, and these were localized for the most part in the region around Kayes, where they had come originally as agents of the French administration or trading companies. Although there were two Wolof deputies in the Soudanese Territorial Assembly, the "Senegalese" populations were certainly not of a size or importance to warrant particular political influence. In addition, Soudan retained a substantial Tukulor population from the invasions of El Hadj Omar, but they had integrated themselves into the local population and retained no particular identification with Senegal or its dominant Wolof culture.

Neither did the more recent immigrant population provide a solid basis of social integration. Although, in 1955, 13 per cent of Dakar's stable African population was born outside of Senegal, only 2.44 per cent were Soudanese. While 15.8 per cent of the transient population came from outside Senegal, only 1.4 per cent came from Soudan.[3] Comparable figures are lacking for Bamako, but the percentage of Senegalese to the total population is probably lower. Although in each case the immigrants were integrated into the life of the town in which they lived, they usually concentrated in particular districts and maintained some remnants of their separate identities.

Normally, open friction between ethnic groups in an urban setting was extremely rare, since, as in traditional society, immigrant groups established more or less formalized patterns of relationships with the dominant population of the city, particularly if the immigrants were a small minority. As long as these unwritten rules of individual and group relationships were observed, there was no cause for difficulty. The creation of the Federation upset some of these relationships in Dakar, the federal capital, however, by both increasing substantially the Soudanese population and giving it a new consciousness of and pride in its communal identity. Many Mande-speaking Soudanese who had long been Dakar residents dropped the Wolof version of their surname (*dyamu*) and resumed the original Soudanese form. Soudanese ethnic, craft, and caste

2. See my "Senegal," Table II and passim. Since the Federation's breakup, a Malinke from the Casamance has been added to the UPS executive bureau.

3. Senegal, Ministère du Plan, *Recensement démographique de Dakar,* Résultats définitifs, 2e fascicule, annex 1, pp. 8–9.

associations either sprang up for the first time, or at least flourished for the first time in the public eye. Particularly well known was the association of Soudanese *griots,* a caste group of traditional minstrels and genealogists, who made it their specialty to lead songs of praise and form a claque for Modibo Keita and other Soudanese personalities in their public appearances in Dakar. This promoted some unfavorable comment, particularly among the low-level UPS party workers whose job it was to whip up popular sentiment for the Senegalese leaders. At the leadership level, both Senghor and Mamadou Dia were believed to be annoyed also. Neither of them had ever gathered a large personal following in the capital city, principally because they had originally come to power in the 1950s by championing the interests of the rural populations against the urban backers of Lamine Gueye. The integration of the Senegalese Socialist party into the UPS had not been accompanied by the transfer of Dakar's popular support to Senghor and Dia.

The Federation's formation, then, had the immediate effect of exacerbating somewhat the social differences between the Soudanese living in the federal capital and their host population. At no time, however, was there any unusual violence or other trouble between Soudanese and native Dakarois. The significance of these differences lay not in that they might make continued political cooperation difficult, but in that no integrated interterritorial social community existed that might mitigate quarrels in the political realm. Rather, the existing perceptions of cultural and social differences might reinforce interterritorial political quarrels by giving each side a righteous faith in its own course and a disdain for the other's point of view.

It is important not to overemphasize these societal differences. In a population only 5 to 7 per cent literate, only 15 to 20 per cent of which is regularly touched by radio, public opinion on any but very local political issues will exist only as it is incarnated in and amplified by political leaders.

Personal Relations between Soudanese and Senegalese Leaders

As Table 10 shows, the political elite of Senegal and Soudan, represented here by the members of the respective territorial assemblies, were exceptionally similar in their professional background.

TABLE 10. Professions of Members of Mali Federation's Territorial Assemblies

	Soudanese Territorial Assembly		*Senegalese Territorial Assembly*	
Occupation	*Number*	*Per cent*	*Number*	*Per cent*
Education	21	26.2	23	28.9
Administration	26	32.5	22	27.3
Railroads	4	5.0	5	6.3
Total government sector	51	63.7	50	62.5
Doctors, veterinarians, etc.	15	18.7	8	10.0
Lawyers	1	1.3	11	13.7
Total professionals	16	20.0	19	23.7
Commerce and industry	7	8.7	8	10.0
Other and unknown	6	7.5	3	3.7
Total	80	99.9	80	99.9

This similarity was evident also in religious composition (about three quarters of the Senegalese deputies and four fifths of the Soudanese were Muslims), and caste background (only three of the Senegalese and nine of the Soudanese deputies were of lower caste). As Seurin has shown for territorial assemblies elsewhere in French-speaking West Africa, Senegal and Soudan shared their similarities with all their partners of former AOF.[4] Because of limited educational and job opportunities and similar political conditions, the political elite of all AOF was drawn from the same strata of the population.

In addition to this high degree of comparability in backgrounds, many of the Senegalese and Soudanese political figures had shared common educational or other experiences. At least ten of the Senegalese and eight of the Soudanese members of their respective territorial assemblies had attended the William-Ponty normal school; and Mamadou Dia and Mahamane Alassane Haidara, the leader of the Soudanese delegation to the Federal Assembly, had prepared for teaching careers there at the same time. In addition, common experience in French legislative politics under the Fourth Republic was shared by most of the top leaders of the two countries. This experience, however, they also shared with political leaders of the

4. J. L. Seurin, "Elites sociales et partis politiques d'A.O.F.," *Annales Africaines* (*1958*), pp. 123–57, esp. pp. 138, 151–54.

other West African territories, and thus, to the degree that it was common to others, this joint heritage was less salient.

Far more important were the links between individual leaders forged by common participation in interterritorial political parties in the days of the Fourth Republic. Although the IOM and its successor, the Convention Africaine, had never made any significant headway in Soudan, both the RDA and the SFIO had been active in both territories. The major RDA link between the Senegalese and Soudanese was Doudou Gueye, late of the MPS–RDA, who was a member of the Senegalese delegation to the Federal Assembly. Doudou Gueye, like d'Arboussier, had originally been one of the most pro-communist RDA members but had followed Houphouet-Boigny when he broke with the Communists in 1950. He had sympathized particularly with the avant-garde positions of the Guinean and Soudanese sections in RDA councils. A good friend of many Soudanese leaders, he became particularly closely associated with Modibo Keita in the early days of the Mali Federation.

Old RDA ties were important also in forging new links between Soudanese labor and youth groups and some of their Senegalese counterparts. Among the labor leaders, many of the Senegalese, as well as all the Soudanese, had originally been associated with the RDA-affiliated UGTAN.[5] In the meeting designed to bring about a united all-Mali labor movement, the Senegalese UGTAN leaders were noticeably closer to the point of view of the Soudanese labor leaders than they were to some of their Senegalese colleagues. Since the Senegalese government had just undergone a massive UGTAN-directed strike which had been broken only by extreme pressure from the Dia government, this reinforcement of UGTAN influence was not entirely appreciated by the top Senegalese leaders.

Similar relations existed between several of the UPS youth movement (MJUPS) leaders and their Soudanese counterparts. Many of the MJUPS leaders had come into Senghor's party from the old Senegalese dissident RDA section, the UDS, and in addition were particularly attracted to some of the Union Soudanaise political positions, notably their insistence on rapid Africanization, or replacement of European civil servants by politically loyal Africans. While the interest of young men just beginning their careers

5. For a summary of the trade union situation, see "Le Syndicalisme en Afrique Noire" in *L'Economie*, No. 711 (December 31, 1959), 19–20.

in such an obvious bread-and-butter issue is understandable, the Dia government's policy was to select technically qualified individuals, whatever their color, for important government jobs.

Finally, completely outside of formal governmental relations, old RDA ties also brought some of the Soudanese into renewed contact with some of the Senegalese opposition PRA–Sénégal and PAI leaders, many of whom had originally been in the UDS or, in Parisian student days, in the RDA youth group. While for obvious reasons these contacts were few and discreet, they almost certainly did not pass unnoticed, and, indeed, led the press of both Senegalese opposition parties to acknowledge the correctness of some of the Union Soudanaise's political options.

The former Socialist party also was a source of personal links that were reinforced by the Federation. Lamine Gueye had been influential in persuading some of the Soudanese Socialists of the PRS initially to moderate their opposition to the Federation and ultimately to join the Union Soudanaise after its March 1959 electoral victory. Lamine Gueye enjoyed excellent personal relations with Fily Dabo Sissoko, the old Soudanese Socialist leader, and in his capacity as mayor of Dakar, had the opportunity of receiving Fily Dabo's new associates many times in both formal and informal meetings. The fact that the dean of African politicians came from an old St. Louis trading family with important connections in the Kayes region of Soudan, and had himself been born in the Soudanese town of Médine, gave him an additional opportunity to reinforce his personal relations with the Soudanese leaders.

However extensive these personal links between Senegalese and Soudanese were, they in no case reached to the core of the UPS, which was dominated by Senghor and Dia and their original followers from BDS days. Doudou Gueye was a very new recruit to the UPS, and Lamine Gueye, for many years before he joined the party in 1958, had been Senghor's prime enemy in domestic politics. Had the UPS been a rigidly centralized party like the Union Soudanaise, this might have made little difference. Since the UPS was, in fact, an alliance of various *clans* grouped around individual leaders, the Senghor-Dia team could not automatically count on the whole rank and file following their orders, particularly if a powerful leader like Lamine Gueye were to have his urban base of old Socialist support strengthened by outside help. Similarly, the alliances of part of the Senegalese labor and youth groups with the

Soudanese could possibly have brought unwelcome pressure on the Dia government of a sort to compromise the success of its economic program. This, too, would not have been a problem if the UPS leaders could have been sure of imposing strict party and national discipline. Without this assurance, the personal and ideological links between the solidly united Union Soudanaise leaders and some of the less politically safe Senegalese served if anything to increase Senghor's and Dia's caution in cooperating with the Soudanese.

The Advantages of Federation

The Mali Federation, it was thought originally, would have significant economic and political advantages for both Senegal and Soudan. During the Federation's short life some of these advantages never materialized, and others were either misunderstood by the political leaders or eclipsed by more readily perceptible and immediate disadvantages.

The case for the economic advantages of the Federation was argued with eloquence by Mamadou Dia, the only trained economist among the Federation's political leaders. As he wrote in 1959:

> The great good fortune of Mali is the complementarity of the Senegalese and Soudanese economies. Although both are predominantly agricultural, they are structurally different. The policy so dear to colonial capitalism, of concentrating capital investments near the ports, explains here as elsewhere the disparity in implantation of industry throughout the Federation's territory. But Senegal is perfectly aware of the fact that in order for its port and its industries to live, it needs the minimum economic space of Soudan, while waiting for a rapid enlargement of this space. The [Soudanese] Office du Niger knows that at the very least it must count on the market of its sister Republic in order to continue to produce its rice and cotton. If there is a structural disequilibrium between the two economies coupled in Mali, it should be noted that the disequilibrium is tolerable, and even useful, in that it will oblige the two states to cooperate for reciprocal development. Thus, the duality of structures, far from being a competitive factor and thereby a source of difficulties, is on the contrary the

source of complementarity, and in consequence, an element of association and motive for cooperation.[6]

The federal economy Dia foresaw was clear in outline. The Dakar area would provide port facilities and a manufacturing potential for the Federation, and Soudan would provide raw materials and food for Senegal, with the hope that at some later date it might develop its own secondary industrial base. The two economies were to be linked together by reciprocal economic advantage and by a common economic plan. Unfortunately, as Dia quickly realized, there were some flaws in his image of coordinated complementarity. First, the common economic planning agency never developed. Senegal had in 1958 contracted with Father L. J. Lebret, a French economist with whom Mamadou Dia had once studied, to undertake a massive study of the Senegalese economy and draw up planning recommendations in a twenty-five year perspective. Soudan had contracted with representatives of another and quite different French school of economic planning to draw up recommendations for its development efforts. These two approaches proved irreconcilable, and all economic planning remained strictly in the hands of the individual states.[7] While this lack of coordination did not seem to concern the Soudanese particularly, it was a serious blow to Mamadou Dia's economic conception of the Federation.

A second economic disadvantage for Senegal lay in depending exclusively on Soudanese rice to make up the 20,000 tons Senegal imported annually. Because of the Office du Niger's inefficiency and the less than optimum Soudanese climate, Soudanese rice delivered in Dakar cost some 15 to 20 per cent more than rice imported from Southeast Asia. While this sacrifice would be a small one for the Senegalese economy, it did weaken the economic arguments for Federation.

Senegal's main economic links with Soudan involved the modern sector of the economy. French trading companies with headquarters in Dakar did an estimated 8.3 billion CFA francs worth of import business with Soudan. Even more important for the Dakar

6. *Nations africaines et solidarité mondiale,* p. 108.

7. Ibid., pp. 113–14. For a good summary of the Senegalese planning effort see Institut de Recherche et de Formation en vue du Développement Harmonisé, "Le Sénégal en marche," *Les Cahiers africains,* No. 5 (Brussels, Editions Créations de Presse, 1962).

region's economy, Senegal's nascent industrial sector sold between 30 and 35 per cent of its production, amounting to approximately 8.5 billion CFA francs in 1959, to Soudan.[8] The Senegalese economy thus had an interest in maintaining commercial links with Soudan, but there is no particular reason why it required close political links in addition.

Another area of economic cooperation between Senegal and Soudan was the Dakar-Niger railway line from Dakar to Bamako. This provided employment for about eight hundred Soudanese in Senegal and did about 1.5 billion CFA francs worth of interterritorial haulage.[9] In the agricultural realm, Senegal's peanut crop gave seasonal employment to about 20,000 Soudanese migrant workers. Their wages represented an addition of some 500 million CFA to the Soudanese economy.[10]

For the Soudanese, participation in the Federation brought them substantial rebates from the federal government. In 1959 these amounted to some 2.2 billion CFA francs out of Soudan's total budget of 6.415 billion CFA. It should be remembered, however, that these represented principally receipts from customs and excise duties collected in Dakar. Whether these were greater or less than what might have been collected had Soudan set up customs barriers at its own borders has never been established.[11]

Economic factors will influence political decisions only if they are perceived as important and relevant by the actual political decision-makers. This perception may come out of a personal interest in economics for its own sake or a commitment to specific economic goals, or out of a concern with the political repercussions of an economic decision as, for example, it would affect politically important individuals or interest groups. As was brought out in Chapter 7, the Soudanese leaders were not at all interested in economics for its own sake. They believed simply that political options should determine all economic decisions. Among the Senegalese

8. "La Conjoncture économique au Sénégal après la rupture des relations avec Bamako," *Marchés Tropicaux*, October 15, 1960, pp. 2257–58 and my calculations. This report was drawn up by the Senegalese statistical service and mysteriously leaked.

9. Estimated from *Comptes économiques du Mali, 1956*, pp. 38, 39, and oral information.

10. République du Mali, Ministère du Plan, *Les Comptes économiques de la République du Mali pour 1959, 1* (Bamako, 1961), 163.

11. Ibid., pp. 121, 131. The author of this economic report feels strongly that Soudan in fact was entitled to considerably more than it received.

leaders, Mamadou Dia was particularly concerned with economic goals; however, despite his early hopes, the Mali Federation did not provide the integrated economic planning approach that he thought necessary. The economic relations between Senegal and Soudan did involve several economic interests: the French commercial houses; the small industries of the Dakar region; the Soudanese who worked in Senegal (and their Senegalese employers); and the Soudanese Dioula traders who redistributed the manufactured goods imported from Senegal. For various reasons none of these groups could or would bring substantial pressure on their respective governments to maintain or strengthen the Federation.

From a purely economic point of view, it made only marginal difference to the French commercial houses whether the goods they imported for sale in Soudan entered Africa through the port of Dakar or through the port of Abidjan, since their offices could handle the trade from either point. The Dakar manufacturing interests had a much more serious interest in maintaining direct economic relations between Senegal and Soudan, since their goods could not hope to compete with European goods were they obliged to transship through another West African port. (As it was, high domestic production costs and high coastal shipping rates made most Senegalese products unable to compete with European goods in Abidjan.) Their interest, however, was in maintaining commercial relations, and political unity was useful only insofar as it guaranteed the Soudanese market. What is perhaps more important in the case of both the Dakar manufacturers and the French commercial houses, they did not constitute major political interest groups within the Senegalese ruling party. They had traditionally remained outside Senegalese politics except in those few instances in which French interests as a whole were at stake.[12] They did not command electoral support or followers within the UPS, and were in the habit of doing their economic lobbying more with the French High Commissioner's office than with the Senegalese government. This did not prevent the Senegalese government from taking their interests into account, if only because their activities gave employment to approximately one fifth of Senegal's salaried African workers and contributed about one third of Senegal's

12. As an indication of how small a role the European population played in Senegalese politics, see André Peytavin, "Les Européens doivent voter," *Afrique Nouvelle,* March 5, 1957.

budget. It did mean, however, that the Senegalese leaders could take political decisions they thought necessary without reference to the preferences of the European commercial and industrial leaders.

The Senegalese peanut farmers who employed some 20,000 seasonal laborers from Soudan were for the most part supporters of the Senegalese ruling party, but were not a cohesive bargaining group. Furthermore, the Soudanese made up only about one half of the migrant workers from outside Senegal (the rest coming from Guinea and the Gambia), and Senegal's reliance on these outsiders had been decreasing steadily, as migrant labor from other regions of Senegal became available. In any case there was no indication that Soudanese labor was essential for Senegal's peanut production, however useful and convenient it might be; nor was it likely that the need for outside labor would increase in the future.

From the Soudanese side, the migrant laborers and their families would have an interest in maintaining good relations of some sort with Senegal, but it is unlikely that they were aware enough of the political situation to have cared particularly whether or not their employment was assured by political unity. Even if they were, such a selfish economic interest of a small, unorganized minority of the population would have had little effect on the fundamental political options of the Union Soudanaise political bureau.

A more serious political interest group was the Soudanese Dioulas, who had been instrumental in forming the Union Soudanaise originally, and who had one of the most prominent of their number, Dossolo Traoré, on the Union Soudanaise political bureau. The main interest of the Dioulas was in the traditional trade with the Ivory Coast region, however, and their main connection with the European-dominated Dakar trade was in the role of distributor in the Soudanese interior of goods imported along the Dakar-Niger railway by European firms. Their interest would have been to decrease the trade with Dakar and augment the trade coming through Abidjan in order more fully to use their commercial network and truck transport system. This is not to say that the Dioulas did lobby for any such change. They were not in a position to foist such demands on the Union Soudanaise decision-makers, but the continuation of the Federation was not crucial to their continuing prosperity, and they accordingly had no reason to back it strongly.

If no conclusive and politically potent economic interests were involved in maintaining or strengthening the Mali Federation, what political interests were likely to be served by Mali's success? The most apparent political advantage of the Federation lay in the realm of international African politics. The international prestige of Mali's leaders was most certainly reinforced by the Federation's formation, and the Federation itself had a profound effect on politics in other French-speaking African territories. Houphouet-Boigny's establishment of the Conseil de l'Entente, grouping the Ivory Coast, Upper Volta, Niger and Dahomey, appeared at first as an ineffective response to the dynamic Mali initiative. In the same way, Mali's early drive for formal independence obliged the Conseil de l'Entente and Madagascar to follow the same path, and it appeared from de Gaulle's warm response to a visit from Modibo Keita in his role of Premier of Mali, that even the French were impressed by what the federalists had done.[13] Unquestionably, this international prestige would be severely weakened if the Federation were not a success.

By the very nature of the political evolution that Mali inspired, however, the significance of this international success was reduced. Although both Senghor and Modibo Keita must have felt great pleasure at having put Houphouet-Boigny on the defensive, their success did not have the direct political advantages it had had when they were all competing for influence within the French National Assembly or the Grand Council of AOF. Furthermore, with the formation of the Conseil de l'Entente and the Ghana-Guinea Union, there were no more recruits that the Federation could easily pick up. Thus, Mali's initial success was unlikely to be augmented by a rapid increase in prestige in the international arena.

The prestige accruing to Mali's leaders was, however, of considerable importance in domestic politics. Senghor, particularly, who had for so long championed the cause of federation, now could hope to silence his domestic enemies both within and without the UPS by pointing with pride to the great creation he had fathered and by obliging Lamine Gueye, leader of the old Socialist *clan* within the UPS, to play a secondary role in his, Senghor's, creation. However, this prestige accrued almost entirely to Senghor; most of the other UPS politicians had been preoccupied either with the domestic political planning of Mamadou Dia, or with the lower-level

13. On Modibo's visit, see *Afrique Nouvelle,* May 22, 1959.

political maneuverings of the *clan* leaders. Those individual UPS men who were appointed to the Federal Assembly were without exception closely aligned with Senghor. Thus, while many might benefit indirectly from Senghor's success, the Federation itself was of concern only insofar as it reinforced the position of their patron.

In addition, some of the former MPS people profited from the Federation's formation in that they got their first chance to participate in any government by joining the Senegalese federalists. This was particularly important for Doudou Gueye, who was given an important job in the Federalist party. It was less so for Gabriel d'Arboussier, who had the personal backing of the grand marabout Seydou Nourou Tall and, with the cooperation of Dia's minister of the interior and political boss of Kaolack, was elected to a seat from that region to the Senegalese Territorial Assembly.

The Soudanese leaders, too, benefited from the prestige accruing to Mali's formation. For them, Mali's success was a vindication of their decision to accept the de Gaulle Constitution in the September 1958 referendum, a decision that had been opposed by some of the younger elements in the Union Soudanaise. Given the political bureau's control over the party, however, and the party's control over the country, Mali's continued existence was not immediately necessary for the Soudanese political elite to remain in power. Rather, the Federation provided a larger forum in which to seek the implementation of their political options.

At a lower level the federal government offered employment for some six thousand people, about two thousand of them Soudanese. While the profit to the Soudanese was obvious, it was less so to the Senegalese, many of whom were in fact displaced from jobs they had held with the former AOF federal administration to make way for their Bambara-speaking colleagues. While it was true that many more might have been displaced had the Government-General disappeared and not been replaced by the Mali Federation, this was of little comfort to the individuals who lost their jobs.

Aside from these specific personal or group interests in the Federation, it is extremely difficult to assess the attitudes of the populations at large toward Mali. In the Soudan, Mali unquestionably was greeted with enthusiasm by the people predisposed to the Union Soudanaise, as would be any initiative in foreign policy that the Soudanese mass party took. The Federation's prestige was also heightened by its symbolic choice of name which revived memories of past imperial glory among the Mande-speakers. It is doubtful, though, that for most people the Federation had any importance aside from that which their leaders chose to give it. In Senegal, too, the Federation and its activities lay outside the realm of popular concern. This was true even for most of the lower-level politicians outside of Dakar who were more involved with local issues and the fight for *clan* interests within the UPS. For them, too, the importance of the Federation was that it marked a success for Senghor and by extension those within the country who identified with him. In Dakar, if any opinion predominated, it was not one of enthusiasm for the Federation, in part because of the new importance it gave to the local Soudanese population, and in part because Senghor had never succeeded in capturing the support of the sophisticated Dakarois. Except in a few cases this did not mean hostility to the Federation, simply lack of interest. Mamadou Dia, writing in retrospect, put the matter neatly, "In truth, the Senegalese people adopted the Mali *mystique* only out of attachment to their leaders; their adherence to Mali had the value only of a new act of faith in the policies of [the Senegalese leaders]."[14] Those who put little faith in their leaders' policies paid little attention to the Federation.

To sum up, the Mali Federation served the economic and political interests of many sectors of the Senegalese and Soudanese populations and most particularly the interests of some top political leaders. With the possible exception of Senghor, however, none of the elite staked his political position on the success of the Federation and, in the larger setting, no single politically relevant individual or interest group was deeply involved in making the Federation a success. For many in Senegal and Soudan it was a convenience, for a few an annoyance; for most of the masses it was irrelevant; and for virtually no one was the Federation a necessity.

Institutions of the Mali Federation

The institutions of the Mali Federation were the federal government, the youth and labor movements, and the new political party established by the federalists. The government structure was of necessity modified after the defections of Upper Volta and Da-

14. *Nations africaines et solidarité mondiale,* p. 140.

homey, but the principle of territorial parity of representation was retained and in some minor senses strengthened.[15] The territorial delegations to the Federal Assembly were enlarged to twenty each for Senegal and Soudan to produce an Assembly of forty members. The Federal Council of Ministers consisted of an equal number of Senegalese and Soudanese, with responsibilities as carefully balanced as possible. Thus, Modibo Keita was named Premier, but Mamadou Dia was made Vice-Premier and in addition was given responsibility for defense. To maintain this approximate equalization of powers, the previous ineligibility of territorial ministers was dropped. (Mamadou Dia was also Premier of Senegal.) This change made the federal government more dependent on the will of the territorial governments than it had been previously when the federal executive could contain no members of territorial executive bodies. A second change, requiring all decrees of the federal government to be countersigned by both the federal Premier and the minister responsible, could also restrict the ability of the Premier to act unilaterally.

The same parity principle was built into the two paragovernmental organizations, the Mali labor and youth organizations. In the youth organization, the Union de la Jeunesse du Mali, this posed no particular problems, since both territories' delegations were simply the youth wings of the dominant political party. The Senegalese labor movement, however, was fragmented into at least four contending factions, all of whom had to be represented in the Mali labor movement, the Union des Travailleurs du Mali. Although there was one faction headed by Alassane Sow, which the UPS had chosen to speak for it, the confusion of voices and responsibilities on the Senegalese side proved too great, and after an initial meeting the Mali labor movement was quietly put on the shelf.

While such an emphasis on representational parity could go far to allay fears of either side's being systematically exploited by the other, it also could decrease the federal government's flexibility of action. In particular, it could lead to a series of permanent stalemates with both sides refusing to budge. Equally serious, if a repeated pattern of unilateral defection from territorial solidarity developed, one side could enjoy a permanent majority on all issues. While a defection of this sort was unlikely to occur in the ranks of

15. On the constitutional revision, see Mali, *J.O., Débats,* No. 1 (Meeting of April 4, 1959), pp. 3–4.

the Soudanese, it was always possible for the less regimented Senegalese.

Parallel to the government, and in theory superior to it, was the new federalist interterritorial party, the Parti de la Fédération Africaine (PFA). This new party, whose existence was made necessary by the fact "that the former political parties of Black Africa, particularly the RDA and the PRA, no longer reflect the present political situation," took as its goal "the realization of African Unity in the form of a Federal Republic, of which the Mali Federation represents the first step."[16] By providing also that "only one section of the Party can exist in each State," the PFA was designed to be the logical culmination of the realignment of political forces that had begun at the time of the referendum and continued at the Bamako and Dakar conferences of December and January.[17] Although the principle was not formally inscribed in the PFA's statutes, the same principle of parity that characterized the institutions of the federal government was present in the federal party. Senghor became the PFA's president, and Modibo Keita was named secretary-general; similarly, too, an equal number of Senegalese and Soudanese held positions on the party's political bureau. There was one main difference with the Federation's governmental institutions, however; the PFA, faithful to Mali's open and expansionist ideals, included representatives from federalist parties in other territories. Among them were the PFA's two vice-presidents, Djibo Bakary of Niger and Emile Zinsou of Dahomey. These outside representatives constituted a third force, capable of breaking a deadlock between the Senegalese and Soudanese should the need arise, and introduced an element of flexibility lacking in the two-party governmental and paragovernmental structures.

Despite this flexible element, all of the formal institutions of the Mali Federation shared one principal handicap. Because they were controlled by the two territorial political parties, there was nothing to stop a quarrel started in one institutional setting from spilling over into all the others. Furthermore, because the decisions taken involved ultimately the policies of a very few political leaders, any dispute in any organizational setting would be forced up to the top for settlement. Since the settlement of any serious disputes at the

16. Conférence des Fédéralistes Africains, "Résolution" in *Semaine en Afrique Occidentale,* March 28, 1959.
17. Ibid.

summit directly involved the prestige and reputations of the top politicians, escalation of a minor dispute into a major interterritorial crisis was highly possible.

Equally important, there were no institutions for cooperation outside of the party-linked structures. Thus the positive "spill-over" effect, by which nongovernmental pressure groups in Europe combined across national boundaries to bring pressure on the international governmental institutions of cooperation and thus reinforced the process of integration, had no chance of working in Mali.[18] In Mali success in one governmental or party sector of cooperation might spill over to reinforce cooperation in another sector, but so, too, might failure.

Willingness of Each Side to Compromise

Ultimately, the success of any cooperative venture depends on the willingness and ability of each side to compromise. While there is no way of predicting how much the Senegalese and Soudanese would have been willing to compromise, we can identify certain objectives of crucial concern for each in which compromise would have been extremely difficult.

For the Senegalese leaders, maintenance of good relations with France was obviously an important point, as much for economic and political reasons as for sentimental ones. A second area of concern, particularly for Mamadou Dia, was economic development. He, and members of the UPS who identified with him, would have opposed any projects that might have jeopardized his development plan for Senegal. But for the Soudanese leaders formal independence was a primary goal and the only compromise possible was with regard to the timing. In addition, they felt that political considerations should dictate policy in other domains.

One overshadowing consideration—the need to retain domestic political power—was a condition of any political action for the leaders of both territories. For the Senegalese leaders, this meant maintaining a free hand to balance and control competing *clan* interests within the UPS. The importance of that freedom was underlined by Senegal's refusal to yield to the federal government control over customary law, an area of prime concern to the Muslim marabouts.

18. On the "spill-over effect," see Ernst B. Haas, *The Uniting of Europe* (London, Stevens and Sons, 1958), p. xiii.

The problem of remaining in power was less acute for the Union Soudanaise leaders, but they too, in a longer perspective, had a definite interest in maintaining a sense of political momentum in federal affairs, in order to prevent a challenge from younger and more radical elements in the party. The Soudanese leaders' study of "the sense of history" made them well aware of the dangers a revolutionary regime faces in being outflanked on the left.

Aside from these few crucial concerns, there were a multiplicity of issues the Federation would have to face on which compromise would be possible under the right conditions. Before people will compromise, however, they must first perceive a need to compromise. This involves an understanding not only of one's own deeper interests, but also of the other side's interests and likely reactions. Despite the many common goals and shared political experiences of the Senegalese and Soudanese leaders, their domestic political situations were quite different. It was primarily in regard to the Federation's effect on each territory's domestic situation that the requisite mutual understanding might be lacking.

10

The Federation's Failure

Independence: A Conflict Resolved

The first great issue the Mali Federation faced was independence, perhaps the most important issue on which the Senegalese and Soudanese leaders differed. The constitution of the Fifth Republic, which established the Community, granted sovereignty over internal matters to the constituent states, but left the domains of foreign affairs, defense, and monetary policy to the Community as a whole, that is to say, to France. This satisfied Senegal's desire for "independence in interdependence," but provided neither the juridical recognition of complete national sovereignty nor the complete domestic political control that the Soudanese sought. The question of independence dominated the PFA's formal constituent congress, held in Dakar during the opening days of July, 1959. As he had done at the Cotonou Congress of the PRA the preceding year, Senghor gave a lengthy political report in which he emphasized theoretical economic considerations and studiously avoided bringing up the subject of independence.[1] Also as at Cotonou, Senghor's report did not suit the mood of most delegates, and the smattering of applause he received came mainly from the Senegalese benches.[2] The Soudanese, speaking through their Minister of the Interior, Madeira Keita, promptly defended the necessity of obtaining immediate independence.[3] This position was rapidly supported by orators from the non-Mali territories, who felt it to be to their domestic political interest to promise independence while the regimes they opposed at home were enthusiastically cooperating with the French.[4] Their speeches also received pointed applause from some

1. Leopold Senghor, "Rapport sur la doctrine et le programme du parti," in *Congrès Constitutif du Parti de la Fédération Africaine*, pp. 7–72.

2. A good account of the proceedings is given by André Blanchet in *Le Monde*, July 4 and 6, 1959.

3. "Congrès Constitutif du PFA, Débats," pp. 40–42.

4. See particularly the speeches of Emile Zinsou and Youssouf Gueye, ibid., pp. 18–30, 48–50.

of the Senegalese UPS youth movement delegates and quiet support from the PFA's organization secretary, Doudou Gueye, late of the MPS–RDA.

The seriousness of the Senegalese-Soudanese dispute on this question was not diminished by the fact that some of the Senegalese seemed to sympathize with the Soudanese; were they and others like them to switch to the Soudanese side, Senghor and his associates would be put in an extremely delicate position within their own territorial party. Fortunately, the very fact that the non-Mali delegations took a pro-independence position blurred the fact that this was fundamentally a quarrel between Senegalese and Soudanese leaders and permitted the Senegalese to yield graciously to a majority, not of the Federation, but of the West African political party. The final compromise resolution, emphasizing that "along with *le fait national,* the other reality of the twentieth century is the *interdependence of Nations,"* and demanding the "transformation of the Community into a multinational Confederation," was a reasonable verbal formula for both sides and one in which neither side lost face.[5] Since the practical details of this resolution would have to be worked out later on the governmental level between the Mali leaders, and ultimately between them and France, the Senegalese leaders were able to accept the resolution in the full knowledge that the opportunity was still open to them to interpret its wording in ways consonant with their territory's interests and their own political positions.

France, fortunately, proved cooperative. After initial tentative soundings had revealed that a request for formal independence might be received by France, Senegal agreed with Soudan to present on September 22, 1959, a formal request that negotiations be undertaken to transfer full sovereign powers from the Community to the Mali Federation.[6] As befits his political style, President de Gaulle chose to make the Malians wait for his response until he visited the Mali Federal Assembly on December 13, 1959. There, speaking with dramatic simplicity, he announced that France would cooperate in granting Mali its national sovereignty, and would furthermore continue to aid and assist the new nation. Negotiations for the transfer of powers lasted from January through March, and June 20, 1960, was set as independence day for the

5. "Résolution sur le programme du PFA," *Congrès Constitutif du PFA,* p. 101.

6. For an initial French reaction, see the editorial in *Le Monde,* September 27–28, 1959.

Mali Federation.[7] Mali agreed to remain within the Community and the franc zone. As a sovereign nation, the Federation was to have its own army, but it agreed that the French army should continue to be its main defense against external threats. Mali also allowed the continued use of French military bases on Mali's soil.

Although the solution of "independence in interdependence with France" was a convenient compromise which satisfied both Senegal and Soudan, much, perhaps most, of the credit must go to de Gaulle's determination not to repeat his Guinean mistake of the previous year. Had France proved difficult, Senghor and his party might have been obliged to choose between France and the Federation. As it was, not just the Mali institutions, but also the French Community proved flexible enough to permit a compromise satisfactory to everyone. Once France's accord and continued help were assured, the problem of independence ceased to be a crucial question for the Senegalese, and compromise became possible.

Unity vs. Federalism: The End of Cooperation

The question of independence was resolved peacefully and with a minimum of hard feelings in part because the world outside of the Federation proved accommodating. No such arrangement could solve the internal problems of the Federation. These quickly came to be cast in the familiar mold of a dispute over governmental centralization vs. states' rights. The Union Soudanaise leaders, faithful to their *mystique* of national unity, sought to concentrate supreme power in the hands of the federal government. The UPS leaders, attuned to the delicate functioning of the Senegalese political system, sought to guarantee, as Senghor had phrased it almost a decade previously, "the autonomy of the Senegalese soul."[8] This difference of orientation was epitomized by a dispute over the powers of the federal president. The Soudanese wanted to concentrate supreme political power in the hands of a single individual, by combining, once independence was proclaimed, the role of chief of state with the office of head of the government responsible for foreign affairs. This would definitely break the parity principle on which the Federation had been founded, since the next highest

7. The text of the Franco-Malian agreements can be found as Document 7, *Chronique de politique étrangère, 14* (January–May 1961), pp. 370–401.

8. *Condition Humaine,* November 29, 1951.

office, that of vice-president of the council of ministers responsible for defense, would equal the presidency in neither power nor prestige. Furthermore, since under the April 1959 agreements Modibo Keita had been named president of the council of ministers responsible for foreign affairs, he would have a head start in the race for the supreme post.

The Senegalese argued strongly that the principle of parity must be upheld, dividing executive functions between a chief of state and a head of government of different nationalities. This quarrel went on behind the scenes during the winter and spring of 1960. It was considered serious enough by the Senegalese that in April their two legal experts, Doudou Thiam and Gabriel d'Arboussier, secretly circulated a proposal that Mali be transformed into a loose confederation with the executive power restricted to an economic and technical coordinating role much like that proposed for Houphouet-Boigny's Conseil de l'Entente. Although Senghor agreed, as he later put it, that "things were not going well at all,"[9] he was reluctant to concede defeat in this quest for an African federation. A meeting of Mali's political leaders was called on April 14 to settle the differences.

The meeting, held behind closed doors, was a stormy affair at which each side accused the other of bad faith and of violating the original agreements. The meeting lasted three days, and although each side subsequently gave a different account of what took place, the following seems to have been agreed upon.[10] First, the offices of chief of state and head of government would be separate, with the latter retaining control over foreign affairs, and secondly, a Senegalese "might be chosen" as chief of state. Whether this "might" was to be interpreted as permissive or exclusive and definitive has never been made clear, and probably each side chose to interpret it as he saw fit. With further progress proving impossible, the details were left to a "conciliation mission" of the Directing Committee of the PFA, in which non-Mali members were included to break the deadlock.

The non-Mali members carried out their conciliation mission

9. Interview, January 6, 1961.

10. The different versions can be found in République du Sénégal, *Livre blanc sur le coup d'état manqué du 19 au 20 août 1960* (Dakar, 1960), p. 5, and Modibo Keita, "Communication à l'Assemblée Législative de la République Soudanaise" (Bamako, August 29, 1960, mimeo.).

with dispatch. They arranged that a president of the Federation would be chosen by a congress made up of an even number of Senegalese and Soudanese Territorial and Federal Assembly members, which would meet before the opening of the fall's United Nations General Assembly, to which the independent Mali Federation expected to be admitted. The mission also persuaded the Soudanese to accept some changes in the federal constitution to grant greater control over territorial affairs like economic planning and internal taxation to the individual territories.[11] This solution was accepted by a new meeting of the Mali leaders on May 21 and 22, and the crisis seemed ended.

The conflict between the Soudanese preference for a unitary political system and Senegalese desire for decentralized political control had its repercussions also on the level of the political party. The Soudanese emphasized the unifying function of the PFA, while the Senegalese sought to maintain control over internal Senegalese politics within the UPS. The immediate issue in dispute was whether a native of one territory residing in the other should join the section of the territorial party of his place of origin, or of his place of residence. While the few Senegalese living in Soudan were quickly included in the Union Soudanaise, the Senegalese were reluctant to include the new Soudanese arrivals in Dakar in the local committees of the UPS. Senghor and Dia were particularly concerned because of the tenuous nature of their hold over the loyalties of the federal (and Senegalese) capital, and because they rightly foresaw that inclusion of even a few of the dynamic and disciplined Soudanese political militants in Dakar local committees could greatly complicate their problem of maintaining control, especially if the Soudanese were to make an alliance with the old Socialist *clans* within the UPS.

The Soudanese based their preference for membership according to place of residence on Article 3 of the PFA statutes which provided that "there can exist only one territorial section of the PFA in each State." At the suggestion of the PFA conciliation mission, however, they agreed not to press the issue, and it was left that those Soudanese who had already joined a local UPS committee

11. The Federal Constitution was revised just before the proclamation of independence on June 20, 1960. See *J.O. Mali, Débats,* meeting of June 18, 1960. For an analysis of Senegal's interest in the changes, see the *Déclaration de Monsieur Mamadou Dia, président du conseil, devant l'Assemblée Législative du Sénégal,* June 19, 1960 (Dakar, 1960), pp. 10–12.

would remain, while the others would not press their case for the time being. Those who had already joined were primarily Soudanese who had lived in Dakar for some time, and a few younger people who had joined the Senegalese party youth movement.

After the meetings in May, the Federation appeared to be back on the track. Whether this was the result of confidence reestablished between the Senegalese and Soudanese leaders or simply of the euphoria created by the proclamation of Mali's independence on June 20, 1960, all friction seemed a thing of the past. At the independence day celebrations, Modibo Keita, speaking in Dakar as premier and acting chief of state of the Mali Federation, brushed over any mention of differences between Senegalese and Soudanese, and pointedly emphasized some of the Senegalese leaders' favorite ideas, notably the importance of economic considerations now that formal political independence had been won.[12] Senghor went even further. In his political report to the UPS congress on July 2, he went out of his way to praise the "brilliant" Soudanese leaders and to "deplore a certain campaign against our Soudanese brothers."[13]

All through the difficulties of the previous few months, and despite the fact that the original Soudanese demands had jeopardized his claim to the presidency of the Federation, Senghor had shown himself most conciliatory toward his Soudanese "brothers." In large part his attitude reflected the peculiar political position in which he found himself. For so long had he been identified with the cause of federation that Mali's failure would have reflected adversely on his whole political career. Nor could Senghor easily accept a transformation of Mali into a loose confederation, as d'Arboussier and Doudou Thiam had suggested and as Dia would have accepted, for this would mean, most simply, that Houphouet-Boigny had been right all along. Houphouet-Boigny's prestige, after being weakened initially by Mali's successful bid for independence within the Community, had been substantially increased when the Ivory Coast leader had demanded and obtained the right to independence without any prior commitment, such as the Malians had given, to joining the Community. In the peculiar context of French-speaking African elite politics, this had been considered a brilliant maneuver

12. "Discours de Modibo Keita," in *Proclamation de l'indépendance du Mali* (Dakar, 1960), pp. 21–28.

13. "Rapport sur la politique générale," Deuxième congrès de l'UPS-PFA, pp. 44–45.

which put Mali and thus Senghor on the defensive for the first time.

Finally, Mali's failure would put Senghor in a very difficult domestic position which Lamine Gueye or perhaps a younger and more radical politician might be able to turn to his profit. The fact that Lamine Gueye and some of his close political associates had been noticeably reluctant to support Senghor in some of the backstage bargaining with the Soudanese did not reassure Senghor as to the old Socialists' intentions. On the other hand, following his understanding of the compromise decided on in April and May, Senghor had had himself invested as the Senegalese nominee for the Federation's presidency at a secret meeting of the UPS executive committee the day after independence was declared. He calculated that, once he had assumed this office, his prestige and influence in African affairs and his control over the UPS would be assured. Everything, thus, led him to support the Federation and to quiet the voices of dissent within his own party.

The position of the Union Soudanaise leaders was equally complex. Part of Mali's attractiveness to them had been its avant-garde status in French-speaking West African politics. As they had argued in urging restraint on their militants at the time of the referendum, provisional acceptance of the Community would permit them to go not only beyond the admittedly retrograde position of the Ivory Coast, but even ultimately beyond that of Sékou Touré's Guinea by accomplishing both independence and African unity. Touré, however, by aligning his country with Ghana, had done at least as much, and now even the Ivory Coast was obtaining independence on slightly more favorable terms than Mali had managed to get.[14] The Soudanese realized the danger to the Federation of pushing the Senegalese leaders too hard in the April–May controversy over the distribution of power within the federal government, and so compromised. This very compromise, however, constrained them to push for rapid advance on other fronts, notably to reinforce the Federation's political unity and the federal party's political control over the federal and the territorial governments.

14. As Immanuel Wallerstein observed, "One of the complex of causes involved in the breakdown of the Mali Federation . . . was Mali's loss of its *avant-garde* status, one of the most important factors holding together two such disparate groups as the Soudan RDA and the Senghor forces in Senegal." "How Seven States Were Born in Former French West Africa," *Africa Report*, 6 (March 1961), 15.

In addition, individual Soudanese leaders did not hide their impatience with what many of them considered to be the Senegalese leaders' truckling to the French on symbolic issues like Algeria and the Saharan atom bomb explosions; and, although the subject was never broached directly, there was considerable pressure from within the Union Soudanaise to demand a revision of the Franco-Malian agreements at the earliest opportunity.

The first public indication of the Soudanese leaders' new resolve to press forward in consolidating political control came at the July UPS congress, to which their "fraternal delegation" had so warmly been welcomed by Senghor. The issue the Soudanese chose to champion at this time was the "Africanization" of all governmental and administrative posts within the Federation. The Soudanese had made their position on this question clear at the PFA's constituent congress the previous year, when, supported by Doudou Gueye, they argued that the construction of the Federation required, not primarily technical experts, but "men politically committed."[15] The Senegalese leaders, whose definition of political commitment differed somewhat from that of the Soudanese, put the emphasis on the need for technical expertise and employed many Europeans, particularly in the finance and planning ministries. Africanization had always been a sore point in Senghor's and Dia's relations with the UPS youth movement, and at the July 1960 congress they were obliged to spend most of an evening getting the younger delegates to approve a party platform that did not include a commitment to rapid and total Africanization. As the meeting was drawing to a close, Senghor asked Modibo Keita, as head of the visiting Soudanese delegation, to say a few closing words. Instead of confining himself to the usual perfunctory expressions of solidarity, Modibo Keita invoked his role as PFA secretary-general and Premier of the Federation to declare that he was not at all in agreement with "Comrade Senghor" on the Africanization question. This threw the meeting into uproar, and it required the better part of the night for Senghor and Dia, who were loudly hooted by some of the youth delegates, to reestablish control and get their resolution reapproved.[16]

15. Doudou Gueye, "Rapport de présentation des résolutions de politique générale," in *Congrès Constitutif du PFA,* p. 93. Madeira Keita, in "Congrès Constitutif du PFA, Débats," p. 42.

16. The incident is alluded to delicately in the Senegalese *Livre blanc,* p. 8.

While the Soudanese leader probably did not foresee the effect his intervention would have, Senghor, and Dia particularly, were thoroughly outraged. They saw this demand simply as an attempt on the part of the Soudanese to create a faction within the UPS and particularly within the UPS youth movement that would be subservient to orders from Bamako. Whether or not this was the Soudanese intent, the whole experience of Senghor and Dia with Senegalese politics made them extremely sensitive to this sort of maneuver.

At about this time, whether before or after the UPS congress I have not been able to determine, the Soudanese leaders learned that Senghor had had the UPS secretly approve his candidacy for President of the Federation. While the Senegalese subsequently defended the action on the grounds that according to the federal constitution and in keeping with previous practice, "it is always the [party] section of the State involved that approves candidates for a political position in Mali,"[17] the Soudanese saw this action as an illegitimate and dishonest way of bypassing the federal political party which should control federal nominations as well as policies. At this point, as one of the Soudanese leaders said afterward in an interview, "We decided that whoever became President, it would not be Senghor." This dissatisfaction was made clear two weeks later when, in talking to a group of French journalists, Modibo Keita indicated simply that the discussions in April and May had decided that the offices of chief of state and head of government would be divided between the two territories, without adding that Senegal was to have the former and Soudan the latter.

Relations between Senghor and Dia and the Soudanese leaders deteriorated rapidly after independence, and in this atmosphere actions that might otherwise have passed unnoticed or have been easily explained took on sinister implications in the minds of the other side. Thus Modibo, invited as chief of Mali's government to pay a state visit to Liberia, took with him an entourage composed entirely of Soudanese and added a Senegalese only when the Senegalese leaders protested. During his stay in Monrovia, the local "Malian" population, composed principally of Soudanese Dioulas, presented him with a big, black Lincoln convertible. Since the Senegalese ministers were at that time undergoing rather reluctantly one of Mamadou Dia's periodic austerity compaigns, and were re-

17. Ibid., p. 6.

stricted to less prestigious Peugeot 403s, Modibo's acceptance of the gift was seen as unwonted arrogance on the part of a Soudanese who had often scoffed at the flamboyant style of living of the "soft" Senegalese politicians. In reply, Amadou Aw, a Soudanese and federal Minister of Public Works, let it be known that he had discovered several instances of Senegalese politicians requisitioning material under his ministry for their own private purposes and furthermore using their position to import items for personal consumption without paying customs duties. While it is doubtful that anyone took this sort of pettiness seriously, the fact that it should have been brought out indicates the breakdown of confidence that had occurred between the two sides.

Of somewhat more relevance to the future policies of the Federation, delicate Soudanese hints that a revision of the Franco-Malian agreements would be desirable were magnified out of all proportion by the Senegalese. Modibo's suggestion in Monrovia that "the establishment of an African monetary zone" might further the cause of a larger African regrouping[18] was taken as an indication that the Soudanese wanted to take Mali out of the franc zone. This possibility was a matter of some concern not only to Mamadou Dia, who saw his development plan threatened, but to French commercial interests and the French government as well. Modibo Keita's avowal of the need to work with France to end the Algerian war was either not noticed or misinterpreted. However, off-the-record allusions by other Soudanese to the desirability of revising the military arrangements with France were interpreted by the French as an attempt to oust them from their important Dakar naval and air force headquarters and by the Senegalese Premier as a threat to the ten billion francs that French military expenditures contributed annually to the Senegalese economy.[19] In fact, it is highly likely that the Soudanese were concerned primarily with obtaining French evacuation of their base at Kati, outside of Bamako.

If Mamadou Dia needed anything more to turn him against the Soudanese and the Mali Federation, the "affair of the colonels" did it. According to the Franco-Malian agreements, Mali was to have its own army, composed of Senegalese and Soudanese soldiers who had been serving in the French army. To command this new mili-

18. Press conference text in *Afrique Nouvelle*, July 27, 1960.
19. Mamadou Dia, *Nations africaines et solidarité mondiale*, p. 115.

tary force two colonels with distinguished military records, and separated by only a few days' seniority, were available. One, Colonel Fall, was a Senegalese, the other, Colonel Soumaré, was a Soudanese, though one who had spent considerable time in Senegal and indeed was distantly related to Lamine Gueye. Mamadou Dia, in his capacity of federal Minister of Defense, preferred the Senegalese. Modibo Keita, arguing his case on the rather tenuous grounds of seniority, chose the Soudanese Soumaré, and when Dia refused to countersign his nomination as chief of the general staff, Modibo Keita had it published anyway in the *Journal Officiel* on July 25. This definitively alienated Dia, who refused to receive Soumaré and cut off all communications with the federal Premier.

Among the Senegalese leaders, now only Senghor, who had spent the second part of July at his summer home in Normandy, remained to be convinced of the need to end the Federation. The "affair of the marabouts" did that. It will be recalled how crucial a role the Muslim religious leaders played in Senegalese internal politics, and how much of Senghor's own political career had depended on the support he had received from these gentlemen whose piety was matched only by their sharp sense of temporal economic and political realities. That Senghor had felt it wise to join in the Mali Federation had been possible only because his government had been able to maneuver most of the marabouts into a position of dependence on the government's financial support, thus permitting the UPS to defeat the PSS, the conservative party animated by one of the more fractious young religious leaders, Cheikh Tidjane Sy.

This same Cheikh Tidjane Sy, after spending a year in jail and, presumably, in response to some consideration by the Senegalese government of his personal interests, had decided to abandon his opposition and at his instigation the PSS dissolved itself. With no resentment over his year's confinement, he joined the UPS in June 1960. The next month Sy went to the Senegalese Premier and told him that he, along with several other religious leaders, had been approached by certain Soudanese who had suggested that Mali's evolution along Islamic lines might better be assured if a Muslim were to be president of the Federation instead of the Catholic Senghor. He, of course, had given no encouragement to such ideas, but he was not so sure that others, such as his uncle who had defeated him in a succession dispute three years earlier, had not succumbed to the Soudanese way of thinking. It is doubtful that either Dia or Senghor took Cheikh Tidjane Sy's statements at their face value, but there is no question that he had touched a sensitive nerve.

Subsequent investigation revealed that emissaries of Modibo Keita had indeed had repeated contact with Cheikh Tidjane Sy's uncle and that Modibo Keita himself, in his capacity of federal premier and acting chief of state, had asked to pay a formal call on Falilou M'Backé, the Grand Khalif of Senegal's 600,000 Mourides and the man who had been the key to Senghor's defeat of the Socialists in the 1950s and his defeat of the PSS in 1959.

Whatever had been the Soudanese leader's motives in making contact with the Senegalese marabouts, Senghor and Dia interpreted this as the most dangerous form of direct meddling in Senegal's internal affairs. Even putting the best possible face on it, Senghor concluded that he could not afford to have Senegal continue in the Federation so long as anyone else outranked him in the federal government's hierarchy. At the very least the Senegalese had to have a veto power, and that only the President of the Federation would have. In a meeting in Paris on August 8, Senghor, Dia, and d'Arboussier concluded that unless it were certain that Senghor would get the presidency and the Soudanese would, in d'Arboussier's words, "behave themselves," they would take Senegal out of the Federation. Even at this point, when most of his close advisors were decided on breaking with Soudan, Senghor clung to the hope that the Federation could be saved.

The Senegalese leaders returned to Dakar on August 12, and went immediately to the great festival of the Mourides at Touba. There, Senghor and Dia clearly announced their position. As Dia said:

> I want Mali, but I want also Senegal. That is our motherland. Before setting up anything else, before consolidating anything else, before consolidating Mali, we must first think of Senegal. We must now watch out that after our liberation from the hands of the colonialists, there is no place for other colonizers.[20]

Lest the Mouride religious leaders misunderstand the situation, Senghor added, "The UPS will not forget the active support it has

20. Speech quoted in *Marchés Tropicaux,* August 27, 1960, p. 1897.

always received, not only from the great religious leaders of Islam, but also from the imams and their disciples."[21]

If this was intended to make the Soudanese back down, it had no apparent effect. On that same day Tidiani Traoré of Soudan, the federal Minister of Information, insisted to the press that the President would be chosen without regard to his territorial origin.[22] On August 14, it became known that the office of the PFA's organization secretary, Doudou Gueye, had been mysteriously burglarized, and the minutes of the April meeting at which the distribution of the top jobs had been decided had disappeared. This sleight-of-hand finally convinced Senghor that the Soudanese would never let him be elected. On August 15, Senghor, Dia, d'Arboussier, and three or four close associates decided that Senegal would break up the Federation.

To understand why Senghor should finally have taken this step, going against the course of his whole political career, we must examine the alternatives with which he was confronted. On the one hand he could yield the presidency to Modibo Keita, but by doing this, he was convinced, he would seal his doom in Senegalese internal politics. Using the prestige of his office and the contacts the Soudanese had established with groups within Senegal and the UPS itself, in particular with Lamine Gueye's old Socialists, Modibo Keita would have every opportunity and indeed every reason to eliminate his major rival and to replace him with a more tractable associate, either one of the opposition leaders like Abdoulaye Ly of the PRA-Sénégal, or worse yet, with Lamine Gueye. If, on the other hand, he chose to fight for the office, he would have to do so before an electoral corps equally divided according to the principle of parity between the Senegalese and Soudanese members of their respective territorial assemblies and the Senegalese and Soudanese delegates to the Federal Assembly. With a two thirds majority required for election, and the absolute certainty that the Soudanese would maintain perfect discipline, Senghor had no chance.

Neither, perhaps, did Modibo Keita, but there was one compromise candidate possible: Lamine Gueye, whose old Socialist supporters within the Senegalese territorial assembly added to the

21. Speech quoted in *Paris-Dakar*, August 17, 1960.

22. "Communiqué du Ministre de l'Information et de la Sécurité du Mali," text in Senegal, *Livre blanc*, p. 48.

Soudanese votes would be almost enough to tip the balance in his favor. With the people of Dakar alerted on Lamine's behalf and demonstrating outside the hall, nothing Senghor could do would stand in his way. Any hopes that Senghor might have had that the Socialist-Soudanese rapprochement had not come off had certainly been quashed on August 3, when the traditional leader of Dakar's Lébou community, a group very closely identified with Lamine Gueye, had taken the unusual step of publicly congratulating Soumaré on his nomination for Army Chief of Staff.[23] If Senghor were to keep Senegal in the Federation, he would be confronted by a choice between Modibo Keita and Lamine Gueye. The election of either would mean not just the end of Senghor's dreams of leading the Mali Federation, but also of his control over Senegal. As every other successful politician we have encountered in these pages has done, he chose to sacrifice his wider aims to preserve his territorial political power.

Why, finally, did the Soudanese not stop before things reached this point, since no immediate fear of defeat at home obliged Modibo Keita to press on as he did? First, the Soudanese did not understand fully how the Senegalese leaders interpreted their actions. The Soudanese thought of their pressure for a unitary state as perfectly logical, indeed historically dictated. They saw no reason why any honest and forthright African politician would not understand this. Secondly, their actions were firmly in accord with their view of the way to get things done. As Modibo Keita said during his trip to Liberia in July, 1960: "The mystical force of African unity is not yet strong enough to bring States together. Only events will do this by putting pressure on African leaders who, by a reaction of self-defense, will all join hands."[24] The Soudanese, as good modern Marxists, saw no reason not to hurry the course of history, to bring about these "events." They did not, however, foresee all the possible "reactions of self-defense" recalcitrant African leaders might have. Finally, the Soudanese simply did not believe that the Senegalese leaders would react violently to their pressure. In this miscalculation, they were undoubtedly following the Soudanese stereotype of the Senegalese, and particularly of the Senegalese politician, as a man of many words and no action. The fact that almost no contact at upper echelons took place between Senegalese

23. Statement in *Paris-Dakar,* August 3, 1960.
24. Press conference text in *Afrique Nouvelle,* July 27, 1960.

and Soudanese leaders during the month preceding the breakup meant that little contrary evidence caused them to revise their estimate. Of those close to Modibo Keita, only Doudou Gueye, himself a Senegalese, warned him of what might happen. He was laughed at for his pains.

The Breakup of the Mali Federation

Events now moved very swiftly, and in a pattern that suggests that neither side was entirely in control of, or responsible for, what happened. The Senegalese leaders made repeated contacts with the French High Commissioner, and evidently explained at least some portion of the situation and of their plans. So far as one can tell, he sympathized with their side of the story and promised at least a benevolent neutrality.[25] In the country outside Dakar, Ousmane N'Gom, the UPS political secretary, took measures to assure that rural party members faithful to Senghor could be brought into the capital on short notice.

Whether by coincidence or from a partial realization of the extent of the Senegalese leaders' activities, Colonel Soumaré, on August 16, called into his office the French commander of the Mali gendarmerie, Lieutenant-Colonel Pierre, and asked him how many gendarmerie platoons were in the vicinity of Dakar and ready to go into action should the need arise. Soumaré further asked Colonel Pierre to notify him of any requisition of the gendarmerie's services which did not come from his office. Colonel Pierre, who was aware of the peculiar state of relations between the Chief of Staff and the Minister of Defense, promptly notified Mamadou Dia, under whose ministry the gendarmerie was placed, and also, one may be sure, informed the French High Commissioner. Mamadou Dia in his capacity of Minister of Defense, then promulgated an *arrêté* on August 17, placing the gendarmerie under the exclusive orders of the governments of the territories in which the units were stationed.[26] That same afternoon, Mamadou Dia brought Senegal's

25. Although there is no indication that France actively sought the breakup of the Federation, once the breakup seemed inevitable there was no question as to which side it would choose. Certainly, a Federation without Senghor's strong moderating influence would not serve France's purposes.

26. This and other relevant documents are reproduced in the annex to the Senegalese *Livre blanc*. Their authenticity has not been seriously challenged by the Soudanese.

regional governors together and informed them that they should be ready in case of trouble from the night of the 19th on. This date was presumably dictated by the fact that the conference of the Mali leaders, which was to attempt to decide on a single presidential candidate for presentation to the corps of electors meeting a week later, was to be held on the 20th.

The next morning Colonel Soumaré asked the gendarmerie to transmit to the Mali army posts at Podor (on the Senegal River) and Bignona (in Casamance) a request for information on how many troops would be ready to move on short notice to Dakar in case they were needed to keep order on the day of the election to the Presidency (August 27). A few hours later, Soumaré presented a second telegram for transmittal to Bignona requesting the army post there to have three sections of from 24 to 30 men each, "all Malians," ready to move on Dakar immediately and provided with a week's rations. The telegram concluded with "departure orders follow."[27] Having been informed of the contents of the telegrams, Dia called Soumaré to his office and ordered him to cancel his messages. This apparently was not done, but neither was the departure order sent, so the army stayed in its barracks. That night and the next morning, the Senegalese leaders alerted a wider circle of party faithful that something was up, and orders were sent to UPS local committees in the interior to mobilize as many loyal men as possible and transport them to Dakar.

On the morning of the 19th, Dia addressed an order to Colonel Pierre, without informing Soumaré, asking him to have eight platoons of gendarmes ready to maintain order in Dakar starting at noon. This precaution and indeed the whole role of Colonel Pierre seem to have passed entirely unnoticed by the Soudanese. It was not until seven that evening, when someone reported seeing dozens of trucks and buses loaded with Senegalese peasants armed with flintlocks and bows and arrows pouring into Rufisque on the way to Dakar, that the Soudanese became aware of how dangerous was their position. Modibo Keita hastily called a meeting of the Federal Council of Ministers, to which only one Senegalese, Boubacar Gueye, the nephew and law partner of Lamine Gueye, came. The Council of Ministers formally revoked Mamadou Dia's functions as Defense Minister, transferred them to the federal Premier, and decreed a national state of emergency. Modibo Keita then called

27. Ibid., p. 51.

in the French High Commissioner to inform him of the Council of Ministers' actions and received assurances that since this was a domestic matter, the French army of the Community would not intervene.[28] Modibo Keita next broadcast a notice of his actions on Radio Mali and announced that the existence of Mali was in danger. Not knowing of the gendarmerie's position, Modibo ordered Colonel Soumaré to deploy the gendarmerie and the Mali army to safeguard public installations.

Modibo Keita's action evidently caught the Senegalese leaders by surprise. At the moment he was being deposed as federal Defense Minister, Mamadou Dia was in Tivaouane, near Thiès, making sure that one of the marabouts there was not going to side publicly with the Soudanese. Senghor was napping at the Federal Assembly building, already surrounded by troops. D'Arboussier, seeing the troops, roused Senghor and took him to Dia's house where they encountered, among others, Colonel Pierre, Valdiodio N'Diaye (Senegalese Minister of the Interior), and Colonel Fall (Senegalese military attaché) who had also been looking for Dia. Leaving d'Arboussier behind to alert the loyal Senegalese territorial assembly members, the others drove to the gendarmerie barracks. While Senghor and Valdiodio whipped up the gendarmes' enthusiasm for their cause, Colonel Pierre telephoned Colonel Soumaré requesting him to come to the gendarmerie barracks on a matter of extreme urgency. Soumaré did so, and was promptly overpowered and put under arrest. With Soumaré out of the way, Colonel Fall, as the next highest ranking officer, ordered the Malian troops to yield their guard of public buildings to the gendarmerie. This they did, and the gendarmes then proceeded to surround the main administrative building, the radio station, and the residence of Modibo Keita.

Mamadou Dia, on his return to Dakar, called a midnight meeting of the Senegalese territorial assembly. Lamine Gueye and his old Socialist supporters were absent, but the 67 members present voted to declare the independence of the Republic of Senegal from the Federation.

By this time, Modibo Keita was aware of what had happened,

28. See the statement of the French High Commissioner, Hettier de Boislambert, to the United Press International, reproduced in Senegal, *Livre blanc*, p. 59. For a somewhat different version, see Modibo Keita, "Communication à l'Assemblée Législative . . . Soudanaise."

and he hurriedly called on the French High Commissioner to demand the intervention of French troops to safeguard Mali's integrity. Hettier de Boislambert informed him that France still regarded this as an internal affair and saw no reason to modify what they "together" had decided earlier in the evening. By morning the streets were full of loyal UPS militants from the interior, all faithful to Senghor, while the Soudanese leaders and some of their Senegalese associates were under house arrest. The Soudanese were sent back home to Bamako by special sealed train on the morning of August 22.

The Senegalese party quickly purged its ranks of those seriously compromised by dealings with the Soudanese.[29] With Senghor and Dia firmly in control, Senegal adopted a new constitution on September 26 and a week later elected Senghor its president. Lamine Gueye was allowed to retain his positions in the party and the government, but was kept very much on the sidelines for another two years. Although he obviously felt personal pain and some embarrassment at the failure of his long fight for federation, Senghor's control over the party and Senegal's political life remained unshaken. Many Dakar intellectuals denounced him for betraying the cause of African unity, but for most Senegalese the Federation's death, like its birth, was a matter of great indifference. Senghor's personal power was further consolidated by Mamadou Dia's elimination from political life after a series of basic disagreements over internal politics led to an armed confrontation between their supporters in December 1962.

The Mali Federation lived a dwindling half-life in Bamako. The first reaction of the Soudanese leaders on returning home was to denounce the complicity of the "French colonialists" and "certain Senegalese traitors" in the events of Dakar and to proclaim that the Federation continued to exist with its government located provisionally in Bamako.[31] "*Le Mali Continue*" was the slogan. In reprisal, the Soudanese cut the railroad with Dakar at the border and refused all Senegalese offers to establish diplomatic relations. But the logic of political events was too strong for the Soudanese leaders. On September 12, France, followed by most other nations, rec-

29. The most important of these were Doudou Gueye, who escaped to Mali, Boubacar Gueye, Lamine Gueye's nephew and the only Senegalese federal minister to appear at the ministerial meeting of August 19, and Patrice Diouf, Lamine Gueye's *directeur du cabinet*. By 1965, all had been brought back into the government's good graces.

30. Modibo Keita, "Communication à l'Assemblée Législative."

ognized the separate independence of Senegal and Soudan and offered to back their admissions to the United Nations. The Union Soudanaise called an Extraordinary Congress on September 22 which, under a banner proclaiming "Death Rather than Dishonor," formally took note of the Federation's breakup and announced that "Mali" would be continued by changing the name of Soudan to the Republic of Mali.[32]

Although political facts were thus given their due, political passions took longer to subside. The Mali Republic maintained its blockade of communications and trade with Senegal at the price of painful economic dislocation for both countries, and for a time charges and countercharges of plots and espionage were hurled back and forth by the leaders of the two countries. It was not until June 22, 1963, that, under the influence of the newly-formed Organization of African Unity, Senghor and Modibo Keita met at the Senegal-Mali border in an emotional embrace to reopen the railroad and usher in a new era of cooperation between two independent states. Federation had failed, and its failure had passed into history.

31. "Résolution de politique générale," in *Congrès extraordinaire de l'U.S.—R.D.A. 22 septembre 1960* (Koulouba, Imprimerie du Gouvernement, 1960), pp. 44–45.

11

Mali and the Problem of Political Union

THIS STUDY has sought to answer two questions: Why was the Mali Federation founded? Why did it fail? In these concluding pages I shall summarize its findings and indicate some of the broader implications of the Mali experience for federations of other new states.

WHY WAS MALI FOUNDED?

Let us begin by looking at some common hypotheses that do *not* explain Mali's formation. First, there is no indication that Mali's founding was in any sense an "historical necessity." If, as many Africans have argued, Africa has a "federal destiny," if history points ineluctably to African political unity, this destiny is so veiled in mystery, and the workings of history are so complex and take such an irregular course, that those who seek Africa's unity might better not rely on history to bring about their ends. Secondly, it cannot be shown that the Federation was dictated by any social, economic, geographic, cultural, linguistic, or other "natural" community, or that it was foredoomed to failure because of this lack. The most that one can say is that the situation was permissive, and that there were no serious nonpolitical obstacles to the Federation. Thirdly, the Federation was not dictated by any constellation of popular or interest-group pressures. The social, economic, and political structures of West Africa simply did not permit pressures of this sort to be effective. Finally, the evidence does not support the contention that either the Federation's formation or its dissolution was dictated by any foreign power. France at various times and in various ways made life difficult for the Federation and at other times and in other ways helped the Federation. The initiatives for both its founding and destruction came from Africans, and ultimate responsibility for the Federation and its failure rests with Africans.

The Mali Federation came about through the actions of a few political leaders who sought what they assumed to be mutually compatible goals in uniting the political bodies under their respective controls. Mali did benefit, however, from one common historical or situational factor, the feeling of people who had recently undergone foreign political rule that political unity was a highly desirable goal. But it took political leaders to translate this diffuse popular feeling into concrete political proposals. It is on the actions and thoughts of these political leaders that this study has concentrated.

The Senegalese political leaders believed that the Mali Federation would be economically useful, both in reinforcing their country's pattern of trade with West Africa and the rest of the world and in opening up new opportunities for economic growth and prosperity. More important than this, however, they saw the Federation as a chance for Senegal to extend the political role it had played throughout the preceding half-century. Furthermore, Mali seemed to them to make good sense in terms of French West Africa's past history. They expected the Federation to give Africa, Senegal, and themselves additional power in dealing with France and to reinforce their and their country's position relative to other African countries and leaders. Unfortunately, once the political framework under which these goals had been inculcated had disappeared, and once independence was achieved, this power and position were no longer as great or important as they had assumed. Finally, one man, Senghor, had identified himself firmly with the idea of federation, and saw its realization in Mali as his own achievement. This was less personal vainglory than a desire for personal prestige that could be used for other political purposes, in particular to reinforce control over his domestic political base as a means to attain specific political goals.

The Soudanese political leaders saw Mali above all as an historically correct decision. As such, it was invested not only with legitimacy, but with a sense of necessity which they could oppose only at their peril. The Soudanese leaders, as they constantly reiterated, appreciated the necessity of bowing before events and facts, and for them the inevitability of African unity was a fact. They saw the Mali Federation as part of a great interrelated complex of political necessities, like mass action, anticolonialism, and, above all, independence. Their faith in Mali was reinforced, as was that of the

Senegalese, by economic interests and historical experiences and by an appreciation of its usefulness in maintaining domestic political unity and control.

Both Senegalese and Soudanese leaders would have preferred a larger federation. Its reduction to Senegal and Soudan alone was the result of forces outside their control, which both sides accepted and tried to make the best of.

Why Did Mali Fail?

The simplest explanation for Mali's failure is that the Senegalese political leaders felt that the continued existence of the Federation threatened their domestic political base and, therefore, their opportunity to continue to play a significant role in African political life. Also, at the crucial moment they were able to mobilize force to break up the Federation.

In a few domains, notably those having to do with economic development and relations with France, the Senegalese and Soudanese leaders had different goals. While these goals were not necessarily incompatible, the rigid, bipolar structure of the Federation turned many disagreements into formal fights between Senegalese and Soudanese leaders in which the prestige of each side was deeply involved. In this atmosphere the feeling of competition frequently obscured the possibilities of compromise. Furthermore, the lack of boundaries between the Federation's political structures made every quarrel between the two partners relevant to every other quarrel. Because, particularly in Senegal, people tended to personalize political power and political choices in terms of an individual leader, problems originating anywhere in the federal political system were forced up to the top and were perceived as involving the prestige and relative standing of Mali's leaders. Also as a result of this personalization of politics and of the fact that the Federation's highest political office was held by a Soudanese, any transferral of popular or individual loyalties to the Federation meant, in Senegal, a transferral of loyalties from Senghor to Modibo Keita.

Since in Senegal there was someone ready and willing to take over political power from Senghor and Dia, and since that person enjoyed the support of the Soudanese federal politicians, reinforcement and, finally, continuation of the Federation appeared to

Senghor and Dia to threaten their domestic political base. Such a threat was particularly severe, since under the political conditions obtaining it was unlikely that they could ever regain political power, even with the support of a majority of the population, once they were out of office.

Continuing the Federation had nothing to offer in compensation for the danger of losing political power. One might hypothesize that had the Federation offered dramatic possibilities for rapid economic growth, Mamadou Dia, at least, might have stuck it out. No such overwhelming advantages were evident. Similarly, had there been special interest groups in Senegal, whether economic, cultural, or traditional, that felt they had a great stake in preserving the Federation and were willing and able to bring pressure on the Senegalese leaders, the Federation might have been preserved. There were no such groups.

Had the Soudanese been willing to moderate their demands, or more precisely had they perceived the need to moderate them, the Federation might have been preserved. The Soudanese, however, saw their demands as legitimate, indeed necessary, and underestimated the possibility of a violent political riposte by the Senegalese. Had the Soudanese known the Senegalese better, or had the personal quarrels at the summit not closed off all effective communication between the two sides in the weeks preceding the crisis, the Soudanese perceptions might have been more acute, and they might have sought to compromise.

Finally, because Senghor and Dia obtained the benevolent neutrality of the French, because they were able to put superior forces in the field at the proper moment, and because the Soudanese were in alien territory, the Senegalese leaders were able to break up the Federation. Had popular passions been aroused, had the Soudanese been able to call on the populace to defend the integrity of the Federation, things might have been different. This was not possible. The Mali Federation was created at the summit; it was also destroyed there.

Some Implications of Mali's Failure

For all its unique elements, the experience of the Mali Federation may point to some broader lessons about the problems of federation in general, and of particular relevance to the formation of wider political groupings in Africa and in other politically emergent areas. It may further point out some consequences of the differences between the political process in most underdeveloped countries and that in the Western world from which we have in the past drawn most of our generalizations about political behavior.

Some of the important factors present in the Mali experience which typify many underdeveloped countries and differentiate them from Europe and the United States are:

(1) the separation of the political process and governmental activity from the life of most people

(2) the lack of outside pressures on government and politicians

(3) the existence of a small, relatively homogeneous political elite

(4) the expectation of continued rapid political change by the elite

(5) the lack of a stable internal political process permitting peaceful and democratic replacement of elites and offering the possibility of a return to political office once a person has lost a political contest

(6) a tendency to personalize political issues and political power

With an awareness of these distinctive characteristics, we can use the Mali experience to reconsider some generalizations about the requirements for successful political union derived from European and American experience. These generalizations are drawn from the study by Karl W. Deutsch and associates of the requirements for political community in the North Atlantic area.[1] They found ten conditions essential for the peaceful voluntary union "of two or more previously independent units into a single larger unit, with some type of common government after amalgamation."[2] I shall briefly take up each condition and show its relevance to the Mali case.

The first two conditions that the North Atlantic data showed to be essential to the maintenance of even the most minimal political community are "compatibility of the main values held by the relevant strata of all the political units involved,"[3] and "mutual responsiveness" leading to the "ability to predict each other's behavior

1. Karl W. Deutsch et al., *Political Community and the North Atlantic Area* (Princeton, Princeton University Press, 1957), pp. 123–54.

2. Ibid., p. 6.

3. Ibid., p. 123.

and ability to act in accordance with that prediction."[4] My study has shown that it is precisely the lack of these two factors that brought on the crisis between Senegalese and Soudanese and led directly to the Mali Federation's breakup. The one possible difference that should be noted is that the "relevant strata" were considerably smaller in the case of Mali, being confined to the political elite itself. This does not mean, however, that compatibility of main values may be easier to come by, for to the extent that the political participants are concerned with transforming society fundamentally, more and more values may become main political values and, as such, subject to serious dispute between the partners of a federation. Similarly, the mere fact that the small politically relevant strata of society have common characteristics and some shared experiences may not be enough to promote the mutual responsiveness required if their domestic political experiences differ. Without the advantages of mass communication and wide popular participation in politics, this responsiveness must be manifested by a very small number of people. Should they for any reason be unable or unwilling to respond, the political community will find no sympathetic responses in the population at large to help it over difficult periods.

Apart from these two fundamental considerations, eight others were found essential. The first of these, a distinctive way of life,[5] was obviously lacking in Mali's case. There was nothing distinctively different about Senegal and Soudan that made their union any more "natural" than if it had included any other members of French West Africa. Perhaps, had the federalists been able to include all of AOF, the necessary distinctiveness based on historical experience would have been present. It is questionable, however, whether even this would have sufficed, and it may be indicative of this dilemma that many Africans interested in political regrouping find they are able to talk meaningfully only in terms of the largest grouping—all of Africa, the one unit that would indeed be distinctive.

The North Atlantic data suggest that more important than the maintenance of a balance of power between amalgamating units is the existence of a strong core area or nucleus possessing advanced

4. Ibid., p. 129.
5. Ibid., pp. 133–37.

economic, political, and administrative capabilities.[6] This may hold true for the underdeveloped nations, too, in the long run. In a shorter perspective, however, the Mali experience and that also of the United Arab Republic suggest that a more equal balance of power—which at least assures the leaders of each unit continued undisturbed control over their own domestic political life—is a necessary precondition. So long as political power is a matter of competitive personal prestige, the dominance of one unit over another will be resented by members of the leadership who may find it in their interest to destroy the community rather than risk a loss of political status at home.

The North Atlantic data indicate that "superior economic growth" and the "expectation of joint economic rewards" are also essential conditions.[7] The Mali Federation unquestionably would have benefited from such economic advantages; however, its experience indicates two necessary qualifications. First, in the underdeveloped countries, economic rewards will be important only as they are perceived as important by the political leaders, and to judge by the Soudanese attitude it is by no means certain that they will be so perceived. Secondly, in the short run at least, political rewards in the form of increased international and domestic prestige may compensate for a lack of economic dynamism. It is unlikely, however, that this will suffice for long or survive the introduction of new groups of the population into the political process.

Two essential conditions found in the North Atlantic study involve relations between the amalgamating units. These are: a "wide range of mutual transactions," and "greater mobility of persons" between the units.[8] Neither of these conditions was present to a significant degree in the Mali case, nor is likely to be present in unions of other underdeveloped nations. It is not clear, however, that either of these would have been essential to maintain Mali, at least for the short run, since it is unlikely that the political elite would have been directly influenced by such relations among the population at large. The fact that a substantial portion of the Mauretanian population crosses the border into Morocco and back each year has not had a notably happy effect on relations between

6. Ibid., pp. 137–39.
7. Ibid., pp. 139–44.
8. Ibid., pp. 144–48, 151–54.

those two countries. Neither did the Soudanese migrant workers contribute significantly to a reinforcement of the Mali Federation.

Two final conditions from the North Atlantic study relate particularly to the politically relevant strata of society. These are a "broadening of the political, social, or economic elites," and "the presence of unbroken links of social communication between the political units concerned and between the relevant social strata within those units."[9] While in the long run these conditions would undoubtedly be extremely helpful, Mali's brief experience points up some of the short-run dangers involved in both conditions. In part it was the very presence of links between the Soudanese and certain Senegalese that led Senghor and Dia to break up the Federation. Unbroken links must exist, but they must be links between top political leaders first and foremost. In like manner, had the Federation lasted long enough to broaden the political elite to include categories not expressly loyal to the leaders of both sides, the Federation again would have been in jeopardy.

From this brief review, it appears that political integration in countries like Mali does share many common requirements with political integration in the Western world. The great exception is that primary short-run emphasis must be given to assuring the existing political elite of continued control over their domestic political base. The only alternative is to replace them with a new political elite, although this may just postpone the problem. This political condition is essential to federations of most emergent nations. Economic advantages and social links by themselves are not enough. It is the *political* interests, desires, and expectations of the *political* elite that are crucial.

Mali and the Future of African Unity

Viewed in perspective, the failure of the Mali Federation appears not as an isolated and unusual incident, nor as a deviation from an historical evolution, but rather as part of a general African trend toward political fragmentation which has progressed steadily since decolonization began in 1956. Since this time, numerous large scale colonial federations have dissolved; French West Africa, French Equatorial Africa, the Federation of the Rhodesias and

9. Ibid., pp. 148–51.

Nyasaland, and Ruanda-Urundi have all split into their component territories. Of African federal states, only the Congo (Leopoldville) and Nigeria, both of which have benefited from unusual conditions, still remain together.

The point is properly made that the units being destroyed are colonial federations, imposed by and for the convenience of the colonial power, and bearing little necessary relation to the interests of their African populations. This does not entirely solve the problem, however, for the federations' constituent units were also based on the convenience of the colonial power. The determining factor in each case seems to be the territorial unit on which nationalist political groups based their organization during the immediate preindependence period. It is this organizational base, formalized eventually by participation in governmental organizations, that has determined the basic African political unit. To the degree that colonial policy determined the territorial basis for nationalist political organization, it can be said that the most enduring legacy of the colonial era is the political boundaries it gave Africa.

Beyond this, Mali's experience, like that of other African federations, makes it clear that independence and international political union are as likely to be conflicting as compatible goals. "Unity" retains its potency as a political rallying cry after independence, but it represents the consolidation of a domestic political base, not a wider, interterritorial unity. Of these two political goals, independence is clearly preeminent and is likely to remain so for some time. Only where it is probable that interterritorial unity will contribute to strengthening domestic political control is an existing political elite apt to welcome it.

It has been argued that the dismantling of colonial federations is necessary for the construction of large political units on true African principles, independent of a colonial heritage. In the very long run this may prove possible; however, Africa's short-run record in building new political unions is not reassuring. Aside from the Mali Federation, the Union of African States—grouping Ghana, Guinea, and eventually the Mali Republic—was disbanded by Sékou Touré's unilateral declaration in 1963. The Conseil de l'Entente has lost whatever political significance it once had, and the much discussed East African Federation of Kenya, Tanganyika, Uganda, and Zanzibar has yet to come into being.

Two political unions, Somalia in east Africa and the Cameroons in the west, have so far proved successful.[10] Somalia has benefited from an unusual degree of ethnic homogeneity and from the fact that traditional authority over lineage groups has not been seriously disturbed by the new national government. At the same time, the presence of a common external enemy, Ethiopia, has submerged domestic differences in the same way that opposition to a colonial regime preserved solidarity elsewhere in the pre-independence period.[11] The reunion of the former British trusteeship territory of the Southern Cameroons with the former French trusteeship territory of Cameroun likewise must be judged provisionally as a successful case of union. This was not quite the union of two independent states, however, since the British-ruled Southern Cameroons, like Northern Somalia, moved directly from dependent status to independence as part of the larger unit. Likewise, the Cameroons benefited from a substantial degree of ethnic homogeneity, at least in the southern areas, and from a strong feeling that the old colonial boundaries established by Germany before World War I were the legitimate ones.[12] Part of the strength of the Cameroonian union also derives, paradoxically, from the fact that the domestic political processes in each of the parts have been kept separate by the different European languages used for politics in each unit. So long as English remains the primary language of politics in the Southern Cameroons, the political leaders from that region will have little to fear from its larger and wealthier French-speaking partner. This same factor could augur well for the future of a union between Senegal and Gambia.

The focus of movements for African unity has now shifted to a much larger scale. The formation of the Casablanca and Monrovia groups, and of the Afro-Malagasy Union of former French colonies were the first such attempts, and were concerned primarily with strengthening the voices of like-minded sovereign states in foreign affairs. All these groups have now disbanded in favor of bringing together all independent African states (except South Africa) in the Organization of African Unity, formed in Addis Ababa in

10. The more recent union of Tanganyika and Zanzibar may be a third example. At this writing it is too early to judge.

11. On Somalia, see A. A. Castagno, Jr., "Somali Republic," in Coleman and Rosberg, pp. 512–59.

12. One of the more interesting aspects of Cameroonian political history is that many of the most active political groups on both sides of the border referred to their country as "*Kamerun.*"

1963.[13] Clearly today the OAU is the embodiment of and the hope for greater African political unity. But this is to be a unity of an entirely new sort. First, it is based on a truly distinctive unit—the whole African continent. Secondly, the OAU is not involved in any way in the domestic political processes of its member states. The Organization's charter goes out of its way to make this clear; four of the seven Principles on which the Organization is based affirm the independence, sovereignty and territorial integrity of each member state.[14] As Modibo Keita proclaimed at the Addis Ababa meeting, "If all of us are truly animated by the ardent desire to achieve African unity, we must take Africa as it is. . . . African unity demands of each one of us complete respect for the legacy which we have received from the colonial system, that is to say, maintenance of the present boundaries of our respective states."[15] Like the medieval empires of the Western Sudan, the central organization will base its continuity on not interfering in local affairs. Whether by example or from introspection, the African states have clearly learned the lesson implicit in Mali's failure.

The OAU is also to emphasize different functions from those originally envisaged by the proponents of African unity. First and foremost, it is to be an actor on the international scene, a means for Africa to make its weight felt in the United Nations and in less formal world gatherings. To this end, members are urged to "coordinate and harmonize" their foreign policies. Secondly, the OAU provides a framework for peacefully settling disputes through negotiation and persuasion among sovereign members. Other functions, like mutual defense and economic cooperation, may at a later date move to the fore. In sum, the new Organization of African Unity is essentially a cooperative regional organization like the Or-

13. The best structured of these, the Afro-Malagasy Union, represented in large part a means of continuing, without France, the cooperative relations of the moribund French Community. After much heated discussion it dissolved itself as a political unit but maintained its organs of economic cooperation.

14. These principles are: "(1) The sovereignty of all member states; (2) noninterference in the internal affairs of states; (3) respect for the sovereignty and territorial integrity of each member state and for its inalienable right to independent existence; (4) peaceful settlement of disputes by negotiation, mediation, conciliation, or arbitration; (5) unreserved condemnation, in all its forms, of political assassination as well as of subversive activities on the part of neighboring states or any other states; (6) absolute dedication to the total emancipation of the African territories which are still dependent; (7) affirmation of a policy of non-alignment with regard to all blocs." Article III of the OAU Charter.

15. Cited by C. L. Sulzberger in the *New York Times*, April 23, 1964.

ganization of American States, whose charter was a model for that of the OAU. The OAU may well fulfill such modest purposes and, in the long run, lay the bases for closer political cooperation. This study can only conclude that more ambitious hopes for quick political amalgamation are likely to be disappointed.

The strength of the OAU is its very size, which permits it to diffuse quarrels among its members and to prevent the polarization of issues and interests that destroyed the Mali Federation. Thus, it is particularly reassuring that ideological divisions between the Casablanca and Monrovia states have not carried over into the new organization. At the same time, the OAU must continue to perform some minimally useful services, whether in the field of foreign affairs or in the field of technical economic cooperation, and this without stepping repeatedly on too many sovereign toes. As with the conquest empires, and as with the Mali Federation, size alone cannot guarantee stability if a strong member feels seriously threatened. Perhaps with regard both to the Mali Federation and to the new Organization of African Unity, it is proper to conclude with the warning of the Malinke proverb: "However great the village where discord reigns, its ruin is the affair of but a single day."

Appendix I "Unity"

THE CONCEPT OF "unity" played a significant role in French West African politics both at the end of the Fourth Republic and in the short experience of the Mali Federation. A great concern with unity and an accompanying fear that obscure centrifugal forces implicit in society will tear a political system apart are common to territories making the transition from traditional or colonial forms of rule to a modern political system. In these transitional societies, concern with unity generally takes the form of rejecting pluralism as an acceptable form of political system. This can be partially explained as a reaction against the traditional system's high degree of pluralism (e.g., division of society into castes, religious groups, clans, tribes, etc.) which inhibited the growth of a national consciousness. Furthermore, the spokesmen for these pluralistic groups, such as chiefs, religious leaders, elders, are rarely accorded legitimacy in the newly evolving political structures. This in turn leads to a lack of what Pye has called "political brokers"—legitimate spokesmen for differing and functionally specific interests within society—which obliges the new political elite to make undifferentiated appeals to wide segments of society and to decry any attempt at bargaining in the name of a subgroup of society.[1]

Concern with unity has been particularly strong in Africa—perhaps because of the extreme fragmentation of traditional society and the tenacity of traditional social and political structures—and especially among the younger elites and radical reformers, that is to say among those with least experience in pluralistic bargaining and those least willing to admit the legitimacy of traditional pluralistic societal structures. Unity has become a rallying cry not only in French West Africa, but throughout the continent as well. In his study of Nigerian and Ghanaian students in the United States, Zalinger found that "slightly more than 90 per cent of the respondents considered that the current tribal or regional differences were

1. See Lucian W. Pye, "The Non-Western Political Process," *Journal of Politics*, *20* (August 1958), 468–86.

the Number One obstacle to immediate self-government," and a decided majority preferred a unitary form of government as the best way of dealing with the problem.[2] Similarly, in his study of East African Swahili materials, Whiteley notes the statement: "We are just now crying out for unity, and we don't listen to any incitement to division. . . . In our aim of nationhood let us forget tribalism." He comments, "Throughout the material examined one is left with a suspicion that writers believe in a kind of causal link between unity and freedom; of the order, given unity, then freedom. There are numerous references of the following pattern, 'We have no weapons but our unity,' 'nothing is beyond our grasp if we are united.' "[3]

Unity is expected to be a potent force at all levels of political action. The mass party, described in Chapter 3, represents unity applied to the political party. Similarly, national unity is seen as the key to a strong nation-state. At the extreme, pan-Africanism demands unity of all African and sometimes all black people. These levels of unity are frequently seen as functionally interdependent: the united single political party is the guarantor of national unity; by a people's seeking the higher ideal of pan-Africanism, local differences will be smoothed out and national unity assured.

Concomitant with the emphasis on unity as part of the battle for independence, there is a tendency to impute a desire to divide and rule to the colonial power. This is often done rather indiscriminately, as when the Indian nationalists accused the British of partitioning their country to "divide and rule."[4] In Africa the Europeans are held responsible for first dividing the continent among themselves, and then for maintaining tribal or other divisions as a means of playing off African against African. While this interpretation is open to challenge on the grounds that such national unity as there is results from colonial rule, it has often enough been the case to reinforce the fears of the African politicians. The position of the MRP during the debates on the Fourth Republic's Constitution

2. Alvin D. Zalinger, "A Study of African Students in the United States," working paper quoted in George H. T. Kimble, *Tropical Africa* (New York, The Twentieth Century Fund, 1960), pp. 377–78.

3. Wilfred H. Whiteley, "Political Concepts and Connotations," *African Affairs,* No. 1, St. Antony's Papers, 10 (Carbondale, Ill., Southern Illinois University Press, 1961), p. 20.

4. See Rupert Emerson, *From Empire to Nation* (Cambridge, Harvard University Press, 1960), pp. 122–23.

and the attitudes taken in the French West African colonialist press are good examples.[5]

The tendency to seek in unity the solution of all problems would perhaps not be so pronounced were it not reinforced on both the sociological and psychological levels. The communalism inherent in much of traditional African society makes the search for unity a particularly acceptable goal of political action.[6] Aside from any predisposing factors toward common or united action carried over from early training, the new African political elite can resolve its ambivalent attitude toward traditional Africa by reasoning that its actions bent on destroying many survivals of traditional political privilege and forms are actually directed toward reemphasizing a (or *the*) crucial value of traditional African society. The personal stresses and constant threat of rootlessness plaguing individual Africans leading the way in the transition from old to new also increase predispositions toward seeking communion with others in the same difficult situation. This is particularly true for the young student cut off completely from traditional associations and thrust into the challenging and sometimes hostile environment of a European university, and for the newly urbanized, cut off from family and friends and confronted with the intricacies of making a living in a monetary economy and a home in a comparatively impersonal

5. See particularly the column "Les Propos de P'tit Jules" in the French West African organ of *petit blanc* opinion, *Les Echos d'Afrique Noire* (Dakar). Many African leaders have of course expressed a more balanced view of European intentions. Thus Nnamdi Azikiwe, "Whilst European nations may be rightly accused of *balkanizing* Africa in the nineteenth century, yet they have atoned for it by federating many African territories, which are now being *balkanized* by African nationalists on the attainment of the independence of their countries." *The Future of Pan-Africanism* (London, Nigeria Information Service, 1961), cited in Colin Legum, *Pan-Africanism, A Short Political Guide* (New York, Praeger, 1962), p. 120.

6. I am aware of the criticisms leveled by anthropologists at those who attempt broad Africa-wide generalizations of this sort, and agree that they can be dangerous. (See Robert A. LeVine, "Africa," in Francis L. K. Hsu, *Psychological Anthropology, Approaches to Culture and Personality,* Homewood, Ill., Dorsey, 1961, pp. 48–52.) I am emboldened to make this qualified generalization particularly because African intellectuals themselves are so insistent upon communalism as a basic and distinctive element of their traditional civilization. See for example, Leopold Senghor, "La Voie Africaine du socialisme," PFA, *Séminaire organisé à l'occasion du Congrès de l'Union Nationale de la Jeunesse du Mali* (Dakar, 1960), p. 84. "Negro-African society places greater emphasis on the group than on the individual, more on *solidarity* than on the activity and needs of the individual, more on the *communion* of persons than on their autonomy. It is a *communal society* (*société communautaire*)." Italics in text.

context. Hence the surprising strength of both student groups and urban workers' unions or protective associations.

The factors predisposing the transitional person to seek a broad form of unity may be the same as those predisposing him to political militancy. Data collected by the Institut Français d'Opinion Publique suggest a strong correlation between political militancy, radicalism, and pan-African group membership among African students in Paris. The Guinean students, in particular, were least well disposed toward the French, most active in "international" African student groups, and most disposed to draw their friends from among many different African "nationalities."[7]

The strength of student emphasis on unity is best brought out in J. P. N'Diaye's thorough study of French-speaking African student opinions. Asked what conditions would have to be fulfilled before they would have complete confidence in Africa's future, 24.5 per cent answered "the realization of unity." The next largest category, economic development, was mentioned by only 12.5 per cent.[8] N'Diaye sums up the students' reasoning:

> Just as recognition of the right to independence is a necessary precondition for negotiation and negotiation for the proclamation of independence, so African students consider African UNITY as being the necessary precondition for a viable political, economic, and humane Africa, englobing a more natural ensemble. Only Unity re-establishes the monolithic structure of ancient Africa and by the same token guarantees security, economic growth, and a political personality in the future.[9]

Finally, it should be noted that in fact experience has shown that Africans, like everyone else, *can* often get what they want when they are united and are frequently exploited when they are divided. When colonialist opposition to any form of African unity is added to this, a dissatisfied African elite draws what is seemingly the only obvious conclusion, that unity is *the* key to political success, and that people, programs, and action may legitimately be judged on the basis of what their attitude or effect is likely to be on construction or maintenance of unity among Africans.

7. "Les Etudiants d'Outre-Mer en France," *Sondages, 3* (1961), 50–79.

8. J. P. N'Diaye, *Enquête sur les étudiants noirs en France* (Paris, Réalités Africaines, 1962), p. 218.

9. Ibid., p. 219.

Appendix II Content Analysis of *Essor* and *Unité Africaine* Editorials

In attempting to understand the political perceptions, predispositions, and thought patterns of the Senegalese and Soudanese leaders, I did very early in my research a systematic content analysis of a major form of political communication, the editorials in political party weekly newspapers, the UPS's *Unité Africaine* and the Union Soudanaise's *Essor*. These editorials are intended to transmit the thoughts of the political party's leaders to the rank and file, and thus may be considered reasonably accurate guides to official party policy. Much of the background for the chapters on Senegalese and Soudanese political ideas is derived from this. As a measure of the usefulness of this technique, I have included some notes comparing UPS and Union Soudanaise political thought that were made after doing this content analysis and before holding interviews with political leaders.

Techniques

The editorials considered were a random selection from one of each four consecutive issues from May 1959 to August 1960. The entire editorial, including the title, was scored. Scoring was by "sense unit," a phrase or sentence expressing a thought about one of the symbols. Where a single thought was developed at some length, a score was marked for each two complete lines.

The analysis concentrated on a small number of symbols (22), which a previous reading of the subject matter had shown to be of importance. They are:

1. POLITICS – including political strategy, doctrine, the "realm of politics," etc.
2. ECONOMICS – economic policies, doctrine, economics in general. See also 14.
3. PEOPLE – the masses.
4. PARTY – the Union Soudanaise or UPS, PFA, party members.
5. GOVERNMENT – formal government structure, officials in government roles.

6. INTERNAL UNITY – national unity, solidarity, homogeneity.
7. AFRICAN UNITY – federalism, confederalism, etc., in Africa.
8. INDEPENDENCE
9. WORK – hard work, increased activity, self-sacrifice.
10. COLLECTIVISM – communal projects or living, opposed to individualism.
11. INDIVIDUALISM
12. DEMOCRACY
13. BOURGEOISIE – capitalists, capitalism, high finance.
14. ECONOMIC DEVELOPMENT – special case of 2.
15. MALI
16. SOUDAN
17. SENEGAL
18. AFRICA – in general or a particular country (not 15, 16, or 17), the agents of such a country.
19. IMPERIALISM – colonialism, colonial system, imperialist or colonialist powers, ideas, etc.
20. FRANCE
21. INTERNATIONAL RELATIONS – as opposed to domestic politics.
22. NON-AFRICA – the world outside Africa, non-Africans (excluding 20).

The scoring system was designed to record relationships between the different categories as well as incidences of mention. Three sorts of relationships were coded: 1. facilitative (+), e.g. "The PARTY promotes AFRICAN UNITY," scored PY + AU; 2. hindering (–) e.g. "IMPERIALISM hurts the PEOPLE," scored IMP – PE; 3. simple relationship (0), e.g. "Many FRENCHMEN are IMPERIALISTS," scored FR 0 IMP. Where + and – relationships are noted, we may also distinguish direction of the relationship by noting which of the categories is the active and which is the passive partner in the relationship, e.g. "INTERNAL UNITY (active) destroys the BOURGEOISIE (passive)" (IU – B). Each category may thus be analyzed by its active/passive ratio, according to whether it is an active force or an instrumental concept, or whether it is passive and a goal in and of itself. Simple mentions of a category are scored +, –, or 0 according to whether the mention is approving, disapproving, or noncommittal. Statements expressing a wish are scored as if they were affirmative statements unless they are clearly contrary to fact, e.g. "We hope MALI will promote AFRICAN UNITY" (M + AU), but "It would be nice if the IMPERIALISTS would help us gain our INDEPENDENCE instead of acting as they do" (IMP – IND). These relationships are plotted on a 22 x 22 matrix where the categories read horizontally are active and those read vertically are acted upon. At the juncture of the horizontal and vertical for each category, I have scored the simple mentions of that category as described above. These simple mentions are not counted in the compilation of the active/passive ratio.

Comparison can be made between the categories mentioned by each newspaper on the basis of frequency of mention, frequency of association, and activity or passivity. Some sample hypotheses tested statistically and found valid at the $p < .01$ are:

a. The UPS sees DEMOCRACY as a more active and instrumental force than does the Union Soudanaise;
b. The UPS sees FRANCE as facilitating its aims more than does the Union Soudanaise;
c. The Union Soudanaise sees FRANCE, IMPERIALISM, and BOURGEOISIE as being more opposed to their aims than does the UPS.

Comparisons of rank-ordered frequencies of all symbols can yield a measure of degree of common attention focus by employing the Spearman test for association. Comparison of rank-ordered frequencies between the two papers yielded a degree of association, $r_s = .76$. Were similar data available for, say, Guinea and Ivory Coast party newspapers, it would be possible to see which patterns of thought and attention were most similar.

Results: Some Major Differences in Political Thought between the UPS and the Union Soudanaise

Elite and Mass

Both the Union Soudanaise and the UPS claim to be at the service of the masses and acting in response to their wishes. In the comparative content analysis, PEOPLE showed up among the more frequently cited categories, more so for the Soudan than for Senegal. (*Essor,* 8.34 per cent of mentions; *Unité Africaine,* 4.89 per cent.) In all cases the actions of the PEOPLE were viewed by both papers as facilitative, although on the balance, both papers saw the PEOPLE as essentially passive. (Active/passive ratios: *Essor,* .50; *Unité Africaine,* .44.) Similarly, in each case the PARTY affected the PEOPLE considerably more than it was affected by the PEOPLE. (*Essor,* PARTY affects PEOPLE, 23; PEOPLE affect PARTY, 10. For *Unité Africaine* the figures are 9 and 5, respectively.) One notable difference, however, lies in the number of times individual leaders are cited in the text, a measure of the degree of elite personalization of politics.

Table 11. Essor

	Pol.			*Econ.*			*People*			*Party*			*Govt.*			*I. U.*			*A. U.*			*Indep.*			*Work*			*Coll.*			*Individ.*			*Dem.*			*Bourg.*		
	+	−	0	+	−	0	+	−	0	+	−	0	+	−	0	+	−	0	+	−	0	+	−	0	+	−	0	+	−	0	+	−	0	+	−	0	+	−	0
Politics	7		10	4			3			3		3			3																	1						3	
Economics				2	2	2																																	
People	2						6		3	9		1			1			1				1																	
Party	2						18		5	6		13	2			2		1	2			5						1				1		1					
Government	1	1					3		4						5	2																							
Internal unity							1			4						6		4							3			2											
African unity	1									3									4		6																	1	
Independence				3			1									1		1	1	2	3	10	1	9										3					
Work							2		2	6												1			1		1												
Collectivism										1						1									1			1											
Individualism								1			1																		1			4	2		1				
Democracy										1																								1					
Bourgeoisie		3												1			1	1		5			2															1	2
Economic development																																							
Mali																1			4			4		2										1					
Soudan																																							
Senegal																																							
Africa																1	1		1	8[a]		2	4[a]	2										1					1
Imperialism		5			1			1			1			1		3				3			4											1			1		2
France		1			1						1									2																			
International relations																																							
Non-Africa																	1				1																		
Passive	6	10		7	2		28	2		27	3		2	2		11	3		8	20		13	10		4	0		3	1		0	2		7	1		1	4	
Total			16			9			30			30			4			14			28			23			4			4			2			8			5

a. From an editorial against the Ivory Coast.

TABLE 11. (continued)

	E. D.			Mali			Soud.			Sen.			Africa			Imp.			France			I. R.			Non-Africa			Active			Total mentions	Active/Passive	% of mentions
	+	−	0	+	−	0	+	−	0	+	−	0	+	−	0	+	−	0	+	−	0	+	−	0	+	−	0	+	−	Tot.			
Politics																1					1							11	4	15	55	.97	6.75
Economics																						1						1	0	1	16	.11	1.96
People													1				2											13	2	15	68	.50	8.34
Party				2		1							1				1			1								36	3	39	99	1.30	12.15
Government																												6	1	7	24	1.75	2.94
Internal unity							1		1																			11	0	11	40	.79	4.91
African unity				1			1			1			6		1		2		1									14	3	17	60	.61	7.36
Independence	1			7									3				3		2			1						23	5	28	79	1.25	9.69
Work	2																											11	0	11	19	2.75	2.33
Collectivism																												3	0	3	8	.75	.98
Individualism																												0	4	4	12	2.00	1.47
Democracy													1						1									3	0	3	13	.38	1.60
Bourgeoisie														4		1		1										1	16	17	30	3.40	3.68
Economic development																												0	0	0	3	0	.37
Mali				2		13							2								4							12	0	12	53	.67	6.50
Soudan									2																			0	0	0	5	0	.61
Senegal																												0	0	0	1	0	.12
Africa					2								4	8[b]	19										5			10	15	25	95	.81	11.66
Imperialism														6	1		8	3								2		5	24	29	54	2.90	6.63
France				1	5	1								7	2				2	4	13					1		1	18	19	52	3.80	6.38
International relations															1						1		2	3			1	0	0	0	10	0	1.23
Non-Africa																									1	1	6	0	1	1	19	.13	2.33
Passive	3	0		11	7		2	0		1	0		14	17		2	8		4	1		2	0		5	3		161	96				
Total			3			18			2			1			31			10			5			2			8			257	815		99.99

b. Five of these are from an editorial against the Ivory Coast.

TABLE 12. Unité Africaine

	Pol.			Econ.			People			Party			Govt.			I. U.			A. U.			Indep.			Work			Coll.			Individ.			Dem.			Bourg.		
	+	−	0	+	−	0	+	−	0	+	−	0	+	−	0	+	−	0	+	−	0	+	−	0	+	−	0	+	−	0	+	−	0	+	−	0	+	−	0
Politics			5									1							5			2																	
Economics				1		4										1																							
People									1	3		2	1									1																	
Party	5		3	1		1	3		6	3		26		1	1	2		1	9		1	4		3										1		1			
Government	2			4			3						3		5				1			1															1		1
Internal unity	3						1						1			3		7	5	1																			
African unity	1			1			2												3		17	2		1															
Independence							1												1			6		8															
Work							3			2			1			2									3		1												
Collectivism	1			1			2														1																		
Individualism																					1																		
Democracy	2		1				1			3			3			2		1	5															1		2			
Bourgeoisie																																							
Economic development							7															4												1					
Mali																1		1	3	1				3															
Soudan																			1																				
Senegal																			2					2															
Africa	2																		3																1	2			
Imperialism		1[a]			1[a]			1[a]																															
France							1												1		2	3	1	1															
International relations																				1																			
Non-Africa																				1																			
Passive	16	1		7	1		24	1		8	0		6	1		8	0		36	4		17	1		0	0		0	0		0	0		2	1		1	0	
Total			17			8			25			8			7			8			40			18			0			0			0			3			1

a. Quoted from a speech by Modibo Keita.

Table 12. (continued)

	E. D.			Mali			Soud.			Sen.			Africa			Imp.			France			I. R.			Non-Africa			Active			Total mentions	Active / Passive	% of mentions
	+	−	0	+	−	0	+	−	0	+	−	0	+	−	0	+	−	0	+	−	0	+	−	0	+	−	0	+	−	Tot.			
Politics										1					1													8	0	8	36	.47	3.91
Economics										1																		2	0	2	16	.25	1.74
People	5			1																								11	0	11	45	.44	4.89
Party				2		1							4				1											31	2	33	91	4.13	9.88
Government	3			2											1													17	0	17	35	2.43	3.80
Internal unity	1			2		1									2							1		2				14	1	15	40	1.88	4.34
African unity				3			1			1			8									3						22	0	22	88	.55	9.55
Independence	2			3		1	2			2			3		1						1							14	0	14	59	.78	6.41
Work	3									2		1																13	0	13	18	∞	1.95
Collectivism				1																								5	0	5	6	∞	.65
Individualism					1[a]																							0	1	1	2	∞	.22
Democracy				1									4		4												2	21	0	21	38	7.00	4.13
Bourgeoisie					1[a]																							0	1	1	3	1.00	.33
Economic development	1		15			1				2		2	1															15	0	15	50	1.00	5.43
Mali	1		1	3		20	2			2			3		2						6	1		4				13	1	14	92	.52	9.99
Soudan				1		1	1		5			4									3							2	0	2	24	.40	2.61
Senegal				2		1			3	3		11							1		4							5	0	5	47	.45	5.10
Africa				3	2								4	1	26						4			8				8	3	11	100	.34	10.86
Imperialism																	1	1										0	3	3	9	1.00	.98
France						3						2	7	1	1		2	1	6	1	20					2		12	6	18	77	4.00	8.36
International relations				2																				8				2	1	3	29	.60	3.15
Non-Africa													1							3							7	1	4	5	16	∞	1.74
Passive	15	0		23	4		5	0		11	0		31	1		0	3		1	3		5	0		0	2		216	23				
Total		15			27			5			11			32			3			4			5			2			239		921		100.02

While *Essor* mentions individual Soudanese or Mali leaders 9 times, *Unité Africaine* mentions Senegalese and Mali leaders 35 times (in about 10 per cent more text). This gives a different coloring to Senegalese political discussions that we might hypothesize carries over into their political thought. A political idea or action is influenced by who presents it, implying that policies are not determined automatically by the "popular will" or a previously worked-out political program.

An intensive reading of the respective texts permits us to elaborate on this difference. The UPS, aside from a few mentions of the principle of democratic centralism and "la Démocratie forte," spends little time discussing the importance of the influence of the masses on public policy. The Union Soudanaise, on the other hand, spends little time on the modalities of assuring popular control over the party's and government's actions, but goes into great detail over the crucial need for public policy to remain in constant contact with the spirit and ideas of the people.

> We must never forget this eternal truth *that the people's aspirations are always revolutionary and the revolution will be effective if the party continually identifies itself with the masses, if it blends into the masses, if it always continually refers back to their possibilities and their desires.*[1]

This becomes an article of faith. When something goes wrong, it is the fault of the party for not having understood the people or for not having guided the people's actions so as best to fulfill their desires. Failures are the fault of the leaders (*responsables*), not of the people,[2] and only disaster can result from "thinking that any problem can be resolved at the summit . . . without being protected by guarantees of popular accord."[3]

This attitude contrasts sharply with that implied in Senghor's statement, "The first condition for the effectiveness of . . . action at the mass level, is the esteem and reciprocal confidence among Mali's leaders."[4] Where the Union Soudanaise counts on interpreting the desires of the masses for promoting the country's interests, the UPS counts on expertise, both political and technical, working

1. *Essor,* December 11, 1959, italics in text.
2. *Essor,* May 27, 1960, p. 3.
3. *Essor,* December 11, 1959.
4. *Unité Africaine,* August 22, 1959.

strictly from the top down. The masses are seen as an executing agent for the leaders' decisions, which they are called on to ratify every once in a while in a formal election. For the Union Soudanaise, every act of public policy is an informal plebiscite. If it is successful, the people are with them; if it fails, the party has somehow misinterpreted the people's will or misinformed the people of its intentions.

Relationship of the Individual to the Group

The position of the individual is a curious one in both the Union Soudanaise and the UPS doctrines. Both groups accept the principle that African society is historically and fundamentally communal and feel that the future development of their societies should be based on communal action. Mamadou Dia, in particular, has written extensively on the advantages of communal economic forms for Africa. In the content analysis, neither COLLECTIVISM nor INDIVIDUALISM appeared among the more burning issues discussed; *Essor* gave them .98 per cent and 1.47 per cent of the mentions respectively, while the figures for *Unité Africaine* are .65 per cent and .22 per cent. The Senegalese, at least, are not in turmoil over the two categories, and about all one can say for sure is that COLLECTIVISM appears clearly an active and facilitative force (5 active facilitative mentions and no passive or hindering mentions). The Soudanese go further, both praising COLLECTIVISM and damning INDIVIDUALISM. The former gets 3 facilitative mentions and the latter 4 hindering mentions. The conclusion to be drawn from this is not that the Senegalese are not interested in collectivism or African socialism, as their opponents have charged, but rather that UPS doctrine does not see individualism as a threat to political control or economic progress.

The Soudanese mince no words about ridding themselves of individualism and individualists, considered among the most dangerous legacies of European occupation. This is brought out clearly in their attitude toward themselves; the Union Soudanaise leaders are always presented as a collegial body. If there are internal differences, they are seldom brought before the public. As noted above, *Essor* seldom mentions names. They do not like prima donnas—at least not in public. An editorial on the new system of justice to be established in the Soudan sums up their attitude perfectly: "Justice . . . as it is conceived in Western countries . . . sometimes takes on the appearance of a preferential defense of the individual against society. In African society, on the other hand . . . justice is always considered as a means for society to defend itself against the excesses of individualism."[5] The task of the party is to root out individualism wherever it is found.[6] They do not see this as an easy task, for individualism is "a consequence of the structure of society based on personal profit which divides men instead of uniting them."[7] Indeed, the fight against the virus of individualism is intimately bound up in the fight for the transformation of the social, economic, and political structures.

The Senegalese, however, see no fundamental disharmony between COLLECTIVISM and INDIVIDUALISM. I suspect the UPS would agree that the problem of individualism is intimately bound up with societal structure, and would then go on to specify that their conception of a society "*à base collective*" does not imply that all individualism must be suppressed. Certainly the influence of individual political leaders, both inside and outside the party, is never minimized in public. Similarly, if the backbone of the economy is to be rural cooperatives, as foreseen in the UPS plan, a large sector will be left to private enterprise, most particularly in the hope of attracting foreign capital. However, one UPS editorialist did go so far as to touch on that most taboo of subjects, the building up of an African middle class "intermediary between producers and consumers." This can be presented under a nationalist light as an attempt to oust the Lebanese and Europeans from their quasi monopoly of retail trade, but the fact remains that this is tantamount to swallowing the poison of occidental economic individualism. It may possibly be good economics, but it is not good dialectics.

Democracy and Internal Unity

This question is intimately connected with the previous one. For both the UPS and the Union Soudanaise the problem of INTERNAL UNITY is important (*Unité Africaine*, 4.34 per cent of the mentions; *Essor*, 4.91 per cent, each in 8th place according to frequency). The Soudanese see INTERNAL UNITY primarily as an end in itself

5. *Essor*, May 27, 1960.
6. Cf. *Essor*, April 24, 1959.
7. Ibid.

(A/P ratio, .79), while the Senegalese see it rather as a means to other ends (A/P ratio, 1.88). For both it is decidedly a facilitative agent (*Essor,* 11+, 0–; *Unité Africaine,* 14+, 1–). The precise character of this internal unity, however, is viewed quite differently by the two sides, as is brought out in the treatment accorded DEMOCRACY. In *Essor,* DEMOCRACY is barely discussed (1.60 per cent of mentions), and when it is, its content varies from "bourgeois democracy" to "democratic centralism." According to the content given the word, it may or may not be facilitative (2+, 1–).

For the Senegalese, on the other hand, DEMOCRACY is among the more important categories (4.13 per cent of mentions, 9th place). It is also highly active (A/P ratio, 7.00) and facilitative (21+, 0–). Whereas *Essor* mentions no connection between DEMOCRACY and unity on either the internal or pan-African levels, *Unité Africaine* mentions 3 and 5 connections, respectively. The Senegalese doctrine explicitly rejects founding internal unity on compulsion, on abrogation of the liberties of the opposition (as long as it is a national opposition). "No African State worthy of the name can aspire to a true unifying role (*une vocation unitaire*) while individuals and the people of that State live under a regime of terror maintained by a police state atmosphere."[8] Needless to say, practice is far from following the doctrinal letter, but the continued existence of an opposition like PRA-Sénégal and the continued employment of dissenters in government posts would be unthinkable in the Soudanese concept of internal unity. In a certain sense, the Senegalese view of unity is an inclusive one, based on acceptance of a few rules of the game, e.g. tolerance of a national political opposition but not one in the service of a foreign power, while the Soudanese view is exclusive; one is either a complete member of the club, or one is cast out from society in the African tribal tradition.

Politics and Economics

Perhaps the most fundamental doctrinal difference between the Union Soudanaise and the UPS is the question of whether the economic or the political realm should be granted primacy. The Union Soudanaise opts clearly for politics and the UPS for economics, with the emphasis on economic development (*Essor,* POLITICS gets 6.75 per cent of the mentions, 7th place, while ECONOMICS gets 1.96

8. *Unité Africaine,* August 6, 1960.

per cent, 15th place, and ECONOMIC DEVELOPMENT gets .37 per cent and 21st place. *Unité Africaine*, POLITICS gets 3.91 per cent, 11th place, while ECONOMICS gets 1.74 per cent, 17th place, and ECONOMIC DEVELOPMENT gets 5.43 per cent, 7th place.)

The Union Soudanaise proclaims in so many words the supremacy of the political and suggests that only imperialists, capitalists, and their lackeys think otherwise. "The political experience of Africa . . . proves that all those who have minimized the role of politics have always been opposed to any social progress and have placed themselves in the camp of the enemies of democracy."[9] The Soudanese do not deny the importance of the economic realm (they are basically Marxist trained, after all), but they feel that the economic and political realms are inextricably bound up and that any economic decision is first and foremost a political one. They have no concept of the nonpolitical, purely technical decision. Every economic decision affects the structure of the state, and every such decision must first be thought through in political terms. Similarly, they explicitly deny the possibility of effective economic development through economic means (i.e. investment, capital formation, allocation of scarce resources, etc.) alone. The entire social structure must be changed, and the old *économie de traite* rooted out through political action.

The UPS are much more relaxed about it all. They aim to attack economic problems through economic means, though of course they are a political party and politics are still important. Senghor's general political report to the second congress of the UPS put the relationship neatly in focus. "[The UPS] puts the accent on *economic and social development;* but . . . political, I should say 'administrative,' *ways and means* are not, however, lost sight of."[10] Senghor's political report itself is eloquent testimony to the importance of the economic realm for the UPS; 40 of its 67 pages are dedicated to economics. We should note further that the UPS talks little of the abstract ECONOMICS, but much of the concrete ECONOMIC DEVELOPMENT. For them this is not a doctrinal area, it is a technical one. With this background it is not difficult to understand the Soudanese contempt for the Senegalese 25-year plan for economic development. What Soudan would want is a plan for

9. *Essor*, March 11, 1960.

10. Senghor, "Rapport de Politique Générale," Deuxième congrès de l'UPS–PFA, p. 4. Emphasis in text.

political development, with the expectation that the rest would be added thereunto.

Imperialism, Capitalism, and the French

Senegal's favored position and Soudan's role as a neglected stepchild under the old colonial system are both reflected in their post-colonial attitudes toward their former masters and their masters' economic and political systems. For the UPS the categories IMPERIALISM and BOURGEOISIE rank 20th and 21st respectively, with .98 per cent and .33 per cent of the mentions. Further, one third of each of these mentions occurred in quoting one of Modibo's speeches. Capitalism, further, is considered mainly an established domestic fact, not a foreign method of exploitation.

For the Union Soudanaise, both categories are relatively important. IMPERIALISM ranks 7th with 6.63 per cent of the mentions and BOURGEOISIE ranks 11th with 3.68 per cent. Both are active forces (A/P ratios, 2.90 and 3.40) and decidedly do not facilitate the aims of the Union Soudanaise (4+, 25–; 0+, 17–). These two categories are particularly opposed to two highly important values for the Soudanese, POLITICS and AFRICAN UNITY, although IMPERIALISM does, by a sort of reverse action, promote INTERNAL UNITY. Indeed, IMPERIALISM is frequently the whipping boy for anything that goes wrong, as when one author cries, "All our misfortunes are the result of colonialism, of the loss of our total sovereignty."[11] For the UPS, these are dead issues, and they refuse constantly to "faire le procès du colonialisme."

The UPS and the Union Soudanaise are most diametrically opposed when they discuss the French and their role in Africa. FRANCE is an important category for both groups (*Essor,* 9th place, 6.38 per cent of the mentions; *Unité Africaine,* 4th place, 8.36 per cent). Both see FRANCE as a highly active and impermeable force (A/P ratios, 3.80 and 4.00 respectively). But here the similarity ends. The Union Soudanaise sees FRANCE almost exclusively in the role of the evil colonialist, opposed to all its legitimate aspirations. It is noted as facilitating Soudanese goals just once, and as hindering them 17 times. The Senegalese party, however, sees FRANCE as facilitating its goals 14 times and as hindering them only twice. FRANCE is even credited with being the enemy of IMPERIALISM!

11. *Essor,* August 14, 1959.

Where the Soudanese see French occupation as a disaster for Africa, the UPS sees it as a good and necessary step in the continent's development. "[France] has realized in part the dream of the old African Emperors. It has done more; it has organized and structured. It has realised their dream of creating a federation out of individual countries and building a common spirit through the French language."[12] Where the Soudanese leaders see their task as one of taking up directly where the pre-French conquerors like Samory and El Hadj Omar left off, forgetting the unfortunate seventy-five-year period of French rule, the Senegalese leaders see their role as beginning where the French left off: "It is up to us Malians to take up where France left off, to give a soul to the spirit created, a little despite itself, by the colonial administration."[13] It is easy to understand how the Soudanese can lay the blame for Mali's failure on the machinations of the French and their Senegalese lackeys.

12. *Unité Africaine,* June 1, 1959, editorial by Senghor.
13. Ibid.

Bibliography

General

Africanus, *L'Afrique noire devant l'indépendance,* Paris, Plon, 1958.

Almond, Gabriel A., and James S. Coleman, eds., *The Politics of The Developing Areas,* Princeton, Princeton University Press, 1960.

Ames, David W., "The Economic Basis of Wolof Polygyny," *Southwestern Journal of Anthropology, 11* (Winter 1955), 391–403.

Amon d'Aby, F. J., *La Côte d'Ivoire dans la cité africaine,* Paris, Larose, 1951.

Angrand, Armand-Pierre, *Les Lébous de la presqu'île du Cap-Vert,* Dakar, La Maison du Livre, n.d.

Arcin, André, *Histoire de la Guinée Française,* Paris, Challamel, 1911.

Balandier, Georges. "Le Développement industriel et la prolétarisation en Afrique Noire," *L'Afrique et l'Asie, 20* (1952), 45–53.

Balima, Albert, "La Migration du travailleur en Haute-Volta," CCTA Conference Document MIG, Feb. 11–15, 1961.

Banque Centrale des Etats de l'Afrique de l'Ouest, *Comptes économiques du Mali, 1956,* Etudes économiques ouest-africaines, *1* (February 1960).

Berg, E. J., "The Economic Basis of Political Choice in French West Africa," *American Political Science Review, 44* (June 1960), 391–405.

———, "French West Africa," in Walter Galenson, ed., *Labor and Economic Development,* New York, Wiley, 1959, pp. 186–259.

Betts, Raymond F., *Assimilation and Association in French Colonial Theory (1890–1914),* New York, Columbia University Press, 1961.

Binger, L. G., *Du Niger au Golfe de Guinée par le pays de Kong et le Mossi (1887–1889),* Paris, Hachette, 1892.

———, *Le Péril de l'Islam,* Paris, Hachette, 1906.

Blanchet, André, *L'Itinéraire des partis africains depuis Bamako,* Paris, Plon, 1958.

Bloch, M. R., "The Social Influence of Salt," *Scientific American, 209* (July 1963), 89–98.

Bodiel, Thiam, "Hiérarchie de la société ouolove," *Notes Africaines,* No. 41 (January 1949), 12.

Boisdon, Daniel, "Préface aux débats sur la réforme constitutionelle," *Marchés Coloniaux, 403* (August 1, 1953).

Borella, F., "L'Evolution des Territoires d'Outre-Mer et la Loi-Cadre Defferre," *Recueil Penant, 642* (August–September 1956).

Boulnois, Jean and Boubou Hama, *L'Empire de Gao: Histoire, coûtumes et magie des Sonraï,* Paris, Librarie d'Amérique et d'Orient, 1954.

Bourcart, Robert, *Le Grand Conseil de l'Afrique Occidentale Française,* Thesis, University of Paris, 1955.

Bourlon, Abel, "Actualité des Mourides et du Mouridisme," *L'Afrique et l'Asie, 46* (1959), 10–30.

Boutillier, J., *Bongouanou, Côte d'Ivoire: Etude socio-économique d'une subdivision,* Paris, Berger-Levrault, 1960.

Bovill, E. W., *The Golden Trade of the Moors,* London, Oxford University Press, 1958.

Brunschwig, Henri, *La Colonisation française,* Paris, Calmann-Lévy, 1949.

———, *Mythes et réalités de l'impérialisme colonial français, 1871–1914,* Paris, Colin, 1960.

Buell, R. L., *The Native Problem in Africa,* 2 vols. New York, Macmillan, 1928.

Capet, Marcel, *Les Economies d'AOF?* Paris, Librairie générale de droit et de jurisprudence, 1958.

Cardaire, Marcel, *L'Islam et le terroir africain,* Bamako, IFAN, 1954.

Cartier, Raymond, "En France noire," *Paris-Match,* August 11, 18, 1956.

Castagno, A. A., Jr., "Somali Republic," in James S. Coleman and Carl Rosberg, eds., *Political Parties and National Integration in Tropical Africa,* Berkeley and Los Angeles, University of California Press, pp. 512–59.

Centre de Hautes Etudes sur l'Afrique et l'Asie Modernes, *Notes et Etudes sur l'Islam en Afrique Noire* (Recherches et Documents I), Paris, J. Peyronnet, 1962.

Chabas, J., "Le Mariage et le divorce dans les coûtumes des Ouolofs," *Revue juridique et politique de l'Union Française, 6* (October–December 1952), 474–532.

Chailley-Bert, Joseph, "La France et la plus grande France," *Revue politique et parlémentaire,* No. 33 (August 1902), 230–62.

Charpentier, C., "Les Anciens combattants dans les états africains d'expression française," *L'Afrique et l'Asie, 53* (1961), 16–19.

Coleman, James S., *Nigeria, Background to Nationalism,* Berkeley and Los Angeles, University of California Press, 1958.

———, "Togoland," *International Conciliation,* No. 509 (September 1956).

Cowan, L. G., *Local Government in West Africa,* New York, Columbia University Press, 1958.

Cros, Charles, *La Parole est à M. Blaise Diagne,* Paris, Chez l'auteur, 1961.

Crowder, Michael, *Senegal, A Study in French Assimilation Policy,* London, Oxford University Press, 1962.

Culmann, Henri, *L'Union Française,* Paris, Presses Universitaires de France, 1950.

Decraene, Philippe, *Le Panafricanisme,* Paris, Presses Universitaires de France, 1959.

Delafosse, Maurice, *Haut-Sénégal-Niger.* 3 vols. Paris, Larose, 1912.

Delavignette, Robert, *Freedom and Authority in French West Africa,* London, Oxford University Press, 1950.

Delval, J., "Le R.D.A. au Soudan français," *L'Afrique et l'Asie, 16* (1951), 54–67.

Deschamps, Hubert, *The French Union,* Paris, Berger-Levrault, 1957.

———, *Méthodes et doctrines coloniales de la France,* Paris, Colin, 1953.

Deutsch, Karl W., *Nationalism and Social Communication,* New York, John Wiley and Sons, 1953.

Deutsch, Karl W. et al., *Political Community and the North Atlantic Area,* Princeton, Princeton University Press, 1957.

Devèze, Michel, *La France d'Outre-Mer, 1938–1947,* Paris, Hachette, 1948.

Dieterlen, Germaine, "Mythe et organisation sociale au Soudan Français," *Journal de la Société des Africanistes, 25* (Paris, 1955), 39–76.

———, "Mythe et organisation sociale en Afrique Occidentale," *Journal de la Société des Africanistes, 29,* fascicule 1 (Paris, 1959), 119–38.

Diop, Abdoulaye, "L'Immigration Toucouleure à Dakar (enquête 1958–1959)," Dakar, IFAN, 1960 (mimeo.).

Diop, Ousmane Socé, *Karim,* Paris, Nouvelles Editions Latines, 1948.

Doob, Leonard W., *Becoming More Civilized: A Psychological Exploration,* New Haven, Yale University Press, 1960.

———, *Communication in Africa,* New Haven, Yale University Press, 1961.

Dugué, Gil, *Vers les Etats-Unis d'Afrique,* Dakar, Lettres Africaines, 1960.

Dupuis, J., "Un Problème de minorité: les nomades dans l'Etat Soudanais," *L'Afrique et l'Asie, 50* (1960), 19–44.

Duverger, Maurice, *Les Partis politiques,* Paris, Colin, 1951.

Emerson, Rupert, *From Empire to Nation,* Cambridge, Harvard University Press, 1960.

Fage, J. D., *An Atlas of African History,* London, Edward Arnold, 1958.

———, *An Introduction to the History of West Africa,* London, Cambridge University Press, 1955.

———, *Ghana: A Historical Interpretation,* Madison, University of Wisconsin Press, 1959.

Foltz, William J., "Senegal" in James S. Coleman and Carl Rosberg, eds., *Political Parties and National Integration in Tropical Africa,* Berkeley and Los Angeles, University of California Press, 1964, pp. 16–64.

Fortes, M. and E. E. Evans-Pritchard, *African Political Systems,* London, Oxford University Press, 1940.

Fouquet, J., *La Traite des arachides dans les pays de Kaolack, et ses conséquences économiques, sociales, et juridiques,* St. Louis, IFAN, 1958.

Fournier, François, "Aspects politiques du problème des chefferies au Soudan présahélien," *Revue juridique et politique de l'Union Française, 1* (January–March 1955), 148–82.

Gamble, David P., *The Wolof of Senegambia,* London, International African Institute, 1957.

Gonidec, P. F., "Les Assemblées locales des territoires d'outre-mer," *Revue juridique et politique de l'Union Française, 5* (1952), 317–55 and *6* (1953), 443–91.

———,*Constitutions des états de la Communauté,* Paris, Sirey, 1959.

Gorer, Geoffrey, *Africa Dances: A Book about West African Negroes,* New York, W. W. Norton and Co., 1962.

Gosselin, M., "Bamako, ville soudanaise moderne," *L'Afrique et l'Asie, 21* (1953), 31–37.

Gottman, Jean, *La Politique des états et leur géographie,* Paris, Colin, 1952.

Gouilly, Alphonse, *L'Islam dans l'Afrique Occidentale Française,* Paris, Larose, 1952.

Guetzkow, Harold, *Multiple Loyalties: Theoretical Approach to a Problem in International Organization,* Publication No. 4, Center for Research on World Political Institutions, Princeton, Princeton University Press, 1955.

Guillemin, Philippe, "Les Elus d'Afrique Noire à l'Assemblée Nationale sous la Quatrième République," *Revue Française de Science Politique, 8* (Dec. 1958), 861–77.

Haas, Ernst B., "Regionalism, Functionalism, and Universal International Organization," *World Politics, 8* (January 1956), 238–63.

———, *The Uniting of Europe,* London, Stevens and Sons, 1958.

Hailey, Lord, *An African Survey,* London, Oxford University Press, 1938, and revised edition, 1956.

Hammond, P. B., "Economic Change and Mossi Acculturation," in W. R. Bascom and M. J. Herskovits, eds., *Continuity and Change in African Culture* (Chicago, University of Chicago Press, 1959), pp. 238–56.

Hamon, Léo, *Introduction à l'étude des partis politiques de l'Afrique française,* Paris, Librairie générale de droit (Extrait de la *Revue juridique et politique d'outre-mer, 2,* April–June, 1959).

———, "La Mise en place des pouvoirs politiques en Afrique Noire," *Cahiers de la République, 7* (May–June 1957), 57–59.

Harding, Richard, "The Survival of the French Community in West Africa," unpublished seminar paper, Yale University, May 1960.

Harmand, Jules, *Domination et Colonisation,* Paris, Flammarion, 1910.

Henry, Paul-Marc, "Pan-Africanism: A Dream Come True," *Foreign Affairs, 37* (April 1959), 443–52.

Herskovits, M. J., *Dahomey—An Ancient West African Kingdom,* 2 vols. New York, J. J. Augustin, 1938.

Hodgkin, Thomas, *African Political Parties,* Baltimore, Penguin, 1962.

———, "After Bamako," *Africa Special Report,* December 1957.

———, "Background on French West Africa," *West Africa,* February 20, 1954.

———, *Nationalism in Colonial Africa,* London, Muller, 1956.

———, "A Note on the Language of African Nationalism," *African Affairs, No. 1,* St. Antony's Papers, 10 (Carbondale, Ill., Southern Illinois University Press, 1961), pp. 22–40.

Hodgkin, Thomas and Ruth Schachter. "French-speaking West Africa in Transition," *International Conciliation,* No. 528 (May 1960).

Inkeles, Alex and Daniel Levinson, "National Character: The Study of Modal Personality and Sociocultural Systems," in Gardner Lindzey, ed., *Handbook of Social Psychology, 2* (Cambridge, Harvard University Press, 1954), pp. 977–1020.

Institut de Recherche et de Formation en vue du Développement Harmonisé, "Le Sénégal en Marche," *Les Cahiers africains,* No. 5, Brussels, Editions Créations de Presse, 1962.

Institut Français d'Opinion Publique, "Les Etudiants d'Outre-Mer en France," *Sondages, 3* (1961), 50–79.

Jourdain, Guy, Marcel Drahon, and Marius Reveillon, "Le Marché du gros bétail dans le Moyen-Soudan," Banque Centrale des Etats de l'Afrique de l'Ouest, *Note d'Information, 59* (June 1960).

Kimble, George H. T., *Tropical Africa,* 2 vols. New York, The Twentieth Century Fund, 1960.

Labouret, Henri, *Colonisation, Colonialisme, Décolonisation,* Paris, Larose, 1952.

———, *Paysans d'Afrique Occidentale,* Paris, Stock, 1953.

Lattre, André de, *Les Finances extérieures de la France,* Paris, Presses Universitaires de France, 1959.

Lavergne de Tressan, M. de, *Inventaire linguistique de l'Afrique Occidentale Française et du Togo,* Dakar, IFAN, 1953.

Le Grip, A., "Aspects actuels de l'Islam en A.O.F.," *L'Afrique et l'Asie,* No. 24 (1953), 6–20, No. 25 (1954), 43–61.

———, "L'Avenir de l'Islam en Afrique Noire," *L'Afrique et l'Asie, 10* (1950).

Legum, Colin, *Pan-Africanism, a Short Political Guide,* New York, Praeger, 1962.

LeRolle, "Contribution à l'étude sur l'évolution des partis africains et la création du Parti de Regroupement Africain," Association Française de Science Politique, Table Ronde, March 1959 (mimeo.).

Leroy-Beaulieu, Pierre-Paul, *De la Colonisation chez les peuples modernes,* Paris, Guillaumin, 1882.

LeVine, Robert A., "Africa," in Francis L. K. Hsu, *Psychological Anthropology, Approaches to Culture and Personality* (Homewood, Ill., Dorsey, 1961), pp. 48–52.

Lévy-Bruhl, Lucien, *Les Fonctions mentales dans les sociétés inférieures,* Paris, Alcan, 1910.

Marty, Paul, *Etudes sur l'Islam au Sénégal,* 2 vols. Paris, Leroux, 1917.

———, *Etudes sur l'Islam et les tribus du Soudan,* 4 vols. Paris, Leroux, 1920–21.

Mauny, Raymond, "L'Etat actuel de la question de Ghana," *Bulletin de l'Institut Français d'Afrique Noire,* Série B (Dakar, 1951), 463–75.

———, *Tableau géographique de l'Ouest-Africain au Moyen Age,* Dakar, IFAN, 1961.

Melnick, Constantin and Nathan Leites, *The House without Windows: France Elects a President,* Evanston, Row, Peterson, 1958.

Mercier, Paul, *L'Agglomération Dakaroise,* St. Louis du Sénégal, IFAN, 1954.

———, "Aspects des problèmes de stratification sociale dans l'Ouest Africain," *Cahiers Internationaux de Sociologie, 16* (1954), 59–65.

———, "Etude du mariage et enquête urbaine," *Cahiers d'Etudes Africaines, 1* (January 1960), 28–43.

———, "Le Groupement européen de Dakar," *Cahiers Internationaux de Sociologie, 19* (1955), 130–46.

———, "La Vie politique dans les centres urbains du Sénégal," *Cahiers Internationaux de Sociologie, 26* (July–December 1959), 55–84.

Milcent, Ernest, *L'AOF entre en scène,* Paris, Editions du Témoignage Chrétien, 1958.

Mission Socio-économique du Fleuve Sénégal (MISOES), *Les Budgets familiaux,* Dakar, 1959.

Mission Socio-économique du Sénégal, "Les Migrations," Paris, mimeo., 1959.

Monteil, Charles, *Les Bambara du Ségou et du Kaarta,* Paris, Larose, 1924.

———, *Les Empires du Mali,* Paris, Larose, 1930.

Monteil, Vincent, "L'Islam noir en marche," *Le Monde,* June 14, 1960.

Moussa, Pierre, *Les Chances économiques de la Communauté Franco-Africaine,* Paris, Colin, 1957.

Murdock, G. P., *Africa, Its Peoples and Their Culture History,* New York, McGraw-Hill, 1959.

Mus, Paul, *Le Destin de l'Union française, de l'Indo-Chine à l'Afrique,* Paris, Seuil, 1954.

N'Diaye, J. P., *Enquête sur les étudiants noirs en France,* Paris, Réalités Africaines, 1962.

Newbury, Colin, "The Formation of the Government General of French West Africa," *Journal of African History, 1* (1960), 111–28.

———, "The Government General and Political Change in French West Africa," *African Affairs,* No. 1, St. Antony's Papers, 10 (Carbondale, Ill., Southern Illinois University Press, 1961), pp. 41–59.

L'Office du Niger, "Note de présentation technique," Ségou, mimeo., 1960.

———, "L'Office du Niger en 1960," Ségou, mimeo., 1960.

Paques, Viviana, *Les Bambara,* Paris, Presses Universitaires de France, 1954.

Pélissier, Paul, "L'Arachide au Sénégal," *Problèmes Agricoles au Sénégal,* St. Louis, IFAN, 1953.

Pierson-Mathy, P., "L'Evolution politique de l'Afrique," *Chronique de politique étrangère, 14* (January–May 1961).

Poquin, Jean-Jacques, *Les Relations économiques des pays d'Afrique Noire de l'Union Française, 1925–1955,* Paris, Colin, 1957.

Praetor Africanus, "Emancipations Africaines II: La Loi-Cadre au banc d'essai," *L'Afrique et l'Asie, 3* (1957), 14–30.

———, "En Marge d'une loi," *L'Afrique et l'Asie, 34* (1956), 55–59.

Priestley, Herbert F., *France Overseas: A Study in Modern Imperialism,* New York, Appleton-Century, 1938.

Pye, Lucian W., "The Non-Western Political Process," *Journal of Politics, 20* (August 1958), 468–86.

Réquin, E., *Archinard et le Soudan,* Paris, Berger-Levrault, 1946.

Richard-Molard, Jacques, *Afrique Occidentale Française,* Paris, Berger-Levrault, 1956.

Roberts, S. H., *History of French Colonial Policy (1870–1925),* 2 vols. London, P. S. King, 1929.

Robinson, Kenneth E., "Constitutional Reform in French Tropical Africa," *Political Studies, 6* (1958), 45–69.

———, "Political Development in French West Africa," in Calvin Stillman, ed., *Africa in the Modern World,* Chicago, University of Chicago Press, 1955, pp. 140–81.

———, "Senegal: the Elections to the Territorial Assembly, March 1957," in W. J. M. Mackenzie and Kenneth E. Robinson, eds., *Five Elections in Africa,* London, Oxford University Press, 1960, pp. 281–390.

———, "The Public Law of Overseas France Since the War," *Journal of Comparative Legislation, 32* (1950), 37–57.

Roche, Jean, "Le Budget général de l'A.O.F.," *Annales Africaines, 2* (1956), 213–57.

———, "La Loi-Cadre du 23 juin 1956," *Annales Africaines, 3* (1957), 97–133.

Rouch, Jean, "Contribution à l'histoire des Songhay," *Mémoire de l'Institut Français d'Afrique Noire, 29* (Dakar, 1953), 141–259.

———, "Migrations au Ghana," *Journal des africanistes, 26* (1956), 33–196.

Sarraut, Albert, *La Mise en valeur des colonies françaises,* Paris, Payot, 1923.

Savage, I. R. and K. W. Deutsch, "A Statistical Model of the Gross Analysis of Transaction Flows," *Econometrica, 28* (July 1960), 551–72.

Saxe, Jo W., "The Changing Economic Structure of French West Africa," *Annals of the American Academy of Political and Social Science* (March 1955), 52–61.

Schachter, Ruth, "Single-party Systems in West Africa," *American Political Science Review, 55* (June 1961), 294–307.

Schapera, I., *Government and Politics in Tribal Societies,* London, Watts, 1956.

Seurin, Jean-Louis, "Elites sociales et partis politiques d'A.O.F.," *Annales Africaines, 4* (1958), 123–57.

Sidibé, Mamby, "Histoire des pays formant le Mali d'autrefois et d'aujourd'hui," Bamako, mimeo., 1960.

Skinner, Elliott P., "An Analysis of the Political Organization of the Mossi People," *Transactions of the New York Academy of Science,* Series II, *19,* 740–50.

———, "Traditional and Modern Patterns of Succession to Political Office among the Mossi of the Voltaic Republic," *Journal of Human Relations, 8* (Spring–Summer 1960), 394–406.

"Le Syndicalisme en Afrique Noire," *L'Economie* (December 31, 1959), 19–20.

Tardits, Claude, *Porto-Novo: les nouvelles générations africaines entre leurs traditions et l'Occident,* Paris, Mouton, 1958.

Thomas, Benjamin E., "Railways and Ports in French West Africa," *Economic Geography, 33* (January 1957), 1–15.

———, "Trade Routes of Algeria and the Sahara," *University of California Publications in Geography, 8* (1957), 165–288.

Thomas, Louis V., *Les Diola: essai d'analyse fonctionnelle sur une population de Basse-Casamance,* Dakar, IFAN, 1959.

Thompson, Virginia and Richard Adloff, *French West Africa,* Stanford, Stanford University Press, 1958.

Trimingham, J. Spencer, *A History of Islam in West Africa,* London, Oxford University Press, 1962.

———, *Islam in West Africa,* London, Oxford University Press, 1959.

Vignon, Louis, *Un Programme de politique coloniale,* Paris, Hachette, 1919.

Villard, André, *Histoire du Sénégal,* Dakar, Maurice Viale, 1943.

Wallerstein, Immanuel, "Ethnicity and National Integration in West Africa," *Cahiers d'études africaines, 3* (October 1960), 129–39.

———, "How Seven States Were Born in Former French West Africa," *Africa Report, 6* (March 1961).

Watt, W. Montgomery, *Islam and the Integration of Society,* London, Routledge, 1961.

Westermann, Diedrich, *Geschichte Afrikas,* Cologne, Greven-Verlag, 1952.

Whitely, Wilfred H., "Political Concepts and Connotations," *African Affairs,* No. 1, St. Antony's Papers, 10 (Carbondale, Ill., Southern Illinois University Press, 1961), pp. 7–21.

Williams, Philip, *Politics in Post War France,* London, Longmans, 1958.

Wolff, Kurt, "Die Entstehung der frühen ful-staaten in Senegambien," *Beiträge zur Gesellungs- und Völkerwissenschaft: Professor Dr. Richard Thurnwald zu zeinen Achtzigsten Geburtsdag gewidmet* (Berlin, Gebr. Mann, 1950), 435–45.

Wright, Gordon, *The Reshaping of French Democracy,* New York, Reynal and Hitchcock, 1948.

Works by African Politicians

d'Arboussier, Gabriel, *Le R.D.A. est toujours anti-colonialiste* (*Lettres ouvertes à Félix Houphouet-Boigny*), Paris, n.d.

Dia, Mamadou, "Contribution à l'étude du mouvement coopératif en Afrique noire," *Le Mouvement coopératif en territoires tropicaux arriérés,* Afrika–Instituut–Rykslandbouwhogeschool (Leiden, Universitaire, 1953), pp. 123–58.

———, *Déclaration de Monsieur Mamadou Dia, président du conseil, devant l'Assemblée Législative du Sénégal, June 9, 1960,* Dakar, 1960.

———, *Déclaration d'investiture prononcée par M. Mamadou Dia, président du conseil, devant l'Assemblée Législative du Sénégal à Dakar . . . le 4 avril 1959,* Dakar, 1959.

———, *Déclaration faite . . . à l'ouverture de la session ordinaire de l'Assemblée Constituante du Sénégal,* St. Louis, 1960.

———, *Déclaration faite par M. Mamadou Dia . . . devant le comité exécutif de l'Union Progressiste Sénégalaise, Section Sénégalaise du P.R.A., à Rufisque le 4 octobre 1958,* Dakar, 1958.

———, *L'Economie africaine, études et problèmes nouveaux.* Paris, Presses Universitaires de France, 1957.

———, *Nations africaines et solidarité mondiale,* Paris, Presses Universitaires de France, 1960.

———, *Réflexions sur l'économie de l'Afrique noire,* Paris, Editions Africaines, 1953.

Diop, Cheikh Anta, *L'Afrique noire pré-coloniale,* Paris, Présence Africaine, 1952.

———, *Les Fondements culturels techniques et industriels d'un futur état fédéral d'Afrique noire,* Paris, Présence Africaine, 1960.

Diop, Majhmout, *Contribution à l'étude des problèmes politiques en Afrique noire,* Paris, Présence Africaine, 1958.

———, "L'Unique issue: l'indépendance totale. La seule voie: un large mouvement d'union anti-impérialiste," *Présence Africaine, 14* (1953), 145–84.

Le Drame de la Haute Volta, Paris, Documents Africains, 1960.

Eboué, Félix, *La Nouvelle politique indigène pour l'A.E.F.*, text found as an appendix to Jean LaRoche and Jean Gottman, *La Fédération Française,* Montreal, 1945.

Gueye, Lamine, *Etapes et perspectives de l'Union Française,* Paris, Editions de l'Union Française, 1955.

Guinée: Prélude à l'indépendance, Paris, Présence Africaine, 1958.

Houphouet-Boigny, Félix, "Black Africa and the French Union," *Foreign Affairs, 35* (July 1957), 593–99.

———, "Réponse à d'Arboussier," in *L'Afrique noire,* Dakar, July 24, 1952.

Keita, Madeira, "Le Parti unique," *Présence Africaine, 30* (February–March 1960), 3–24.

Keita, Modibo, "Communication à l'Assemblée Législative de la République Soudanaise," Bamako, mimeo., August 29, 1960.

Keita, Modibo and Léopold Senghor. "Conférence de Presse," Paris, mimeo., May 21, 1959.

Ly, Abdoulaye, *Les Masses africaines et l'actuelle condition humaine,* Paris, Présence Africaine, 1956.

———, *Mercenaires noirs: notes sur une forme de l'exploitation des Africains,* Paris, Présence Africaine, 1957.

Le Rassemblement Démocratique Africain dans la lutte anti-impérialiste, Paris, 1948.

Senghor, Léopold, "L'Avenir de la France dans l'Outre-Mer," *Politique Etrangère, 4* (October 1954), 419–26.

———, "Confédération et fédération," *Condition Humaine,* April 14, 1956.

———, "Conférence de presse sur la situation politique au Niger," Sénégal, Service de la Documentation, mimeo., 1958.

——, "Création de deux grands territoires en AOF," *Condition Humaine,* January 26, 1956.
——, *Pierre Teilhard de Chardin et la politique africaine,* Paris Editions du Seuil, 1962.
Touré, Sékou, *Congrès général de l'UGTAN,* Paris, Présence Africaine, 1959.
——, *Expérience guinéenne et unité africaine,* Paris, Présence Africaine, 1961.

French and African Government Documents

Afrique Occidentale Française, *Conseil de Gouvernement, Session de décembre 1945,* St. Louis, 1946.
——, Gouvernement-Général, *Annuaire Statistique de l'Afrique Occidentale Française 1950 à 1954,* 5 vols.
——, Gouvernement-Général, *Journal Officiel.*
——, *Grand Conseil de l'AOF: Procès-verbaux.*
——, Haut Commissariat, *AOF 1957, Tableaux économiques,* Dakar, 1958.
——, Haut Commissariat, Etudes et coordination statistiques et mécanographiques, *Recensement démographique de Dakar (1955),* Résultats définitifs, 1er fascicule.
——, Haut Commissariat Général à Dakar, *Comptes économiques de l'Afrique Occidentale Française en 1956,* 5 vols.
Côte d'Ivoire, Direction de la Statistique, *Inventaire économique de la Côte d'Ivoire, 1947–1956,* Abidjan.
——, Direction de la Statistique, *Recensement d'Abidjan 1955,* Abidjan.
——, Direction de la Statistique, *Recensement des centres urbains d'Abengourou, Agboville, Dimbokro et Man, 1956–1957,* Abidjan.
France, Ambassade de France, Service de Presse et d'Information, *French Africa, a Decade of Progress, 1948–1958,* New York, 1958.
——, Caisse Centrale de Coopération Economique, *Les Investissements publics français dans les états d'Afrique noire et de Madagascar, les territoires et les départements d'Outre-Mer: Opérations de l'année 1960,* Paris, 1961.
——, *La Conférence Africaine-Française, Brazzaville, 30 janvier–8 février, 1944,* Algiers, 1945.
——, Institut National de la Statistique et des Etudes Economiques, *Annuaire statistique de la France, 1961.*
——, *Journal Officiel: Assemblée Nationale; Assemblée Nationale Constituante; Assemblée de l'Union Française; Conseil de la République.*
——, Ministère de la France d'Outre-Mer, Service de la Statistique, *Enquête démographique 1957–1958. Rapport provisoire de la mission socio-économique du Soudan,* Paris, 1958.

———, Ministère de la France d'Outre-Mer, Service de la Statistique, *Enquête démographique 1957. Résultats provisoires de la mission socio-économique de la basse vallée du Sénégal,* Paris, 1957.

———, Ministère de la France d'Outre-Mer, Service de la Statistique, *Inventaire sociale et économique des territoires d'outre-mer,* Paris, 1957.

Mali, Fédération du, *Journal Officiel.*

———, *Proclamation de l'Indépendance du Mali,* Dakar, 1960.

———, Ministère des Finances, des Affaires Economiques et du Plan, Service de la Statistique et de la Mécanographie, *Bulletin Statistique et Economique Mensuel.*

Mali, République du, Chambre de Commerce d'Agriculture et d'Industrie de Bamako, "Eléments du bilan économique de l'année 1960," Bamako, mimeo., 1961.

———, Ministère de l'Economie et du Plan, Service Statistique, "Population de la République du Mali par cercles et subdivisions d'après les recensements administratifs," Bamako, mimeo., 1960.

———, Ministère du Plan, *Les Comptes économiques de la République du Mali pour 1959,* Bamako, 1961.

Sénégal, République du, Assemblée Législative Sénégalaise, "Procès-Verbaux" (mimeo.).

———, *Livre blanc sur le coup d'état manqué du 19 au 20 août 1960,* Dakar, 1960.

———, *Plan Quadriennal de développement, 1961–1964,* Dakar, 1961.

———, Ministère du Plan, *Recensement démographique de Dakar,* Résultats définitifs, 2e fascicule.

Soudan, République du, Assemblée Législative Soudanaise, "Procès-Verbaux (typescript).

———, Assemblée Territoriale Soudanaise, "Procès-Verbaux" (typescript).

———, Ministère de l'Economie Rurale et du Plan, "Etude sur l'économie agricole du Soudan," 2 vols. Bamako, mimeo., 1959.

United Nations Department of Economic and Social Affairs, *Enlargement of the Exchange Economy in Tropical Africa,* Doc. E/2557/ST/ECA/23, New York, 1954.

———, *Scope and Structure of Money Economies in Tropical Africa,* New York, 1955.

United States, Bureau of the Census, *Statistical Abstract of the United States, 1961,* Washington, 1961.

African Political Party Publications

Bloc Démocratique Sénégalais, *Condition Humaine,* Dakar (weekly).

Bloc Populaire Sénégalais, *Unité,* Dakar (weekly).

Convention Africaine, *Congrès interterritorial de regroupement des partis politiques africains, Dakar le 11, 12, et 13 janvier 1957*, Dakar, 1957.

Parti Africain de l'Indépendance, *La Lutte,* Dakar (irregular).

———, *Momsarev,* Dakar (irregular).

Parti de la Fédération Africaine, *Congrès Constitutif du Parti de la Fédération Africaine,* Dakar, 1959.

———, "Congrès Constitutif du PFA, Débats," Dakar, mimeo., 1959.

———, *Le Mali,* Dakar (monthly).

———, *Séminaire organisé à l'occasion du Congrès de l'Union Nationale de la Jeunesse du Mali,* Dakar, 1960.

Parti du Regroupement Africain-Sénégal, *Bataille pour les positions du Congrès P.R.A. de Cotonou. Les tâches du P.R.A.-Sénégal au lendemain du référendum,* Dakar, Impr. Diop, 1958.

———, *Indépendance Africaine,* Dakar (monthly).

Section Française de l'Internationale Ouvrière (Senegalese branch), *AOF,* Dakar (weekly).

Union Progressiste Sénégalaise, "Deuxième Congrès de l'UPS-PFA," St. Louis, mimeo., 1960.

———, *Unité Africaine,* Dakar (weekly).

Union Soudanaise, "Cinquième Congrès de l'Union Soudanaise-R.D.A.," August 13–17, 1958 (typescript).

———, *Congrès extraordinaire de l'Union Soudanaise-RDA, le 22 septembre 1960,* Koulouba, 1960.

———, "Deuxième conférence territoriale de l'Union Soudanaise-RDA," October 2, 1958 (typescript).

———, *Essor,* Bamako (daily).

———, "Les Travaux du quatrième congrès territorial, 22–24 septembre 1955," Bamako, mimeo.

———, *Troisième conférence de l'Union Soudanaise RDA, Section du PFA,* Koulouba, Imprimerie du Gouvernement, n.d.

Parti Progressiste Soudanais, *Vérité,* Bamako (weekly).

Periodicals

Abidjan-Matin, Abidjan (daily).

Africa Report, Washington, D.C. (monthly).

Afrique Nouvelle, Dakar (weekly).

Agence France Presse, Bulletin, Dakar (daily).

Annales Africaines, Dakar (yearly).

L'Année politique; revue chronologique des principaux faits politiques, économiques, et sociaux de la France, Paris, Presses Universitaires de France, 1945–59.

Bulletin de la Chambre de Commerce d'Agriculture et d'Industrie de Dakar, Dakar (weekly).

Chroniques d'Outre-Mer, Paris (monthly).
Combat, Paris (daily).
Les Echos d'Afrique Noire, Dakar (weekly).
Encyclopédie Mensuelle d'Outre-Mer, Paris (monthly).
France Observateur, Paris (weekly).
Marchés Coloniaux, after September 1, 1956, *Marchés Tropicaux*, Paris (weekly).
Le Monde, Paris (daily).
Paris-Dakar, Dakar (daily).
Présence Africaine, Paris (quarterly).
Réalités Africaines, Dakar (semi-monthly).
Semaine en Afrique Occidentale, Dakar (weekly).
La Semaine Sénégalaise, Dakar (weekly).
West Africa, London (weekly).

Index

YALE STUDIES IN POLITICAL SCIENCE

1. Robert E. Lane, THE REGULATION OF BUSINESSMEN. Out of print
2. Charles Blitzer, AN IMMORTAL COMMONWEALTH: THE POLITICAL THOUGHT OF JAMES HARRINGTON
3. Aaron Wildavsky, DIXON-YATES: A STUDY IN POWER POLITICS
4. Robert A. Dahl, WHO GOVERNS? DEMOCRACY AND POWER IN AN AMERICAN CITY
5. Herbert Jacob, GERMAN ADMINISTRATION SINCE BISMARCK: CENTRAL AUTHORITY VERSUS LOCAL AUTONOMY
6. Robert C. Fried, THE ITALIAN PREFECTS: A STUDY IN ADMINISTRATIVE POLITICS
7. Nelson W. Polsby, COMMUNITY POWER AND POLITICAL THEORY
8. Joseph Hamburger, JAMES MILL AND THE ART OF REVOLUTION
9. Takehiko Yoshihashi, CONSPIRACY AT MUKDEN: THE RISE OF THE JAPANESE MILITARY
10. Douglas A. Chalmers, THE SOCIAL DEMOCRATIC PARTY OF GERMANY: FROM WORKING-CLASS MOVEMENT TO MODERN POLITICAL PARTY
11. James D. Barber, THE LAWMAKERS: RECRUITMENT AND ADAPTATION TO LEGISLATIVE LIFE
12. William J. Foltz, FROM FRENCH WEST AFRICA TO THE MALI FEDERATION
13. Fred I. Greenstein, CHILDREN AND POLITICS